TORRANCE PUBLIC LIBRARY

3 2111 01269 0563

P9-DMI-513

Katy Geissert
Civic Center Library
3301 Torrance Blvd.
Torrance, CA 90503

WITHDRAWN

THE CATCH

THE CATCH

ONE PLAY, TWO DYNASTIES, AND THE GAME THAT CHANGED THE NFL

GARY MYERS

 Crown Publishers   New York

Copyright © 2009 by Gary Myers

Foreword copyright © 2009 by Joe Montana

All rights reserved.

Published in the United States by Crown Publishers, an imprint of the
Crown Publishing Group, a division of Random House, Inc., New York.

www.crownpublishing.com

CROWN and the Crown colophon are registered trademarks of
Random House, Inc.

Library of Congress Cataloging-in-Publication Data

Myers, Gary, 1954 July 1–

The catch / Gary Myers.—1st ed.

p. cm.

1. National Football League Championship Game (16th: 1982: San Francisco) 2. San
Francisco 49ers (Football team)—History. 3. Dallas Cowboys (Football team)—History.

I. Title.

GV956.2.N38M94 2009

796.332'640979461—dc22

2009014961

ISBN 978-0-307-40908-9

Printed in the U.S.A.

Design by Leonard W. Henderson

10 9 8 7 6 5 4 3 2 1

First Edition

To Allison, my greatest catch.
To Michelle, Emily, and Andrew, my championship team.
And to Mom and Dad, for everything.

Contents

THE CATCH

Foreword

BY JOE MONTANA

I WAS FORTUNATE enough to play in four Super Bowls with the 49ers, and they are all very special. But who really knows if that great run would have even happened if we hadn't had that incredible Sunday in January of 1982? That's when Too Tall Jones and what seemed like the entire Cowboys defense was chasing me and Dwight Clark was trying to lose Everson Walls running across the back of the end zone. I threw it and Dwight caught it.

It was exhilarating. It was unforgettable. It was history.

As I go around the country, people always ask me if I was throwing the ball away. The question mainly comes from Cowboys fans. That's no surprise. The answer is no, but it really doesn't matter now, does it? Dwight made The Catch.

To this day, the Cowboys still think I was trying to toss the ball into the upper deck of Candlestick Park. I knew it was high when I let it go, but I still thought it was going to be a touchdown. I just had no idea what a great catch Dwight made until somebody told me he jumped out of the stadium to grab it. I was on my back after running for my life and only knew he caught the ball because of the crowd reaction.

I didn't see Dwight's catch until I watched the replay when I got back to the locker room. But here's one thing I know: The history of the NFL can't be told without a good, long conversation about The Catch. It is one of the most spectacular plays in league history. How many times do you still see it on television? If it didn't mean so much, you wouldn't see it over and over again.

There was a great feeling of excitement on our team before the game. The 49ers won 13 games that season and we had the best record in the NFC, but going into the season, nobody expected us to be in the NFC Championship Game, not even us. We had won only 2 games in 1979, my rookie year and Bill Walsh's first year in San Francisco. We improved to 6–10 in our second season. But this was a building process, and Bill still had some major construction to complete as he entered his third season. I was hoping he felt he had his quarterback. I was confident he had.

And now here we were, one step from the Super Bowl, going against America's Team. We took the Cowboys apart during the regular season 45–14, the game that eventually earned us the home field for the title game. We heard all the talk before the rematch about how the real Cowboys hadn't shown up in October and it would be different this time. It put a chip on our shoulder and led to spirited trash talking before and during the game, some of which, believe it or not, even came from my mouth. Sorry about that, Too Tall.

Gary Myers rekindles so many great memories in *The Catch*. I can close my eyes and imagine being back in Candlestick that day, our championship-starved fans cheering wildly, only 58 seconds on the clock, we were down by 6, and after coming so far as a team and on that drive, we had to find a way to get into the end zone. It was high stakes, but it was fun. This is what you dream about as a kid playing touch football in the backyard with your friends. The championship on the line, the ball in your hands, you have to make a play.

Dwight was a great athlete. He had pretty good leaping ability. When I finally saw The Catch, I was shocked to see how high I made

Dwight jump to go get that pass. To be able to get up that high and stretch and then still catch the ball—that was an all-timer.

It was a great game, maybe the greatest game I ever played in. The Catch was so memorable that's all you have to say, and everybody knows what you are talking about. It allowed a team of young guys and veterans, rookies who didn't know any better and old guys just trying to hold onto a dream, to bond together forever.

I was rolling to my right with the Cowboys defense closing in on me. I saw Dwight in the back of the end zone and let the ball go. He went up and got it, and a lifetime of memories was born.

SPRINT RIGHT OPTION

J OE MONTANA completed his meeting on the sideline with Bill Walsh and jogged back to the huddle. His anxious teammates were waiting to hear the play that would send them to the Super Bowl. The 49ers were down 6 points to the Cowboys and needed 6 yards and only 58 seconds remained.

"Sprint Right Option," Montana shouted.

The primary receiver was Freddie Solomon. The secondary receiver was Dwight Clark.

"We had practiced it so many times," Clark said.

Solomon lines up in the right slot, flares out to the flat. Clark lines up just outside of Solomon, starts out trying to set a pick for Solomon, then angles sharply to his left, reaches the back line of the end zone, then pivots and quickly cuts back to his right. But even in practice, if Solomon was not open, Montana-to-Clark never connected on that play.

"Joe would either throw it too long and it would get picked off, or he would throw it over my head," Clark said.

Candlestick Park, dilapidated and fit to be condemned, was the unlikely site for the NFC Championship Game on January 10, 1982. It was full of energy before what was about to become one of the most memorable plays in NFL history, one that dramatically changed the fortunes of two franchises—one dynasty born, one dying a slow, excruciatingly painful death whose ultimate victim was the legendary coach in the fedora. The torch was being passed. Legends were about to be created, and a classic play was about to be labeled with a simple yet distinctive name:

The Catch.

The Dallas Doomsday II defense had played soft in the dreaded prevent, designed to guard against the big play, all the way down the field to its own 6-yard line, a strategy that caused Cowboys veteran safety Charlie Waters to stage a mutiny on the sidelines before the drive even began. Too much time remained to give up on San Francisco running the ball, he argued to defensive coordinator Ernie Stautner, the decision maker. The 49ers had started on their own 11, and 4:54 was still on the clock—an eternity in the NFL, especially with three time-outs and the two-minute warning. Make Montana earn his way. Make him pay for it with body shots. Waters knew it was the last game of his twelve-year career if the Cowboys lost, and he also knew the strategy he was hearing from Stautner was not the way for him to have a storybook finish in the Super Bowl. Stautner was not happy with Waters's attempt at a sideline coup and reacted by showing him up. He was a Hall of Fame defensive lineman who had played fourteen seasons with the Steelers and was an affable but inflexible man. He was having a fit as the pressure mounted during the television time-out, and he cryptically offered to abdicate the throne and let Waters make the defensive calls—and answer to Tom Landry if it all went wrong.

"Look, we'll get out of the nickel, but it's going to be all on you," Stautner said.

"No thanks," Waters said.

Waters resented being put in that position. Landry didn't interfere, even though at one time he was a defensive genius. He gave Stautner complete autonomy. Linebackers Bob Breunig, D. D. Lewis, and Mike Hegman remained on the sidelines after Danny White's punt pinned the Niners deep. Into the game came defensive backs Ron Fellows and Benny Barnes and smallish linebacker Anthony Dickerson, who was inserted to watch for running backs flaring out of the backfield. He was not sent in to be a run stopper.

Walsh had countered by calling end runs for journeyman back Lenvil Elliott and quick passes by Montana that frustrated the Cowboys. Elliott was shredding the Cowboys defense. The 49ers moved the ball in huge chunks, and Dallas never adjusted. Stautner never went back to his base defense as Montana marched downfield on the first twelve plays of the drive. By the time he adjusted on the thirteenth and final play, it was too late. This was almost too easy for Walsh. "We tried to methodically cut them apart," he said.

Now, with the 49ers all the way down to the Dallas 6-yard line and facing third and 3, the Cowboys defense was finally back in its normal four-three alignment for the first time on the drive. It was ready to plant the skinny quarterback six feet deep in the chewed-up turf, which hadn't had time to recover from torrential rain that dumped six and a half inches of water on the Bay Area the previous week. The rain was so bad, the 49ers abandoned their drenched facility in Redwood City and moved their operation to Southern California to practice in Anaheim at the headquarters of the hated Rams.

It had been nearly ten years since the 49ers' last appearance in the playoffs. Back then, Dallas had eliminated them three years in a row, twice in the NFC Championship Game and the third time when Roger Staubach came off the bench late in the third quarter in the 1972 divisional round with Dallas trailing 28–13 and hit Billy Parks and Ron Sellers with touchdown passes in the final two minutes to win 30–28. Every year, it seemed, Dallas left broken hearts all over San Francisco.

The Cowboys were arrogant and egotistical and had no fear of Montana and Walsh and the 49ers, even at this franchise-defining moment. They were sure they were going to make a play to send themselves to Detroit for Super Bowl XVI to face the Bengals, who had just defeated the Chargers in arctic conditions in Cincinnati in the AFC Championship Game. These weren't the Steelers, the Cowboys' nemesis and tormentors, who beat them twice in the Super Bowl. Poor Jackie Smith. The acrobatics of Lynn Swann. Thomas Henderson saying Terry Bradshaw couldn't spell *cat* if you spotted him the *c* and the *t*. How would Henderson know? He was doing coke on the sidelines.

It was only the 49ers. The Cowboys had never lost to them in the playoffs. But now the 49ers were one game away from playing for their first championship since joining the NFL in 1950.

Dallas had humiliated the Niners 59–14 early in the 1980 season, Walsh's second year. Some genius. "We just got slobbered on," guard Randy Cross said. But the spanking also convinced Walsh it was finally time to elevate Montana to full-time starter after sharing snaps with Steve DeBerg. He started the next week against the Rams. But even when the 49ers shocked the Cowboys 45–14 in week six of the 1981 season at Candlestick, the Cowboys took turns telling the 49ers that the real Cowboys weren't there that day, as if Landry had left them behind at the airport in Dallas and instead took a bunch of high school kids wearing the metallic silver and blue with the star on the helmet. A 31-point aberration? That's how the Cowboys rationalized it—an insult to the 49ers and their wine-and-cheese fan base. "If there was an offensive game that I take pride in, it was that game," Walsh told NFL Films. "Because we took that great Dallas defense and just took it apart. We knew just how to play against it. We beat them 45–14, and we could have scored more."

"We thought it was a fluke. We really did," Waters said.

"They didn't respect us," Montana said.

The Cowboys were distracted before the blowout game when teammate Don Smerek, who was on injured reserve, was shot in the chest early that October morning outside Café Dallas, a popular club in the trendy section of Greenville Avenue, during an argument over a parking spot. Even though Smerek was a fringe player, he was still one of them. And it was on the players' minds as they sat in the locker room before the game.

The Cowboys' angst over Smerek and the beating they took on the field was magnified when they were told after the game that a caller had phoned in a bomb threat to blow up their charter flight home. The call came in just after halftime. It wasn't bad enough that the Cowboys were losing 24–7. The bomb squad went to Candlestick to inspect the team's luggage, its equipment, and the bus taking them to the airport. Dogs sniffed the plane. The flight returned safely. It was the only thing that went right on the trip.

Now the Cowboys were back in San Francisco three months later for another shot at the 49ers, and this time it was game on with Montana 6 yards away and Clark hoping Sprint Right Option would work better than it had in practice. These gut-wrenching playoff moments were not new to the 'Boys. Just the year before, it was Danny White, in his first year replacing the iconic Staubach, throwing two touchdown passes to Drew Pearson in the last three minutes to beat the Falcons in Atlanta. The 'Boys had two Super Bowl trophies, but they also knew the anguish of the Ice Bowl and Smith's dropped pass and Jim O'Brien's kick. The 49ers had no history of success to help them prepare. It was considered a success if they simply won more than they lost. How were they going to beat Dallas?

"They had always beaten the crap out of us," Cross said.

The Niners hated the Cowboys. This, however, was a case of unrequited hate. The Cowboys didn't care enough about the 49ers to hate them back. Not even with the Super Bowl at stake. "The 49ers had a thing for the Cowboys," said Dallas tight end Doug Cosbie, who grew up in the Bay Area going to Niners games at old Kezar Stadium, sitting in the end zone for $1. "I remember being at Fisherman's Wharf the day before the championship game and people were wearing, FUCK DALLAS T-shirts. You don't see people in Dallas wearing, FUCK SAN FRANCISCO or FUCK THE 49ERS T-shirts."

The last 6 yards were going to be the hardest. The Niners trailed the Cowboys by 27–21 and by five Super Bowl appearances. There was a lot of history to overcome.

Walsh gave Montana a play for third down, and just in case, a play for fourth down. The 49ers could also pick up a first down without scoring a touchdown. Walsh still had a time-out in his pocket.

Montana had not played a great game. He'd thrown three interceptions, two of them to rookie cornerback Everson Walls, and he lost one fumble. The 49ers led the NFL with the fewest turnovers during the regular season. They had six in this game. Two plays earlier, Montana sailed a pass over the head of a wide-open Solomon, who had lost Walls in the left corner of the end zone. But Montana was not nervous. He was never nervous. He just threw a bad ball that ruined a great play. The night before, at the team dinner at the old low-rise Hyatt Burlingame at the San Francisco airport, Walsh elected to replace the standard buffet with a fancy sit-down dinner. The 49ers were one step from their first Super Bowl, and that was reason enough to celebrate. "The guys had steak and lobster," owner Ed DeBartolo said.

That was the main course. For Montana, the dessert was more fun. "There were balloons filled with helium," DeBartolo said. Montana, the team's practical joker, untied the balloons. "Joe inhaled the helium," DeBartolo said. And when he spoke, he sounded like Donald Duck. "Bill was there, all the coaches were there, everyone was really loose. Joe was always the one pulling pranks."

Montana was the leader, and he set the mood with the helium hijinks. "I was just being me," he said. "I never tried to do something to intentionally loosen everybody up. One thing that makes people more nervous is when they see somebody acting like they don't normally act. I always just tried to be myself. I was more of a clown."

He had a reputation for short-sheeting the beds in training camp. That summer in roasting hot Rocklin, California, he would hide teammates' bikes in the trees during evening meetings. "He was good at that kind of stuff," Clark said with unmistakable admiration.

The dorm at camp was a quarter mile from the practice field, and everybody rode bicycles around the campus of Sierra College. "Joe never had a bike, but he would steal everybody's," Clark said. "He used to love it when Walsh would leave his unlocked, because he would always steal it and ride to the cafeteria and leave it there. And then Bill would have to walk or take a golf cart or whatever."

"He was always screwing around, doing things with Dwight," DeBartolo said. "They were like a bunch of college kids."

When Montana returned to the huddle after his meeting with Walsh, he had ten pair of eyes on him. His voice was clear. The helium was gone from his lungs.

"Sprint Right Option," he said.

The Cowboys did not have to be the team that began the legend of Joe Cool, the only three-time Super Bowl MVP.

Landry, Tex Schramm, and Gil Brandt were sitting in the Cowboys offices at 6116 North Central Expressway in Dallas in their 1979 predraft meeting. The building was owned by Clint Murchison Jr., who also owned the Cowboys. It had two main attractions. The the love 'em or hate 'em Cowboys were on the eleventh floor. The Playboy Club, with the beautiful women in the skimpy bunny outfits, was on the second floor.

They were both very popular Dallas attractions.

The Cowboys had an unusual setup. Their executive offices, which included Landry's, sat right off a major highway, which was either crawling with bumper-to-bumper traffic at rush hour or had cars zooming at Indy 500 speeds south to downtown Dallas or north to the expanding suburbs. The traffic presented a challenge for Landry to get to his home on Rockbrook Drive for dinner with his wife, Alicia. And he always wanted to have dinner with Alicia before going into his study for a little extra film work. The practice facility was a few miles away on Forest Lane in a run-down old blue metal shack where the cockroaches outnumbered the players three to one. There was a motel that sat right behind the end zone of the practice field. Landry was so paranoid about Redskins coach George Allen sending spies to rent rooms on the second floor overlooking the field that when the Cowboys played the 'Skins, he had Schramm buy out all the rooms on the second floor to prevent Allen from sending in surveillance teams. If Landry had been in charge of the Watergate Hotel, the Republicans never would have broken in.

As they prepared for the 1979 draft, the Cowboys were coming off another Super Bowl loss to the Steelers. They were loaded at every position, particularly at quarterback. That allowed them to draft with the future in mind without having to fill immediate needs. That gave them the freedom and flexibility to take players they wouldn't need to get on the field for a year or two. Even with that philosophy, there was little sense of urgency when Landry, Schramm, and Brandt opened their draft notebooks to the section dealing with the class of '79 quarterbacks.

Roger Staubach was thirty-seven years old, up there for an NFL player, but he sat out five years while fulfilling his Navy commitment after Brandt invested a throwaway tenth round pick on him in 1964. He still had plenty left in his legs, his right arm, and especially his heart. The Cowboys drafted Danny White in the third round in 1974 and considered his decision to start his pro career playing for Memphis in the World Football League a positive. The NFL didn't have a developmental league, and White had no chance to play right away in Dallas anyway. If he'd signed with the Cowboys, the most he would have gotten would have been the third-team reps in training camp. "He would have been our punter," Brandt said.

He was better off in Memphis. "I did go to Phoenix to try and sign him. He picked me up at the airport," Brandt said. But White had an offer from the WFL. Brandt and Schramm discussed their strategy. "We thought it would good for him to go get the experience by playing," Brandt said.

White demoted himself to the minor leagues for a few seasons to get ready to replace Staubach. And just in case White didn't come back or wasn't any good, the Cowboys protected themselves by drafting Glenn Carano in the second round in 1977. Brandt, a former baby photographer, had been hired by Schramm along with Landry when the Cowboys joined the NFL as an expansion team in 1960. When he lined up the players on the Dallas draft possibilities board, they could not rationalize taking another quarterback, even if Landry really liked that skinny Montana kid from Notre Dame and quarterback-rich western Pennsylvania. Montana was ranked number thirty-three on the Cowboys draft board, which means he would have been a reach with their first-round pick and would have been a bargain if he was still available in the second or third round. In their own backyard, three months earlier on New Year's Day, the collegiate version of Joe Cool emerged when he battled the flu in the Cotton Bowl in Dallas, drank some chicken bouillon and some coffee in the locker room, and led the Fighting Irish to a stirring 35–34 victory over Houston after they had trailed by 22 points in the fourth quarter.

"It was the coldest game I played in," Montana said. "I never come from the sidelines to the heater very often. I always felt I was colder when I left the heater. That day I ran to the heater as soon as I came off the field. I had hypothermia."

Brandt was always finding a way to get close to college coaches in the hope they would give him inside information on their players. The Cowboys emptied their equipment room and supplied Notre Dame with cold weather gear to combat an ice storm that had paralyzed the city.

Landry would have enjoyed coaching Montana and would have altered his system to capitalize on his unique skills. "He would have been fun to play for," Montana said.

But Landry looked at him as a wasted draft pick. "If we take him, I'll probably cut him in training camp," Landry declared in the draft room.

Montana laughed when he heard that. By the time he was 6 yards from the Super Bowl, nobody was laughing anymore—especially not Landry, who desperately wanted to get his team back to the Super Bowl.

Passing up Montana broke every golden rule for the Cowboys: Take the highest-rated player. Never stray from the draft board. Don't worry what position he plays. Replenish the roster with the best players, and then let Landry figure out how to get them on the field. The great ones always find their way.

But then the coach announced that Montana wouldn't even make the team. Brandt loved Montana but agreed with Landry that he was a luxury the Cowboys didn't need. "I just think we'll cut him in camp," Landry said again. "I don't know if initially he will be better than the guys we got."

The Cowboys studied Montana, and he reminded them of White, who by now had returned from the minors and had three years in Landry's system. Montana would be redundant. Walsh didn't have those kind of draft problems in his first year as the 49ers head coach. He could take the third-string cornerback from Appalachian State, and it would be a talent upgrade for his sorry team. Sitting in his tiny office 1,700 miles from Landry in Redwood City, off the Whipple Avenue exit south of San Francisco on the 101,

Walsh knew he needed a creative and resourceful quarterback to implement his system, the West Coast offense. It would later become the most copied offensive approach in NFL history. He didn't need a quarterback with a rocket arm like Terry Bradshaw's or running skills like Roger Staubach's. He needed a game manager to run his precision offense and distribute the ball.

Walsh had agreed to leave Stanford after the 1978 season and coach a 2–14 team whose record reflected its talent. The record was no mistake. The 49ers of '78 were bad.

DeBerg, a Cowboys castoff, started eleven games at quarterback. Scott Bull started the other five. If Walsh was going to evolve into The Genius, neither DeBerg nor Bull could be his quarterback. In the months prior to the 1979 draft, Walsh loved Morehead State's Phil Simms. And with the worst record in the NFL, Walsh should have inherited the first pick in the draft to get his rebuilding off to a quick start. But there was an issue: The previous 49ers regime had traded the choice to the Bills for a washed-up running back named O. J. Simpson. Walsh targeted Simms in the second round. But when the New York Giants stunned the NFL by selecting Simms with the seventh overall pick, Walsh had to call an audible. At the top of the second round, he now felt it was too early to take a quarterback, even Steve Dils, who played for him at Stanford. Instead, Walsh selected UCLA running back/wide receiver James Owens, who was a bigger name in track, finishing sixth in the 110-meter hurdles at the 1976 Olympics in Montreal. "Bill really liked Joe," said John McVay, whom Walsh brought to San Francisco to run the front office while he was on the field coaching. "There were rumors he didn't have a strong arm, didn't have a gun. But he had touch. He had the magic about him."

McVay had been the head coach of the Memphis Southmen in the WFL, and his quarterback was Danny White. When McVay later moved to the Giants as an assistant coach, he kept an eye on White's career. Halfway through the 1976 season, McVay was promoted to Giants head coach after Bill Arnsparger was fired. McVay held that job for three years and might have had it longer if he had been able to complete the one trade he was desperate to make. "I tried to move heaven and earth to get Danny," McVay said.

That would have created an opening on the Dallas quarterback depth chart that did not exist in 1979 when the Cowboys were on the clock in the second round and took cornerback Aaron Mitchell after selecting center Robert Shaw in the first round. The 49ers didn't have their own third-round pick, the first overall in the round. They had sent that to Seattle in a deal for safety Bob Jury. Along with Jury, the 49ers received a third-round pick that originally belonged to the Cowboys, the eighty-second overall, the last pick in the third round. Seattle got it when they swapped third-round picks with the Cowboys in addition to receiving defensive end Bill Gregory. The deal did not make big headlines.

When the Cowboys were back on the clock in the third round, Montana was by far the highest-rated player left on their board. Out in Redwood City, Walsh was nervous. Montana was number thirty-three on the Cowboys board. The draft was all the way up to number seventy-six. Montana was great value. But why take a player Landry was going to cut? Instead, the Cowboys selected Santa Clara tight end Doug Cosbie, projected as the eventual replacement for Billy Joe DuPree.

Six spots later, it was Walsh's turn. He still needed a quarterback. He was selecting with the pick that originally belonged to the Cowboys.

Right up until two weeks before the draft, Walsh intended to use his third-round pick on Dils. Coaches love to jump-start their program with players they have coached who are familiar with their system, and Dils would have shortened the transition period. Walsh's plan was to take Owens in the second round and Dils in the third. He made that known in the 49ers offices. And with just ten days left before the draft, Walsh dispatched Sam Wyche, the 49ers' passing-game director, to work out Owens at UCLA. The scouting department heard through the grapevine that Montana was living in Manhattan Beach, right next to Los Angeles, and Wyche arranged for him to join Owens for the workout. It made sense. Owens needed someone to throw him the ball. And it would give Wyche an opportunity to see Montana in person.

"We were going to take Dils," Wyche said. "The advantage being he knew Bill's offense. Steve Dils was a good quarterback." But then . . .

"Joe had a terrific workout," Wyche said.

It happened pretty much in solitude. No other teams were there. No other players were there. "Joe's girlfriend at the time was in the stands," Wyche said. "James and Joe and I were pretty much it."

Wyche reported back to Walsh. "I told him Steve Dils was a very good player and I liked him, but there was something special about this kid from Notre Dame," he said. "He threw a very catchable ball. It arrived soft. He was very accurate, he had very quick feet and had natural instincts."

A few days later, Wyche went back to Los Angeles to work out Owens and Montana again. This time Walsh went with him. "James Owens had a poorer workout the second time, and Joe Montana looked as good or better," Wyche said.

Walsh and Wyche went to the airport for the short flight north to San Francisco. They sat across from each other in aisle seats. Walsh leaned over to whisper to Wyche. "I'm going to tell the staff we are going to take Owens in the second round and Montana in the third," Walsh said.

"After Joe's workout, I'd hate to see us lose him," Wyche replied.

Walsh gambled that Montana would not be taken in the first eighty-one picks. Years later, Wyche was told by friends from teams drafting right ahead of San Francisco that there were fights in their draft rooms over Montana. They all passed. Jack Thompson, Simms, and Steve Fuller were the only quarterbacks picked in the first round. No quarterbacks went in the second or the third rounds until Montana was taken by the 49ers, with the choice originally belonging to the Cowboys, on the round's last pick. How does this happen? How can the player who turns out to be among the greatest in NFL history last so long unclaimed? How do the scouts miss so badly? How do the Steelers cut Johnny Unitas?

"Paul Brown told me never to use the word luck," Wyche said. "It's good fortune."

The Patriots know about that kind of good fortune. In 2000, Tom Brady, a Montana clone, was the 199th player picked. He lasted until the sixth round. Six quarterbacks were selected ahead of him. Where was four-and-one-half-year-old Tom Brady on January 10, 1982? The Bay Area native from San Mateo was in the Candlestick stands watching Joe Montana, his hero, drive the 49ers to the Super Bowl.

"I don't remember much from the game other than I cried when Dwight Clark made The Catch," Brady said. "Not because I was happy or excited, but because everybody stood up and I couldn't see! It is pretty cool to think I was at that game . . . [Montana] was and will always be the greatest quarterback ever to play."

Montana was a product of Walsh's system. He was born to play in the West Coast offense. He became the NFL's all-time best quarterback playing for Walsh. Could he have made it in another system playing for a different coach?

"It was a great fit for me," Montana said. "On the whole, as skinny as I was, I was still pretty resilient when it came to going through changes and fighting through different obstacles. I still felt I would have made it somewhere. Maybe not to the degree of the success, but I still think I would have made it. When I was in college, I had no clue. I was just hoping for an opportunity to make it in the NFL, never thinking that I would."

In the tenth round in 1979, Walsh figured he had nothing to lose and took Clemson receiver Dwight Clark, who looked more like a basketball player. He liked what he saw when Clark did him a favor and caught passes as Walsh was working out Fuller, the Clemson quarterback. The Steelers and Chiefs were the only other teams that bothered to put Clark through a workout. The Cowboys had Drew Pearson, Tony Hill, and Butch Johnson, the best group of receivers in the league. Landry didn't have to bother announcing to Brandt and Schramm that he would cut Clark, too.

The Cowboys' grade on Clark: "Undraftable," Brandt said.

"I've heard that," Clark said.

The 49ers fell in love with Montana when they needed someone to throw the ball to Owens. Walsh fell in love with Clark when he needed someone to catch the ball from Fuller. Montana and Clark would soon be playing catch with each other.

Sprint Right Option.

It was one of the standard plays of Walsh's complicated passing game. The 49ers scored the first touchdown of the game on it when Montana hit Solomon at the 7-yard line and he burst into the end zone through cornerback Dennis Thurman's weak tackle attempt at the 4 to complete the 8-yard score. They practiced it all the time. Now, after Elliott ran the ball to the Dallas 6, Walsh called time-out with 58 seconds left. Montana came over to the sideline and stared intently at Walsh. Solomon would be option number one.

"We're going to call a Sprint Option pass. He's going to break up and break into the corner. You got it? Dwight will clear," Walsh said.

"OK," Montana said.

"As soon as you see the angle he's breaking, then just drop the ball up there. If you don't get what you want, simply throw the ball away. You know what I mean?" Walsh said.

"OK."

"Hold it, hold it, not there, away it goes."

"OK."

"Be ready to go to Dwight. You got it?"

Montana then walked back to the huddle, and Walsh momentarily turned his back to the field. He then quickly spun around and yelled to Montana, "Sprint Option."

Montana was too far away to hear him. He already knew the play.

The way the play was drawn up, Clark would be open if Solomon wasn't and if Ed Jones didn't flatten Montana first. "Everybody was worn out," Clark said. "It had been a grueling game. We all had our hands on our knees."

Montana didn't flinch. "When Joe came into the huddle, he was pretty matter-of-fact," Clark said. "He was very calm."

Montana took the snap from center Fred Quillan and immediately rolled to his right. Clark's first assignment was to set a pick on Thurman. But Solomon slipped as he angled to his right behind Clark, ruining the timing of the play. All hell broke loose. Montana kept rolling to his right, kept rolling with Too Tall Jones, Larry Bethea, and D. D. Lewis chasing after him like wild dogs. Montana knew where Clark was going to be. They'd practiced this play all season, going all the way back to training camp. Too Tall had his arms up and with that wingspan as wide as the Golden Gate Bridge; Montana had an obstructed view, as in those seats behind all the poles in the lower deck at Candlestick.

Clark lost sight of Montana, who was running for his life with over seven hundred pounds of crazed Cowboys in pursuit. Montana never lost sight of Clark running along the back line of the end zone. Then Clark saw the ball come flying out and knew this was going to have to be the catch of his life. Bethea pushed Montana down to the turf just after he let go. Montana had no idea what happened next until the sound of the crowd told him. Once the ball left his right hand, he never saw Clark again—had no idea how he caught it, just that he caught it. Right then, nothing else mattered.

There have been other great catches, of course. Franco Harris's Immaculate Reception to beat the Raiders in the 1972 AFC Championship Game, Lynn Swann's leaping 53-yard catch against Dallas in Super Bowl X, Roger Staubach's Hail Mary to Drew Pearson, and then years later, David Tyree's helmet catch to set up the Giants' winning touchdown against the undefeated Patriots in Super Bowl XLII, followed the next year by Pittsburgh's Santonio Holmes's terrific corner-of-the-end-zone catch to beat the Cardinals in Super Bowl XLIII.

But when you say The Catch, there is only one. It's Montana to Clark. Montana was sprawled on the turf, Clark jumped higher than he ever had in his life or ever would again.

Franchises, careers, lives, and dynasties all changed with one play.

1

"RESPECT THAT . . ."

BILL WALSH stood on the sidelines minutes before the kick-off of the 1981 NFC Championship Game and pulled his headset into place, the biggest moment of his professional life about to play out in front of him. Tom Landry's dark gray fedora sat so perfectly on his bald head that it looked permanently attached. Landry's stoic game-day demeanor and public image were a source of constant ridicule—he was emotionless, a stone face, or "plastic man," as Duane Thomas once called him—but he truly had an underrated, though not life-of-the-party, personality.

Walsh possessed a huge ego, and once he became a Super Bowl champion, he never protested too hard when he was declared The Genius. So what if he spoke as if he'd invented football rather than just advanced the game with his innovative offensive system? He retired with three Super Bowl rings in ten seasons and could have won at least a couple more if he didn't walk away less than one week after winning his third championship. He lived the final eighteen years of his life regretting that emotional decision to leave with his career and his team in its prime. Coaching was still a part of him. That's why he returned to Stanford in the early nineties and coached three more years. That core group of 49ers won two more championships for George Seifert, completing the run that Walsh set the foundation for when he was hired in 1979.

Landry had a rather large ego himself, but it was much more

understated. His self-assuredness came through in his stubbornness. It was the Landry way or go play in purgatory for the Falcons or Cardinals. He was slow to adapt to the changing game and a new generation of players through the eighties, one of the main reasons for the Cowboys' demise. Either way, these two Hall of Fame coaches were outwardly calm moments before Ray Wersching kicked the ball off to Timmy Newsome, setting off three hours of frantic football and putting an exclamation point on a week with some of the best trash-talking the NFL had ever seen.

The Cowboys were the establishment. They were in five of the first fifteen Super Bowls, winning two of them. And when the 49ers followed up their two championship-game losses in the early seventies with another loss to the Cowboys the next year in the divisional round, they went into a free fall, failing to make the playoffs for the next eight seasons and only once managing to win more games than they lost. They switched coaches as often as Landry had changed his fedora. And Landry had a lot of fedoras. When Walsh was hired, he was their sixth coach in five years, including interims.

This was not a true blood-and-guts, down-and-dirty NFL rivalry. The 49ers played in the NFC West, and the Rams were the team they went into overdrive working themselves up to play twice a year. Dallas showed up on their schedule every now and then, but when one team is good and the other is bad, the game doesn't generate much passion. The Cowboys played in the NFC East. They faced snowballs in Philly. In Washington, the two most popular souvenirs were FUCK DALLAS pins and T-shirts that said, I ROOT FOR TWO TEAMS: THE REDSKINS AND WHOEVER IS PLAYING DALLAS." In New York, the fans would drop an f-bomb or two, but a noticeable chunk of Cowboys fans still managed to scoop up tickets every year when Dallas played at Giants Stadium.

The Cowboys were more insulted than impressed when Montana and the 49ers tarnished the glitzy star on their helmets with a

45–14 beating in the sixth game of the 1981 season. It was 21–0 after the first quarter. The 49ers had 440 yards offense and held the Cowboys to 192. The 49ers ran 80 plays. The Cowboys just 53. It was a complete butt-kicking. That didn't make the Cowboys respect the 49ers or even hate them, which infuriated the Niners. All Dallas did was rationalize the loss by saying the real 'Boys didn't show up. From that point forward, the 49ers had one wish for January: We want Dallas.

The 49ers quickly learned to hate Ed "Too Tall" Jones. He worked the 49ers into a rage during the week before the NFC title game by belittling them and their quarterback. But at one point, Montana faked Jones into running right by him, then completed a long pass to Clark. Montana, normally a mild-mannered choirboy then became a foul-mouthed trash-talker whenever Jones got close enough.

Jones, an imposing figure at six nine, was in his second season back with the Cowboys after taking a one-year sabbatical to pursue his real love—professional boxing, of all things. Jones had been the first overall pick in the 1974 draft, and he combined with Harvey "Too Mean" Martin to provide Dallas with a fearsome pass rush. But Jones gave the Cowboys a one-year notice that when his contract expired after his option-year season in 1978 that he was leaving to give the sweet science a shot. The Cowboys drafted Michigan State defensive lineman Larry Bethea in the first round in '78 with the idea that he would be groomed in his rookie year by Jones and then take over, assuming Jones didn't have second thoughts about getting his ass kicked for a living.

Jones did leave the Cowboys for the ring but wasn't gone long: one NFL season. He retired with a 6–0 record with five knockouts against a bunch of tomato cans. With his height, 88-inch reach, and freakish athletic ability, the measurables were certainly there for him to work his way up the rankings to get a shot at heavyweight champion Larry Holmes. Unfortunately, he didn't have the skills that would ever make him more than a curiosity, if not a freak show, because of his immense size and NFL stardom. All six of his fights were nationally televised. He took boxing seriously even if boxing didn't take him seriously. "I loved every minute of it," he said. "I played football at 274 pounds. When I went to New York to continue my boxing training, I weighed 254. I went down to 236. I conditioned myself as well as I could."

The Cowboys were playing on the road against the Giants the day after Jones's first professional bout on November 3, 1979. The team set up a television in a meeting room of their New Jersey hotel, and the players gathered around to watch their former and future teammate take on Yaqui Meneses in Las Cruces, New Mexico, a venue that was not to be confused with Madison Square Garden or Caesars Palace. Unfortunately, Jones's teammates were more amused than impressed. His pass rush carried a bigger wallop than his left hook. He won a six-round majority decision, even though he was knocked down in the final round. "This is not going to last long. Ed has no chance of becoming heavyweight champion," Dennis Thurman said. "He will be back with us."

Nobody argued with Thurman. Jones looked awkward in the ring, even against a bunch of nobodies and stiffs lined up for him to throw out with the trash. His Cowboys teammates supported him at ringside at a fight in Dallas, but it was clear the big guy was much more at home on a football field chasing Terry Bradshaw, and they were sure he would be back with them in 1980. He left boxing after registering a one-round knockout of somebody named Rocky Gonzalez on January 26, 1980, in Jackson, Mississippi. His six opponents had a career record of 37–86–1. He was more effective teaming with Randy White, Martin, and John Dutton to form the NFC's best front line, second only to that of Pittsburgh in the NFL. Then and even now Jones refuses to divulge the reason he quit boxing, as if he were protecting a government secret. He didn't even tell his teammates why he gave up his dream of wearing the heavyweight championship belt. He was a big man who had a very small inner circle. "Nobody has come close to figuring out why I gave it up," Jones said. "I can't wait to set the record straight. But not yet."

Thurman doesn't know why there is such a mystery. "I just figured his boxing career wasn't very good," he said.

In boxing, Jones could say whatever he wanted about an opponent, knowing he was responsible only for himself. He didn't have to worry about the Niners going for Randy White's knees in retaliation for something Too Tall said. Back in football, his words affected the entire team—which made his comments that appeared in the *Dallas Times Herald* five days before the championship game in San Francisco even more surprising. Jones was not loud in the locker room, and he was not loud on the field. He was not a trash-talker. He was more likely to beat you up and then help you up. He was a gentle giant and a real ladies' man, although he never married. So the comments attributed to him regarding the regular season loss were out of character: "To be really honest, I didn't have a whole lot of respect for the 49ers before that game," Jones said, speaking of the 45–14 embarrassment. "I played hard. But I still didn't think they could beat us regardless of what happened. I didn't know half the names of the whole team. Things started happening so fast that we couldn't get control of the game."

It was understandable for Jones to feel that way before the loss. But after it, too? "Believe it or not, I didn't have a whole lot of respect for them after it was over," he was quoted in January 1982. "I didn't think there would be any rematch in the playoffs. Even though they beat us that day, they didn't beat the real Cowboys." Then, just to make sure the 49ers were paying attention, Jones insulted Montana: "All you have to do against that guy is throw off his timing and you blow his game."

The Bay Area newspapers picked up the story, and it provided instant bulletin-board material for a young 49ers team that really didn't require any more motivation. But it was right there in black and white for them to read. "C'mon, gimme a break," Cross said, still angry at Jones years later. "We knew we had to prove a point."

Montana thought he did in the championship game when he ran a Naked Bootleg with Jones bearing down on him and he connected with Clark on a 38-yard completion on the 49ers' fifth offensive play of the second quarter. "He came in and it was him and I," Montana said. "He tried to cut me off and I stepped up and then underneath and I threw about a 30-yard pass to Dwight. He kind of shook his head."

After Clark caught the pass, Montana turned around and saw Jones. They were alone for a second. "Respect that, motherfucker," Montana said.

Cross said Montana's gibe at Jones didn't please the man who was blocking him. "Keith Fahnhorst is going, 'Joe! Joe! Joe!'"

Jones said he doesn't remember saying anything derogatory about the 49ers or Montana before the game. "I don't understand how that got out," he said. Even on a segment on the CBS pregame show on the trash talk, Brent Musburger mentioned, "Surprisingly, the most outspoken player has been Too Tall Jones of the Dallas Cowboys."

Montana wasn't doing Fahnhorst any favors by insulting Jones, who was already frustrated by not getting his hands on the quarterback before he threw the pass to Clark. Why make him mad, too? Before he could retaliate against Montana, he would have to get through Fahnhorst. Montana had just given Jones more incentive. Montana also decided to take on Martin, the Cowboys other dynamic pass rusher. "I don't want to say he was having a tough day, but our guys played pretty well," Montana said. "He finally came in and sacked me or knocked me down, and he said, 'I will be back.' I said, 'I hope so. I was beginning to think you weren't in the game.' Randy [Cross] goes, 'Why do you have to say that to my guy.' I said, 'Randy, you've been playing well all day. What difference is it going to make?' There was a lot of battling back and forth, wordswise. They said some crazy things during the game."

Well, Cross didn't really have to worry too much. He was lined up against Larry Bethea, the weakest of the Cowboys' four linemen. Bethea was subbing for John Dutton, who was injured.

Dallas wide receiver Drew Pearson, who was never reluctant to get in the middle of any verbal warfare, even went on the CBS pregame show and recited a poem that he taped during the week and aired fifteen minutes prior to kickoff. It's a shame the 49ers were too busy at that point to be watching television or they surely would have enjoyed Pearson's grammar-school-quality composition:

Nothing will be finer
Than to get another chance at the San Francisco 49ers.
We'll teach them not to toy
With the Dallas Cowboys.
I know the mud will be thick,
In Candlestick.
But on Sunday,
All they'll say,
Is that it's D-day on the Bay.

Pearson then looked in the camera and laughed. "Heh, heh, heh." Robert Frost must have been turning over in his grave.

The mind games even extended to the owner's box. Eddie De-Bartolo, the 49ers brash owner, who was younger than many of his players, put himself right into the middle of it. He was just thirty years old in 1977 when his father, Ed DeBartolo Sr., purchased the 49ers for $17 million and put his son in control. Ed Jr. was beloved by his players. He was generous with them, flying them to road games on wide-body DC-10s, serving them gourmet meals in flight, and later taking them to lavish vacation getaways to celebrate Super Bowl championships, before such excursions counted against the salary cap. It was a sad day around the 49ers when a casino licensing scandal forced him to relinquish control of the team in late 1997 to his sister Denise and her husband, Dr. John York. He was suspended by NFL commissioner Paul Tagliabue for the 1999 season and by 2000 had reached an agreement with his sister that severed his ties to the organization.

In the locker room after the Niners beat the Giants in the divisional round to set up their showdown with Dallas, Eddie was being interviewed on national TV when he said, "I heard [Tony] Dorsett on the television saying that if they come out here it's going to be vindictive. All I can say to him is, 'They ate it once. They can eat it again.'"

Dorsett then shot back at DeBartolo: "I'm surprised to hear an owner even talk that way. I thought they were a little bit more classy organization than that." He was just getting warmed up. "This is a players game, not the owners game," Dorsett continued. "The owner will sit up there in his box and drink his champagne and his caviar and all that and sit and try to watch his team. It doesn't make a difference to me what he says."

Walsh made sure his players didn't say anything inflammatory about the Cowboys. But he couldn't tell the owner what to say. "Eddie said everything we wanted to say," Dwight Clark said. "He was talking junk to them: 'We'll see if the real Cowboys show.' We should have blown them out in the championship game, too. We had six turnovers. I think about that all the time. We should have beaten them by four touchdowns. That's the sign of a good team. Overcoming adversity."

When DeBartolo was reminiscing more than twenty-five years

later, he laughed about an owner trash-talking with an All-Pro running back. "First of all, I don't drink champagne," he said. "And I hate caviar."

It was a gorgeous day in the Bay Area, fifty-five degrees and sunny, the rain of the past week long gone, and virtually no wind. The field had patches where the sod had been replaced, easily spotted by different shades of green, but the rain the previous week compromised the footing, and players would slip all afternoon.

The Cowboys won the coin toss and elected to receive. For the next three hours and thirteen minutes, NFL fans would witness a classic, more for its dramatic moments than for its artistic beauty: six lead changes, nine turnovers, two huge pass-interference calls on Ronnie Lott, the greatest catch in NFL history, a dynasty dying in the dirt on a last-second fumble, and Tom Landry and Bill Walsh, coaches who would later be enshrined in the Pro Football Hall of Fame, trying to outthink each other.

Landry was dressed for the occasion, as always: blue sports jacket, gray slacks, striped tie, playsheet in hand, dark gray hat, no headset. Walsh was wearing a white sweater with the 49ers logo on the left breast, over a white shirt with tan pants. Unlike Landry, he used a headset to be in constant communication with his assistants sitting in the coaches' booth upstairs. He was also wearing glasses.

Ray Wersching got the game off to a sloppy start by sending the kickoff out of bounds. But then the 49ers picked up where they left off in the regular season game. After the Cowboys went three and out on the first series, with Dwayne Board sacking Danny White for an 11-yard loss on third down, the 49ers started at their own 37-yard line. Montana, with his dirty blond hair long enough in the back that it curled up outside his helmet, set the 49ers agenda right away: They were going after Everson Walls, the rookie left cornerback. He made the Cowboys as a free agent and quickly became a heartwarming story. He was a native of Dallas, went to Grambling, played for the great Eddie Robinson, but was not among the 332 players drafted by the twenty-eight teams during twelve rounds. He went on to lead the league with 11 interceptions as a rookie, outplaying Lott, who was the eighth overall pick in the same draft that overlooked Walls.

Montana connected with Mike Shumann, with Walls covering him, on the right sideline for 11 yards. Later, with Too Tall's hands in his face, he hit tight end Charle Young for 17 yards, then another 24 to running back Lenvil Elliott, quickly setting up the 49ers with a first and goal from the Cowboys 8. Walsh sent in the play that would put the 49ers on top 7–0.

It was called Sprint Right Option.

Solomon was the primary receiver. He was a second-round pick of the Dolphins in 1975 from the University of Tampa, where he played quarterback. Don Shula converted him into a wide receiver, and he was traded to the 49ers in 1978, the season before Walsh's arrival. The 49ers dealt running back Delvin Williams to Miami for Solomon, safety Vern Roberson, and first- and fifth-round picks in the 1978 draft. Solomon had a charmed career playing for a pair of Hall of Fame coaches: three years in Miami for Shula, the NFL's all-time winningest coach, and then five years in San Francisco for Walsh. He was one of only nine players remaining from the team Walsh inherited.

"They were two great coaches," Solomon said. "Their records speak for themselves. I enjoyed the experience with both coaches. As a young player, there were a lot of things I didn't know that I picked up. Playing for Bill was a great experience. His mind was more passing oriented. Don Shula was more run, then pass. Run on first and second down and maybe pass on third down. Bill would pass on any down. He would also run the football on any down. Coach Shula was more control the football, like the old style. Three

yards and a cloud of dust. Bill was more wide open, and he would attack the defense."

Solomon would play a significant role in the 49ers championship-
game victory over the Cowboys. With not even five minutes gone in
the first quarter, Solomon came in motion behind Montana from left
to right. He flared out, and Montana, who was rolling to his right, hit
him with a short pass at the seven. He was wide open. Thurman moved
into position to make the tackle at the four, went low, and threw his
body at him, never trying to use his hands to bring him down, and
Solomon ran right over him and dived into the end zone.

Counting the game from October, the 49ers had now out-
scored the Cowboys 52–14. Candlestick was partying. The 49ers
were motivated to get to the Super Bowl, of course, but also to prove
to the Cowboys that October was no fluke. The 49ers had been rooting for the Cowboys to make it to the title game with them. They
wanted to humiliate them again. Dallas had shown so little fight in
the first game you had to wonder if the players were beginning to
think there was no way they were going to stop Montana. But this
was the championship game. The Cowboys had too many proud
players to get blown out again. Besides, Walsh predicted before the
game, "The winning team will score four touchdowns and the losing team will score three touchdowns."

So there was a long way to go.

Dallas had made a seamless transition from Roger Staubach to
Danny White at quarterback in 1980. Landry prepared White to
take over, and Staubach abruptly retired not long after a playoff loss
to the Rams in 1979. He had suffered at least ten concussions in his
football career, so many that he lost count, but he knew it was too
many to keep playing.

White was only 8 of 16 for 60 yards with 2 interceptions in the
regular-season loss to the Niners. Landry benched him late in the
third quarter with the game out of reach. But now he had to

prevent what happened last time when the 49ers took a three-touchdown lead after the first quarter. He had to find a way to put points on the board to let the 49ers know they were going to be here all day.

On the fifth play of the Cowboys' second possession, Dorsett went around the right side for nine yards. But as safety Dwight Hicks was moving in to help on the tackle, Dorsett slipped and Hicks went flying by. The heel of his left foot nailed Dorsett in the left eye. Hicks was the veteran presence in the 49ers secondary to go along with cornerbacks Lott and Eric Wright and safety Carlton Williamson, who were all rookies. He was the calming influence among a bunch of kids.

"Dwight Hicks and the Hot Licks," McVay said.

Walsh took Lott from Southern Cal in the first round, Wright from Missouri in the second, and Williamson from Pitt in the third. He filled 75 percent of the starting jobs in one shot, ending a comical revolving door in the secondary. "I want to say it was Bill's first year, in 1979, we were at Santa Clara for training camp," Cross said. "We went through so many defensive backs—we had a dozen or so that never had two meals. They never even got their names written on tape on their helmets, they were there for such a short period of time. The number I heard at the time was thirty-something defensive backs. It was amazing. For no other reason than these three guys were drafted so high, they weren't going to cut them. So just to see some talent and some stability—they looked good."

Hicks was a sixth-round pick of the Lions in 1978 but wound up playing that season for the Toronto Argonauts in the Canadian Football League. He was one of the ten thousand defensive backs Walsh ran through the organization in 1979 trying to discover anybody who could play. "I found Dwight Hicks working at a health food store in Detroit," McVay said. "We were looking everywhere for players."

He inadvertently kicked Dorsett out of the game. Hicks was an impact player, but the biggest impact he made in this game was with Dorsett's left eye. "I got caught with a shoe," Dorsett said. "I'm on the ground. It's like a free play. A shoe came and hit me just perfectly right up under my eye. I got blurred vision and it blackened my eye. I can be on the ground about a zillion times and would not get hit in the eye like that."

Dorsett was down for awhile, walked to the sidelines, applied an ice pack to his eye, and James Jones came in to replace him. On the first play after Dorsett was sidelined, White completed a 20-yard pass to Butch Johnson to the San Francisco 34. But with Dorsett missing the rest of this series and the next three, it was up to Jones to carry the load. He was a poor man's Dorsett. In spurts, he could be effective. Over the long haul, he was not. After Johnson picked up the first down, the ball went to Jones three consecutive times: a 2-yard loss on a draw play, a 6-yard gain on another draw, and a 3-yard reception to the 49ers 27 that left the Cowboys 3 yards short of the first down.

That brought Rafael Septien into the game to attempt a 44-yard field goal. He had an excellent season, hitting all but two of his field goal attempts, but like most kickers, he had a fragile psyche. And he was playing with a physical ailment the team knew about but decided it was in his best interest not to tell him about. Septien was diagnosed with a hernia early in the season after hurting himself lifting weights in training camp, but when the Cowboys doctors determined he could not injure himself further by continuing to kick, they elected not to let him in on their secret. They told him he had a pulled groin muscle. The team doctors work for the team, and that raised an ethical issue. Should the doctors' first responsibility be to the team or to the player? Of course it should be to the player.

But the Cowboys were worried that if they told Septien about the hernia, he would go headfirst into the tank.

"Everybody, Landry included, knew I had a hernia. They've admitted it," Septien said after off-season surgery. "But they just told me, 'You pulled a groin.' Then when the season is all over, they change their minds and tell me I have a hernia, too, and I have to have an operation."

Landry said it was his decision not to tell Septien after he gathered information from the team doctors. "I became aware sometime during the season that it was probably a hernia," Landry said. "Doctors said it was something that could be handled after the season. In that case, you go ahead and let him play. You tell him, and he worries and doesn't kick well. We just didn't tell him. It's no big deal. It was my responsibility to decide what to do once I had the opinion of the doctors. It's nothing to me. If I had to do it again, I'd do the same thing."

What Septien didn't know would not hurt him. Ignorance is bliss. "Even if they had told me, I would have kept playing," Septien said. "You cannot afford to be hurt because then they get somebody else."

Septien drilled the 44-yard field goal, and the Cowboys moved to within 7–3.

The game took a quick turn moments later. On a third and 2 from their own 28, Montana handed off to running back Bill Ring trying to pick up the first down. Ring fumbled. The 49ers led the NFL with a plus-23 turnover ratio during the regular season. The Cowboys were second at plus-18. But the first one went to Dallas. Mike Hegman recovered Ring's bobble at the 29-yard line. Jones, still in the game for Dorsett, managed to pick up three yards on first down. Then White hit Tony Hill in stride at the goal line for the Cowboys' first touchdown. It was a perfectly thrown ball with Hill hugging the left sideline just by the pylon. Hill beat Wright, who would make up for it much later in the game. Wright, whose bump and run technique barely bothered Hill at the line, never looked back for the ball as it came sailing down into Hill's arms.

Hill also beat Pearson and Johnson as the first of Dallas's wide receivers to score. The three of them were extremely competitive with each other. Johnson was the best number-three receiver in the league, and he was always lobbying Landry for more playing time. He wanted Pearson's job. He wanted Hill's job. That caused friction among all three of them. Pearson told Johnson to forget about getting his job. And Hill wasn't giving up his, either. So Johnson sulked.

And now that Hill was in the end zone, the score was Dallas 10, San Francisco 7, Hill 1, Pearson 0, Johnson 0.

2

THE GENIUS

TOM LANDRY was the only coach the Cowboys ever had for their first twenty-nine seasons. Even when he was 13–38–3 in his opening four years after Dallas entered the NFL as an expansion team, and the football-crazed fans in Texas were calling for him to be fired, owner Clint Murchison quickly ended any speculation that he was going to dump Landry. With one year left on his contract, Murchison gave Landry an unprecedented ten-year extension, the ultimate vote of confidence and commitment.

"That was the most significant thing that ever happened to me," Landry said. "Everybody thought Clint was going to make a coaching change. From then, I really dedicated myself to be a football coach. Clint Murchison was so important to the long streak we had. He never put pressure on me, never asked me a question in all those years. Anytime we got in a slump, he was the first to write a note with something clever on it."

Ed DeBartolo Jr. was looking for that kind of stability when he sat down in a one-bedroom suite on the eleventh floor of the Fairmont Hotel in downtown San Francisco. He set up a meeting with Stanford coach Bill Walsh as the 1978 season, another dismal one for the 49ers, was mercifully coming to an end. Eddie D was still shuttling between the family's business base in Youngstown, Ohio, and San Francisco and hadn't yet moved into the small apartment down the street from the Fairmont that would soon become his West Coast home.

While DeBartolo was talking business with Walsh on the eleventh floor, his wife, Candy, and mother, Marie, were having lunch downstairs in the hotel restaurant with Walsh's wife, Geri. As the ladies chatted away, it didn't take long for DeBartolo to figure out he'd found the perfect match. "Honest to God, within ten minutes, I knew he was the guy," DeBartolo said. Five minutes later, they shook hands on a deal.

DeBartolo was an intense competitor with a boyish charm who was willing to provide the organization with anything it needed to win: money, wide-body planes, a new training facility. But these were the days before free agency, so he could only do so much to upgrade the talent on the field. He had to use the conventional methods: the draft, rookie free agents, trades, and veterans cut by other teams. His checkbook was no factor. He could not buy himself a Super Bowl. The best players were not for sale. Sure, he wanted to keep his core guys happy once the 49ers started to win, but the best plan was to hire a football man who knew what he was doing and let him find the right personnel to make a run at a championship. Walsh planned the most creative offense in the business, but it took intelligence to grasp his system. He wanted resourceful players, intelligent players. He wanted impact players. Nobody coming up with single digits on the Wonderlic Personnel Test, which is the indicator teams use to find out if a player has the smarts to devour and comprehend the playbook.

Walsh was forty-seven years old, and although that certainly didn't mean his window of opportunity for becoming an NFL coach had closed, his silver hair made him look at least ten years older. Across the bay in Oakland, Al Davis hired John Madden when he was just thirty-two. Don Shula got his first head-coaching job in

Baltimore when he was thirty-three. Walsh had more than paid his dues. Now it was time to cash in after years of disappointment. Just a year earlier, it looked as though the Rams were going to hire him, but they went for Ray Malavasi instead. Malavasi took the Rams to the Super Bowl in his third season, despite just a 9–7 record; they lost to the Steelers. Walsh never got over the heartache of NFL legend Paul Brown passing him up when he retired after the 1975 season and naming another Bengals assistant, the less-heralded offensive-line coach Bill "Tiger" Johnson, to replace him. There were reports that Walsh was so upset he even cried.

He saw men of lesser ability jumping over him in line and becoming head coaches. He heard that he wasn't tough enough, that he was too scholarly, that if he was in charge of an entire team, the players would walk over him.

"If there is an intellectual side of football, I was heavily entrenched in that, because I was calling the plays, putting the game plan together, things of that nature," he once told NFL Films. "People had come to the conclusion nobody can have that kind of an intellectual approach to the game and be tough.

"I recall Al Davis calling one day and saying to me, 'Bill, are you tough enough to be a head coach?' I said, 'Al, just look, if you want to talk about toughness, I was an amateur fighter, had seventy bouts. What do you need?' "

Walsh had no interest in remaining with the Bengals to work for Johnson and immediately left to run the Chargers offense. Looking back, Brown made a horrible mistake. Walsh paid Brown back by twice beating his Bengals in the Super Bowl. But at the time, Johnson was considered a solid choice. He was 10–4 in his first season, 8–6 in his second year, and he resigned or was fired after an 0–5 start in 1978 that was a direct result of quarterback Ken Anderson breaking his throwing hand on a helmet in the final preseason game and missing the first two games of the regular season.

"Tiger Johnson was a hell of a football coach," Bengals guard Dave Lapham said. "Obviously everyone wanted [Walsh] to stay, because he was talented. I honestly think the reason Bill left is because he thought Tiger was going to be here 10, 15 more years."

Brown had hired Walsh in the Bengals expansion year in 1968 to coach tight ends. Two years earlier, Walsh had been the Raiders running-backs coach, but in 1967 he coached the San Jose Apaches, a semipro team. Taking a job with Brown was a no-brainer for Walsh, who was very ambitious. Brown was a legend, and Walsh had a chance to be part of a start-up company. If Brown could get the Bengals going in the right direction, it would enhance Walsh's chances of becoming an NFL head coach, his ultimate goal. And who knows? Depending on how long Brown stuck around, he might even be in line to replace him.

Seven months before Walsh died of leukemia on July 30, 2007, he did an interview with the *Los Angeles Times*. He claimed that Brown "worked against my candidacy," to be a head coach anywhere in the NFL. "All the way through I had opportunities, and I never knew about them," Walsh said. "And then when I left him, he called whoever he thought was necessary to keep me out of the league."

Walsh was asked if it was jealousy. "I can't say," he said. "He did that to other people, too, it wasn't just me. But I was probably the most blatant one."

It was in Cincinnati that Walsh established the groundwork for the West Coast offense that Montana would run to perfection. Walsh was strongly influenced by Brown and another legend, Sid Gillman. The offense was predicated on a short passing game doing the job of the running game—especially if one didn't exist—to keep the ball and the chains moving. "It was born of an expansion franchise that just didn't have near the talent to compete," Walsh once said. "That was probably the worst-stocked franchise in the history of the NFL."

Walsh needed to keep the Bengals defense off the field, too, and that meant eating up the clock on offense. "We couldn't control the football with the run. Teams were just too strong," he said. "So it had to be the forward pass, and obviously it had to be a high-percentage, short, controlled passing game. So through a series of formation-changing and timed passes—using all eligible receivers, especially the fullback—we were able to put together an offense and develop it over a period of time."

Walsh helped develop Greg Cook in Cincinnati, and when injuries curtailed what looked like a very promising career, his next project was Anderson. In Walsh's final season working with him in 1975, Anderson threw 21 TDs and was voted second-team All Pro and first-team All AFC and made the Pro Bowl for the first time. Brown still passed on Walsh and promoted Johnson. Walsh was frustrated. Even his own boss didn't think he was worthy of succeeding him. He had something in common with Montana, who years later was slipping through the draft despite his special talents, until Walsh rescued him at the end of the third round. The desire to show all those who didn't think they were good enough drove these men.

Walsh went to San Diego for one year and had the good fortune to inherit Dan Fouts. In his one season with Walsh, the future Hall of Fame quarterback threw 14 touchdown passes after a total of 16 his first three seasons. And it was no coincidence that three of the four starting quarterbacks in the conference championship games following the 1981 season were Walsh disciples: Montana, Anderson, and Fouts. Only Danny White of the Cowboys didn't have a Walsh connection.

"Walsh made me," Anderson said.

"Bill Walsh made all the difference in the world," Fouts said.

Walsh parlayed his one year with the Chargers into the head coaching job at Stanford, where he had been the defensive backfield coach on John Ralston's staff in 1963. In his two years in charge at Stanford, he had a 17–7 record, including victories in the Sun Bowl in 1977 and the Bluebonnet Bowl in 1978. He was born in Los Angeles in 1931, but he was basically back home working in northern California, having spent most of his youth in the Bay Area and then attending San Mateo Junior College and San Jose State.

Whether Walsh was being paranoid about Brown blackballing him or not, the drought ended in the Fairmont Hotel. DeBartolo looked at Walsh, saw a state-of-the-art coach, and determined that this would be the one and only interview he would conduct with any candidate. "I had the names of other coaches, but truthfully, I just wanted to interview Bill," DeBartolo said.

He picked Walsh to revive his team and make the 49ers important in the Bay Area. After firing GM Joe Thomas, he gave Walsh full control of the entire football operation as well. He would get to pick the players and cut the players. His fate would be in his own hands. It was a big job. Even though nobody questioned Walsh's intelligence, the previous highest level he had risen to in the NFL was offensive coordinator for the Chargers. But he soon proved to be one of the best personnel men in the league. He drafted Montana. He found Dwight Clark in the tenth round. In the 1981 draft, he decided he would fix the 49ers secondary in one shot by drafting Ronnie Lott, Eric Wright, and Carlton Williamson, and they all started, from the first game of their rookie season. He acquired future Hall of Fame defensive end Fred Dean during the 1981 season from San Diego, and shortly after joining the Niners, Dean had a dominant game against the Cowboys in San Francisco's 45–14 victory, with three sacks and two passes knocked down.

This was Walsh's chance to end all those years of frustration. He sat on the edge of the hotel bed. DeBartolo sat in a chair by a little round table in front of the window. DeBartolo had owned the 49ers for just two years and had already been through three coaches: Ken

Meyer, whom he inherited and fired, then Pete McCulley, who was 1–8 and fired after nine games, and Fred O'Connor, who finished the season on an interim basis and went 1–6. DeBartolo needed to put an end to the turmoil and find a way to create stability in his organization. Constant change was not the way to win championships. In contrast, Chuck Noll was hired by the Steelers in 1969, won four Super Bowls, and stayed around until he retired and was replaced by Bill Cowher in 1992.

Landry was the perfect example of continuity as the key to success—as long as the right coach is hired, of course. He went to five Super Bowls, winning two. In the twenty-nine seasons he coached the Cowboys, his twenty winning seasons came consecutively from 1966 to 1985, and he made the playoffs eighteen times. On January 9, 1979, three years and one day before Walsh took the 49ers to the NFC Championship Game against Landry's Cowboys, he was introduced as their new head coach.

"It's quite possible in the first year for things to look promising and then level off again the next season," he said at his introductory news conference. "It depends so much on personalities." He would not comment on the players, or rather the lack of players. "I'm not about to remark on a team I haven't had a chance to observe," he said.

Clearly, there was nothing remarkable about the 49ers of 1979. They were lacking personality and personnel. They went 2–14 again. This was not going to be an overnight success story. But DeBartolo and Walsh were in it for the long haul, and Eddie was trusting his instincts and the legwork he'd done before he hired Walsh. "It was just that personality, his deep intuitive thinking," he said. "I saw how really brilliant he was. He always seemed to be a step ahead when you were talking to him. His number-one key was to have players who could think on their own, that were easily coachable."

Walsh pretty much had DeBartolo the moment he walked into the room. DeBartolo set up the interview through a radio friend of his in the Bay Area, and from the start, it was Walsh's job to lose. "He had done some research on the roster," DeBartolo said. "He said, 'We've got a lot of older guys. We're going to have to reshape probably the entire roster.' He said he would have a three- to five-year plan and we absolutely had to be on the same page. He said there are times it's going to look bleak and times when things will look positive. We had our draft, we started the process."

The process got off to a good start. "Joe came in 1979," DeBartolo said.

DeBartolo and Walsh were each taking a chance. Walsh was entering new territory with responsibilities he never had before. DeBartolo was making the hire that would either get his franchise straightened out or send it deeper into the San Francisco Bay. They liked each other. But could they work together? They talked about it.

Walsh: "You have to be sure about this."

DeBartolo: "You know what? I've been with a lot of people. Unfortunately, we've gone through some coaches. We had Joe Thomas here. He was a nice man, but he alienated the fans. Good personnel man, but very difficult to work with. I certainly don't know football like I need to know."

Walsh: "That's my job, too. I will spend the time with you. I will mentor you. I'll have you with me, and we'll go through this thing together."

DeBartolo: "Bill, I think we can make a good team. I would like you to come on board."

The first brick in the construction of a dynasty had been laid.

Walsh needed a right-hand man to oversee the operation while he was coaching the team. He considered Ernie Accorsi, the assistant general manager of the Colts, but Accorsi was looking for a job with more authority. George Young's name came up too. But he had virtually the same job working for Shula in Miami, and there was no need to relocate all the way across the country for a lateral move. One month later, Young was hired as the general manager of the New York Giants. Accorsi later became the GM of the Colts, Browns, and Giants. Walsh turned to John McVay, who had just been fired as the Giants head coach. They'd gotten to know each other years earlier when McVay brought Walsh to Giants training camp to work with his offense, which needed a GPS to find its way into the end zone.

Walsh quickly put together his 49ers staff. But it was going to take time before he could turn the roster over. The 49ers won two games his first year. They won just six games his second year. Walsh was so discouraged, he considered quitting and kicking himself into the front office. You can say the positive is he had Montana, but even at the end of that second season in 1980, Walsh was not sure he had found his long-term quarterback. Montana had proven he had special leadership qualities besides his natural ability. He wouldn't quit. And he would never let the players around him quit. That was evident in an incredible late-season victory against the Saints at Candlestick, when he brought the 49ers back from a 35–7 halftime deficit to win 38–35 in overtime. Walsh was muttering to himself, "Pathetic," as New Orleans was embarrassing his team in the first half. The Saints had come into the game 0–13. This was already the fourteenth game of Walsh's second season. He expected much more.

Walsh was clueless when he stepped in front of his team at the half. Should he appeal to their pride as professional athletes? Should he kick their asses? Threaten their jobs? Cut the entire team? He never had to do any of that. The Saints soon provided all the motivation Walsh needed.

"We really played good in the first half," Saints quarterback Archie Manning recalled. "We don't look like we're an 0–13 team."

This was the second game for the Saints with Bill Stanfill as their head coach. He had been promoted from offensive-line coach after the Saints fired Dick Nolan, the former 49ers coach. "We go into the dressing room, and we're not there very long," Manning said. "The 49ers dressing room is right across the hall. And now we're heading back to the little tunnel leading to the field."

Years later, Manning and Walsh got together. Walsh, when he got back into coaching at Stanford after he left the 49ers, recruited Archie's son Peyton, who wound up going to Tennessee. "Bill says he wants to tell me a funny story," Archie said. "He is in there trying to figure out what to say to a team getting beat 35–7 by an 0–13 team. He conferred with his coaches and didn't come up with anything. About this time, he hears the Saints going by the dressing room."

Then one New Orleans player fired up the 49ers by shouting right by their locker room door, "Let's beat these guys 80–7!"

No need for a Walsh speech. "He didn't need to say anything," Manning said.

That comeback might have been the turning point. The 49ers became a team that day, and Walsh told them after the game that the comeback was so positive, the 49ers would benefit from it for the next decade.

Even though Montana had positioned himself late in the season as the number-one-ranked passer in the NFC after taking over for Steve DeBerg, it was apparent that Walsh had not seen enough of a sample to support him fully. "I believe it would be too soon to change my perspective about the draft," Walsh said with a couple of games remaining in the season. "Not that we don't really appreciate his accomplishments. He very well could with a couple of big plays win the passing title, which would be quite a feat. But with two games remaining, it's probably just as well that I remain relatively calm about it until the season is completed. I can say that he has certainly played well for the amount of experience he has."

In the 1981 draft, Walsh did select a quarterback—Joe Adams of Tennessee State in the twelfth round. Adams was the 322nd player off the board.

The Montana era had arrived in San Francisco.

The 49ers moved their training camp in 1981 to Rocklin, about an hour from the state capital, Sacramento. They reported without any illusions about who they were and what they could accomplish. "Everybody thought we were going to be better," Clark said. "Nobody thought we were going to win the Super Bowl."

Walsh had made nice strides in his second season, tripling his victory total from two to six, but the Eagles were the defending NFC champs, the Falcons were the defending NFC West champs, and even the most enthusiastic 49ers loyalist wouldn't have said this was going to be a playoff year. There was no reason for the 49ers to hold back on making vacation plans in January.

"But we were really feeling positive after the 2–14 season in 1979 because we actually started scoring points. Even though we were 2–14 for the second straight year, we were positive we were a much better team," Cross said. "After being one of the worst teams ever, we were probably one of the best 2–14 teams that ever played in the league. We started out good in the 6–10 year but then went on a long losing streak."

The Niners began the 1980 season 3–0 for the first time since 1952 with victories over the Saints, Cardinals, and Jets. But none of those three teams finished better than 8–8 in 1979, and they would combine to win only ten games in 1980. After the promising start, the 49ers lost eight in a row, including a humiliating 59–14 loss at

Dallas that gave them indigestion—Walsh told the team that Landry ran up the score on them—that didn't go away until they got revenge during the regular season one year later.

"That might have been, next to the '82 strike year, the hardest one of Bill's early years," Cross said. "He remarked to us a couple of times in small groups, 'I don't know how much longer I can do this. Losing is just killing me.'"

Walsh did some boxing in college, and the players would look over and see him shadow boxing in the middle of practice, to relieve stress during the day. "He did it all the time," Clark said. "I'm sure there was some psychology to this. One day, I'm in the weight room working out, and Bill comes in there with his workout stuff on and his boxing gloves on. He loved his players. He'd say, 'Clark, come over here and hold this bag for me.' So I went over there and held the heavy bag, and he's pounding this bag."

Clark was due for a new contract.

"Do you think we are going to get this contract done?" Walsh asked.

"What, are you going to kick my ass if we don't?" Clark answered.

Clark said it "was hilarious. I knew there was some kind of psychology to it, but I wasn't smart enough to figure that out."

Walsh had waited so long to get this opportunity, but less than two years into it, the lows by far outweighed the highs and were eating him up. "Then we came out of it and ended our season on a high note," Cross said.

They beat the Giants and Patriots and had the amazing comeback against the Saints to get to 6–8, but they lost by three to the Falcons and four to the Bills to finish up the season.

If things followed the natural progression, the 49ers could win eight games in 1981. But that would depend on Montana continuing to improve and rewarding the faith Walsh was showing in him.

Walsh had the track record with Cook, Anderson, and Fouts, but that didn't mean Montana would overcome the inconsistency he showed at Notre Dame, which prevented him from being drafted any higher than the end of the third round. He didn't have a big arm, and he was not considered a sure thing to be an NFL starter. Notre Dame didn't even know what they had, because Montana went into his junior year third on the depth chart. The 49ers had not had a winning season since 1976, which was their only one since 1972. But the Walsh influence was taking hold.

"We were starting to establish Bill's way of playing football," Cross said. "But we were beating the hell out of each other. I remember the first couple of times I ran into Ronnie Lott in practice. I was given the opportunity to figure out he was pretty special. I mean, seriously, most people were made of flesh, and other people's muscles were made of lead. And he was in the lead category. We were pulling out on a sweep and I blocked him, hit him, but it was like, 'That doesn't feel very good. I'm glad I don't have to do that in a game.' "

Clark, who owed his NFL career to Walsh taking a chance on him, said the players knew, "Bill Walsh was going to make us better. We were throwing the ball all over the place and having success. We just couldn't stop anybody."

Walsh drafted Lott, Wright, and Williamson to fix the secondary. He brought in veteran middle linebacker Hacksaw Reynolds before the '81 season to give the defense an edgy attitude. Reynolds lived in San Mateo, just off the 101, and would buy "old junked-out cars and keep them in this guy's lot and work on them," Cross said. "He was wired a little differently. He would put cars together and help the guy out, and he let him live upstairs over the garage, and he didn't have to pay rent. That was Hacksaw."

Reynolds set the tone for the 49ers the morning of the championship game against the Cowboys by showing up for the team breakfast in full uniform. "The message that was sent was, Hacksaw had been in that situation with the Rams. What he was saying was, 'I'm ready,'" Ronnie Lott said. "Hacksaw had a way of intensifying moments that needed to be intensified. People say, 'Why do you bring in an old veteran?' You bring him in for those kinds of moments. He came in letting everyone know that's a moment that is special."

Reynolds then arrived at the stadium very early in a cab at the same time Cowboy safety Charlie Waters and linebacker D. D. Lewis were showing up in a limo. They were dropped off in the same parking lot near the locker room. Reynolds was in uniform. Waters took notice.

So did DeBartolo when he saw Reynolds earlier at the team breakfast. "I was with my dad," he said. "We were at the hotel and we were so damn nervous. It was six-thirty or seven o'clock in the morning. We were going to have breakfast. You know the columns they have in hotels with little mosaics on them? That's what they had near the players' dining room. Hacksaw Reynolds was fully dressed, had on his bootblack, and was hitting the column. He was fired up."

Once the Cowboys took the 10–7 lead, the game began to settle down. The 49ers could not move the ball on their next possession and went three and out. Then the Cowboys went three and out as well, and Dallas held a 3-point lead into the second quarter. The Cowboys felt good about taking the early shot from Montana and the 49ers, then forcing a turnover and coming up with a defensive stop on the 49ers next two possessions.

The Cowboys were not staggering from the 49ers' early score in the title game. They had all that championship-game experience, and other than the few veterans Walsh had brought onto his roster, the 49ers were playoff virgins. They had dominated the Giants the week before in the divisional round of the playoffs, but now they were in deep with the Cowboys, the conference's dominant team for a decade.

The second quarter began with the grounds crew filling in the chunks of grass that the players had kicked up on the soft field. Then Montana finally got the 49ers offense going again. Starting from their own 20, they moved to their own 35. Montana rolled right after a play action fake. Jones came in charging hard from Montana's right, but Joe quickly stopped short, watched Jones fly by him, stepped up in the pocket and fired a 38-yard pass to Clark, who had beaten Walls with a double move, faking to the outside and then cutting inside, spinning Walls around. Once the play was over, Montana looked back at Jones and let him know, with some x-rated language, how he felt about his pregame putdowns. After Montana was sacked for a 5-yard loss by Harvey Martin, he connected on a 10-yard pass to Clark, putting San Francisco at the Dallas 22. A good part of Walsh's genius was his feel for the game and for his team. Right at that moment, his instincts told him to go for it all. The 49ers had moved nearly 60 yards down the field without much of a problem. The corners were having trouble covering Clark and Solomon.

But the plan backfired. Walsh sent rookie wide receiver Mike Wilson into the game. Wilson had been drafted in the ninth round from Washington State by Landry and the Cowboys that year but didn't make it out of training camp. Even if he had made the team, when exactly would he have gotten an opportunity to play? Dallas had Pearson, Hill, and Johnson and had just drafted Ohio State's Doug Donley in the second round. Wilson was better off getting cut and being picked up by Walsh, who was still looking for warm bodies.

Now Wilson was going against Walls. They had been together in Thousand Oaks in camp that summer, fighting for spots on the Dallas roster. Wilson lined up to fullback Earl Cooper's left in the backfield behind Montana, then went in motion to his right, Montana dropped back and fired a pass down the right sideline. It was Wilson versus Walls. You can say this about Walls, the rookie free agent from Grambling: He gave up big plays. But he also made big plays. He set the Cowboys' single-season interception record while just a rookie. He had inside position on Wilson and easily picked off Montana's pass, which floated right into his arms. His momentum carried him into the end zone, but the officials ruled he was down at the San Francisco 2.

It was a crucial decision by the officials not to call it a touchback and give Dallas the ball at the 20. The 49ers had turned the ball over, but the Cowboys were backed up deep in their own end.

On the next series it wouldn't take long for Montana and Clark to turn that battle for field position into seven points.

It was at the end of the second day of training camp in 1981 that Walsh called Montana and Clark over for a quick meeting on the field. Montana feared the worst.

"We're both thinking we're in trouble for something," Montana said.

"I want you to work on this," Walsh told them.

It was Sprint Right Option. Walsh had run it his first two years, but the play was always designed to go to Freddie Solomon. "We would try to get it to Freddie, but the guy who was always open was Dwight," Montana said. "We never threw it to Dwight."

So in camp, Walsh had Montana and Clark practice the secondary part of the play. Clark would first pick off Solomon's defender, then run to the end line, pivot, and reverse field, going left to right. If Montana had not yet thrown to Solomon, then Montana was supposed to throw to Clark. His target spot was over Clark's head. The one warning Walsh gave Montana: If there was any doubt, throw it away, don't risk an interception.

"The funny thing in practice is, the ball never went to that spot right where Joe threw it in the game," Clark said. "It was always too high, where I couldn't get it. Or it was chest level. In practice, it was never in the exact perfect spot. But in the game, under duress, he put it in the exact perfect spot."

It was the genius of Walsh. The play was so well designed and so well executed that the Cowboys, to this day, are convinced Montana was throwing the ball away rather than just following Walsh's instructions that the pass was supposed to be thrown high.

"Bill, in fact, was a genius," McVay said. "He had a regal air about him. He wore the mantle."

The 49ers offense soon became known as the West Coast offense. As Walsh's assistants were hired around the NFL, they took it with them. Two things were always missing from the copycat version, though: Walsh and Montana. They had a tremendous chemistry on game day. Walsh would not burn out Montana with late-night film sessions, but he would drill the nuances of the game into him.

"He depended a lot on fundamentals," Montana said. "Not only the fundamentals of the positions, but the fundamentals of the offense. He had an uncanny ability to do that. So when you are behind or running a two-minute drill, everything you are doing is everything you have done from day one."

When Walsh would install a new play to run against a specific defense, invariably the 49ers offense had trouble making it work in practice. "It would be the worst play," Montana said. "It would never, ever, be open in practice."

But that wouldn't stop Walsh from calling it in a game. He drew it up. That meant it had to work. "OK, guys, here we go," Montana would say in the huddle.

"No, no," his teammates moaned.

"So you call the play and all of a sudden, bang, it's wide open," Montana said. "Then you start going, 'Wow.' There was always something a little different about Bill. He didn't make a lot of changes for people. If there was a specific blitz, or you had a guy like LT, who is very rare, or you had a defense like the Bears, he would make changes. Otherwise, he said, 'I'm going to do what I'm going to do and somebody has got to change me. I'm not going to change for them unless we can't handle something.'"

Sid Gillman is credited with the early development of the West Coast offense, but Walsh refined it and took it to another level when he was in Cincinnati working for Paul Brown. The West Coast offense differed from the traditional offenses that relied on a strong running game to set up the passing game. In Walsh's system, the five-yard run was still a desired end result when he elected to give the running back the ball, but his offense featured a short passing game that put the ball in the hands of his playmakers in space. The short-yardage run was replaced by a 3-yard pass to a back or wide receiver, who then would use his running skills and shiftiness to turn the play into a big gainer. It required an accurate quarterback, skilled position players with escapability and good hands, and a creative playcaller. Montana was the best ever at the short three-step drops and then getting rid of the ball on quick slants. Nobody was better than Montana at deciding where to go with the ball. Walsh was the best playcaller in the business.

"We demanded that everyone be a good receiver and that everyone have great discipline," Walsh once said. "I think those are still the foundations of the offense."

The West Coast offense relies on timing, and the required routes are so precise that when it is run correctly, it looks as choreographed as a ballet. But Walsh was also smart enough to adjust to his personnel and not completely adhere to his system. When he drafted Jerry Rice in 1985, a whole new set of possibilities opened up for Walsh. Rice wasn't a flat-out burner, and some scouts thought he would have trouble getting off the line of scrimmage in the NFL. It was those reasons, more than coming from tiny Mississippi Valley State, that he wasn't taken until number sixteen in the first round. The 49ers were coming off a 15–1 regular season and a Super Bowl victory over the Dolphins and Dan Marino. It might have been the best team Walsh had in his ten years coaching the 49ers. They were loaded.

That season Walsh was sitting in his hotel room watching television the night before a 49ers road game. College football highlights from the day were about to come on. "In a few minutes, you are going to see the phenom of the South," the television announcer said. Walsh sat up on his bed. He had heard of Jerry Rice, but had never seen him play. "He caught like five touchdown passes and ran the length of the field every time," Walsh said. "So that was enough for me."

After winning the Super Bowl, the 49ers had the twenty-eighth and last pick in the first round. Rice fell right out of the top ten and was still on the board after the Jets took Wisconsin receiver Al Toon and the Bengals took Miami receiver Eddie Brown. Walsh started dialing the phone and tried to move up to get Rice. The Patriots, picking sixteenth, were happy to trade down, and Walsh got his guy. "He has been the best player in all of football in our era," Walsh said on the day Rice retired in 2005. "If you include [all-time], he's certainly been in the top two or three. It's time to celebrate one of the greatest careers in the history of the NFL."

Rice didn't have sprinter's speed, but when the ball was in the air, nobody was faster. Walsh incorporated Rice's ability to get down the field and make big plays into the 49ers offense. Although it's hard to believe now, Rice struggled early in his career holding on to the ball.

Walsh also was a big believer in scripting the first twenty-five plays in a game and practicing them repeatedly. He would vary the script, depending on down and distance, but generally stuck to it. As the leaves scattered off the Walsh coaching tree, scripting plays became as common as the West Coast offense around the NFL.

Cross feared he might outlast another coach when the 49ers hired Walsh. The 49ers had turned into a burial ground for coaches. As it turned out, Cross and Walsh retired from the 49ers in the same year. "He was at Stanford, so it wasn't like we didn't know who he was," he said. "Being a UCLA guy, I also had the other pre-conceived built-in prejudices against Stanford guys. We always talked about pseudo-intellectuals—people that thought they were a lot smarter than everybody else. We talk about athletic arrogance in successful athletes; he had intellectual arrogance. When he put things on the board and said, 'This is going to work, and here's why,' it didn't take doing it too many times and having it work and you'd go, 'These guys are in trouble.' It always worked. Even when we weren't winning games, like in 1980, we were scoring points."

Cross remembers Walsh as being "a conflicted deep thinker in that he loved military guys. He would quote military heroes. He'd quote philosophy, he would quote political leaders. He would talk about the bombing in London and Churchill under fire and stuff like that. But he's the same guy that would be silently off to himself shadow boxing. He'd be over there punching, be covering up with the right hand, throwing the left. He had such confidence."

He also had a dry sense of humor that was very entertaining. Before the big regular-season game against the Cowboys in 1981, Walsh stood in front of his players at a team meeting outlining how he needed them to be at their best for Dallas.

"We got to have everybody fresh for this ball game," he said.

Then, in a deadpan delivery that would made any comedian take notes, he said, "Somehow you got to be fresh. In some cases, it may mean a lot of sex. In others, I don't know."

He once told his players what he thought of the Cowboys. "I'm sick of them. I hope you guys feel the same way I do."

Walsh, more than any coach since Lombardi, left a lasting impact on the game. He was instrumental in establishing the minority coaching internship program that the NFL named in his honor in 2009. He learned not long into his job with the 49ers that it was counterproductive to run the players into the ground in practice. It served little purpose to have them pound each other and then not have key players available on Sunday. He made sure the 49ers got their work done, and they were always prepared, but once word spread around the league how Walsh didn't often make his players wear pads, that he was saving their bodies Monday through Saturday to help the team win not only on Sunday but also prolong careers, then San Francisco was where they all wanted to play. He didn't push it too hard in camp. On one of his first days with the 49ers, ex-Cowboys receiver Tony Hill was not on the practice field. Walsh had told him to go for a swim in the campus pool instead.

Cosbie, the former Cowboys tight end, went into coaching after he finished his playing career. He was a Bay Area guy and returned to Santa Clara, where he went to school, and began his coaching career. But Santa Clara dropped football a couple of years later, and he needed a job. Cosbie and Walsh, who was then back at Stanford, had a mutual friend named Al Matthews, who had coached one of Cosbie's Santa Clara players. Matthews called Walsh to recommend Cosbie. He was hired to assist Monte Clark coaching the offensive line. He also worked with tight ends and special teams.

"I recruited the southwest and part of Orange County," Cosbie said. "Texas was one of my territories. One year we signed three of the best players in the state of Texas, and Bill went with me to go do the home visits. We spent a couple of days together flying around Texas and staying in hotels."

All these years later, Cosbie was curious about The Catch. "Was Joe really not throwing it away?" he asked.

"We worked on it all the time," Walsh said. Sprint Right Option was in the Stanford playbook.

Cosbie worked for Walsh for two seasons until Walsh retired again. After being around Landry and not having many memorable conversations with him, Cosbie saw another side of coaching with Walsh.

Walsh drew up the play that cost Cosbie and the Cowboys a trip to the Super Bowl, but "I didn't feel like I was a traitor working for Bill," Cosbie said. "It was really a unique experience being a young coach getting to work with Monte and Bill. Having coached with Bill for two years, he was truly amazing. His system and his organization and his teaching ability and his ability to get people open and create new things. There is no one who has that whole package."

As far as Xs and Os, Walsh's West Coast offense became the dominant system in the NFL in the nineties and carried right over into the new millennium. The attack required great timing. Montana didn't have a weak arm, but he didn't have an arm like John Elway or Dan Marino or Brett Favre. But in Walsh's system, it didn't matter. Montana was incredibly accurate, and the idea of the offense was to complete short passes to the receivers in stride. Once Jerry Rice arrived in San Francisco, he and Montana perfected the art of YAC—yards after the catch.

But for the West Coast offense to be spread so effectively around the league, there had to be coaches teaching it. Walsh's coaching tree was actually more like a forest. Future NFL head coaches who worked directly for Walsh included Mike Holmgren, George Seifert, Dennis Green, Sam Wyche, Bruce Coslet, and Ray Rhodes. Paul Hackett went on to become a head coach in college.

Then when Holmgren was hired as the Packers' head coach, he hired future head coaches Jon Gruden, Andy Reid, Steve Mariucci, and Mike Sherman. Mike Shanahan and Gary Kubiak worked for Seifert. Green went to Minnesota and hired Tony Dungy, Mike Tice, and Brian Billick. Dungy's coaching tree produced Herm Edwards, Lovie Smith, Mike Tomlin, Rod Marinelli, and Jim Caldwell. Even though Dungy and four of his assistants who later became NFL head coaches were all raised on the defensive side of the ball, somewhere in there, the teachings of Bill Walsh exist.

In fact, Walsh and all of the coaches connected to his tree account for twelve Super Bowl victories.

"I always said that he was an artist and all the rest of us were blacksmiths pounding the anvil, while he was painting the picture," Holmgren said.

The Cowboys were in denial once the Landry era was over, regarding the impact of that loss to the 49ers and how it was the impetus for the dynasty of one team and the collapse of another. Not Charlie Waters. "It was not so much that we went down. It was the confidence that we gave to San Francisco in that attack, in that style, in that quarterback, and in that coach and their belief in that system," he said. "It started something. They dominated the decade."

But Walsh had bigger problems than worrying about how The Catch sent Dallas reeling. What happened to his team in 1982? The 49ers were 3–6 in a season shortened by a players strike. It was probably not a good sign that Cross dislocated his foot, broke his leg, and tore all the ligaments on the inside of his ankle at an off-season March of Dimes charity event at Marine World in Redwood City. He fell off a structure on a kid's obstacle course and landed with his foot underneath him. Walsh visited Cross in the hospital. "In Bill's mind, that might have been the start of that horrendous year," Cross said.

The 49ers also were not mature enough to handle success. Walsh realized he had to take a step back in his relationship with the players. He couldn't convince them that what they did in 1981 had no bearing on how they were going to do in 1982. Walsh and his wife, Geri, used to join the players for postgame celebrations following victories in the first Super Bowl year. "It's one of the reasons that our whole experience the next year in 1982 was so hard on Bill," Cross said. "He trusted everybody so much. And we proved that trust misplaced." It was a loose group that "literally had more fun than allowed by law, and we paid for it the next year."

Walsh, however, set the tone in 1981, and it was conducive to winning. When the 49ers players arrived at the team hotel in Detroit for the Super Bowl, there was a silver-haired man in a bellhop outfit greeting them at the door. Walsh had arrived at the hotel ahead of his players and planned to loosen them up before the week got started with all the media attention that came with the Super Bowl. They got a good laugh out of it, and pictures of Walsh in his bellhop uniform were printed in just about every newspaper in the country.

The 49ers had the early practices at the Silverdome, but that didn't stop them from staying up all night partying. It was the first cold-weather Super Bowl, and if the players couldn't be out playing a round of golf or sitting by the pool, they were going to find ways to enjoy themselves in frigid Detroit.

"We were doing donuts in the parking lot," Cross said. "We were a bunch of idiots from California. I'd never been in snow and ice. We had rental cars that we weren't responsible for, and we'd be sliding across the parking lot with the wheels doing 360s and slamming into a snow pile. Then we would get out of the car, turn it off and walk into the hotel."

Walsh did not set a curfew the first few days. Cross called a team meeting on Thursday: " 'We're having a great time, but, guys, this is the Super Bowl. We might want to get some sleep.' We had guys that were getting two or three hours of sleep every night."

If the nights were long and taxing, then the practices were not. Walsh gave his assistants a song list to have piped into the stadium to simulate crowd noise. The Niners had the field from 9:00–11:30 A.M.; then the Bengals took over. "At about 11:15, I looked down at the other end of the tunnel, and there's Bengals coach Forrest Gregg standing in the end zone and the team is in full pads and they got their chin straps buckled up and they are ready to start practice," Cross said. "We're back there playing air guitar to the music and dancing around."

Walsh had to change after 1982 when the players he trusted so much didn't have his back. He started with The Talk, as the players called it. He would bring each player into his office, review the previous season and tell him how much longer he could play with the 49ers. It was a way to wake them up. When a player returned to the locker room, his teammates knew if he just had The Talk. "You'd come down and be working out and see somebody sitting at their locker, and you'd go, 'Did you have The Talk? Did you have your appointment yet? What did he say?' " Cross said.

"Shit, he said I've got four years left in the league, but I only got two years left here," was the response.

Walsh trusted his guys in 1982. It didn't work. Now he was going to put all trust in himself. The 49ers made it to the NFC title game in 1983 and might have defeated the Redskins if not for some questionable officiating calls. They won the Super Bowl in '84 and again in '88, and then Walsh made the biggest mistake of his coaching career.

He walked away.

3

THE LEGEND

THE MAN sat solemnly in his office at Valley Ranch in the Dallas suburb of Irving on an otherwise beautiful Sunday afternoon. It was February 26, 1989, one day after he was fired. He was packing twenty-nine years of memories into boxes and transporting them out the door to his car. He looked like anybody else who'd been canned, but he wasn't anybody else, that's for sure.

He was Tom Landry.

It was just eighteen hours after the famed Saturday Night Massacre in which the only head coach the Cowboys ever had became the only head coach the Cowboys ever fired. Hundreds of times over nearly three decades, Landry told players to turn in their playbook, and despite his icy exterior and his ability to butcher the easiest names, which gave the false impression that he thought his players were just a bunch of interchangeable numbers in metallic silver and blue, it deeply hurt him to let a player go.

It hurt to take away the playbook, even from a long shot who had been around just a few days. He knew he was ending a dream for the player, his family, and those counting on him. Landry was not a robot, he was not without a heart, but in the days when Gil Brandt would sign 65 rookie free agents, hoping to find just one who could play like Everson Walls, and the Cowboys would bring 120 players to training camp, Landry knew on the first day of practice that he would have to let more than half of them go.

"One time he came in, it was 1975, he had to cut a bunch of guys, and he cried in the meeting," Drew Pearson said. "It's a tough business."

Now Landry had been told to turn in *his* playbook to an oil tycoon he'd never met and couldn't have picked out of a lineup, a guy who never showed up on the Cowboys draft board after an undistinguished career as an offensive guard at Arkansas, although he was a cocaptain on the Razorbacks 1964 national championship team. This guy was firing Tom Landry? But it wasn't the same coach who had been to five Super Bowls. He was coming off a 3–13 season and had not taken the Cowboys to the Super Bowl in ten years. His best shot was in 1981, but Montana and Clark took care of that in the NFC Championship Game. If the Cowboys had won that game, they might have won two or three more Super Bowls before Landry was done. Danny White might have become Joe Montana.

Dallas was in part shock and part mourning when Landry was fired. He and the Cowboys eventually had helped erase the stigma of being the city where President John Kennedy was assassinated in 1963.

The Cowboys entered the NFL in 1960 and were dreadful in their first six seasons, winning only twenty-six games. But it all turned around in 1966 when they went from a Texas-size joke to the NFL Championship Game. Of course, it's ludicrous and insensitive to believe that a football team could lessen the impact of one of the darkest days in American history. That would never change. But there is no doubt the Cowboys helped in the city's healing process and in the rehabilitation of its self-esteem. Instead of the Grassy Knoll and the Book Depository and Lee Harvey Oswald, at least when people now thought about Dallas, there was a positive alternative: Landry. Bullet Bob Hayes, an Olympic hero. Don Meredith. Bob Lilly. Lee Roy Jordan. A collection of winners soon to be known as America's Team.

Even though the Cowboys finished 3–13 in 1988, the most losses in Landry's twenty-nine years, he still wanted to coach at the age of sixty-four. He had one year left on his contract, and quitting never crossed his mind. But his team had been taken away from him. He went through his drawers like a college kid cleaning out his dorm room after collecting four years of junk. Only Landry earned his degree and icon status with a Phi Beta Kappa body of work going back three decades. Some items he looked at and smiled and stuffed them into a box to keep. Others he tossed into a garbage can. That's where he would have liked to put brand-new Cowboys owner Jerry Jones, who the day before had flown to Austin, where Landry owned a vacation home in the exclusive Lakeway section outside of town, and awkwardly informed him that he was making a coaching change and replacing him with Jones's former teammate at Arkansas, Jimmy Johnson of the University of Miami. Johnson was the hottest college coach in the country after winning the national title at Miami in 1987.

"It was the most inadequate I've ever felt in my life," Jones said. "If you grade Jerry Jones for his words, he gets an F."

Landry, Alicia, and their son Tom had boarded Landry's single-engine plane at Love Field in Dallas at nine-thirty earlier that Saturday morning for their usual off-season weekend getaway of golf and dinner and more golf the next day. Landry, a bomber pilot who flew missions over Germany in World War II, owned and piloted his own small plane and was at the controls when it touched down on an airstrip near Lakeway at eleven A.M. After lunch, Landry and his wife, son, daughter, and son-in-law kept their two P.M. tee time at Hidden Hills on Lake Travis. Meanwhile, Schramm was frantically trying to find Landry to inform him that Jones had just completed his $140 million purchase from Bum Bright and that he and Jones needed to see him. He called his home in Dallas. He called his home in Austin. He called the golf course. Landry knew he was in the final hours of being the Cowboys coach after the story of Jones's intentions broke on a Dallas television station two days earlier. But he had not been told officially, so there was still hope in his mind. He stepped up to the first tee and let it rip.

"Dad had an excellent drive," Tom Jr. said.

After that first shot, however, the club pro chased Landry down the fairway to tell him he had an urgent call from Schramm. Landry went to the pro-shop telephone.

"Am I OK? Is everything alright?" he asked Schramm.

"No," Schramm said.

Jones and Schramm were soon on their way for the official execution. No blindfolds or cigarettes. Landry didn't smoke anyway. He played another fifteen holes before it got dark. Hit the ball well. Jones's personal jet, which already had a silver and blue Cowboys star painted on the tail, landed in Austin at five P.M., and thirty minutes later, Jones and Schramm, who was fighting back tears, were sitting in a sales office at the country club with Landry and his son. It took forty minutes to do the unthinkable—fire Landry.

"I'm here and so is Jimmy," Jones told him.

At least Jones wasn't being literal. Johnson wasn't with him in Austin. He was back in Dallas constructing his coaching staff. When Jones's plane returned from Austin, Johnson was waiting at Love Field. He then flew home to Miami. Johnson had already asked Dolphins coach Don Shula for permission to hire Dave Wannstedt, who was Johnson's best friend. Wannstedt had just left Johnson's staff at Miami to take a job as Shula's linebackers coach. He would be the Cowboys' defensive coordinator. In return for letting Wannstedt leave so soon after getting there, Johnson also hired Shula's son, David, as his offensive coordinator. The younger Shula, who was Miami's quarterbacks coach, needed to get out of his father's shadow to establish himself in the NFL and escape the cries of nepotism in Miami. Shula's best friend in the NFL was Schramm, but he never called Tex to tell him about Johnson's hiring of his son and Wannstedt or even to ask him what the hell was going on in Dallas. Schramm didn't have a clue, anyway. Bright had left Schramm in the dark during the later portion of the sales process because every time a potential buyer surfaced who planned to be actively involved in the team, Schramm managed to scare him away. He was protecting his own interests. After twenty-nine years of hands-off owners Clint Murchison and Bright, who each let him run the team any way he pleased and never cared much about the bottom line, Schramm had no interest in bringing in anybody who could erode his power base. So when local television reporter Tom Murray broke the story on the ten o'clock news on Channel 5 in Dallas on February 23 that Jones and Johnson were in and Landry was out, Schramm issued a vehement denial, pretty much telling Murray that he was risking his career by going with such bad information. But Murray was so sure he was right, he did his live report standing on the campus of the University of Miami.

But those words from Jones to Landry ended a Hall of Fame coaching career. Jones was so rattled and felt so guilty, he discussed a job with Landry in the organization, which would potentially buy some goodwill in Dallas for Jones and also enable Landry to work off the $1 million he had remaining on the final year of his contract. If Landry wasn't such a gentleman, if he wasn't so religious, if for once in his life he had just dropped an f-bomb, he might have had a colorful way of telling Jones where he could stick his job and how he really felt about this intruder from Arkansas crossing state lines and dismantling the organization. The best he could do was not give him an answer that day. Landry, of course, never worked for Jones. How could he have? The oilman had burst into town like a Texas tornado and blown Landry right to the unemployment line. Adding indignity to embarrassment, Jones sneaked Johnson into Dallas, and they dined on that Friday night at Mia's, the popular

Tex-Mex restaurant near the hotel where they were staying. Everybody except Jones knew that Mia's was Tom and Alicia Landry's favorite spot. The picture of Jones and Johnson in the *Dallas Morning News* the next day having dinner and a couple of cold ones gave the appearance they were stomping on the legend's grave. Or at least eating his nachos and burritos.

Jones and Johnson were friends and teammates at Arkansas, but they were hardly inseparable. Now they were in charge of the Dallas Cowboys. Jones would pay the bills. Johnson would make them winners.

"I think Tom's emotion was disappointment," Brandt said. "He felt we had turned this team around, and we knew we were getting Troy Aikman in the draft. There were some players there, guys like Ken Norton and Michael Irvin. We thought we had some pretty good players. But the biggest disappointment for Tom is it wasn't done in a different manner. If Bum had just come to him and said he was selling the team and [Jones] wants to bring in his own guy. Bum was so happy to get out."

Jones was clumsy in the days before and after he fired Landry. Bright, all of a sudden feeling empowered because he was leaving after doing next to nothing in the five years he owned the team, stepped up and told Jones he would do the dirty work for him and fire Landry himself. He would have taken great joy in getting revenge on the coach he felt disrespected him by ignoring him at team functions. Bright knew Jones was going to fire Landry because Jones told him that Johnson would be his coach through the process. Bright would have liked to have fired Landry years earlier himself but knew that was not going to happen while Schramm was in charge. Even though Bright owned the team, he deferred to Schramm on all football matters. But now that he was selling, if he fired Landry, that would be his legacy. Instead, Jones was the bad guy, and *his* ownership got off to a rocky start. Jones actually was going to give Landry the opportunity to walk away with his dignity intact by saying, "We have a new ownership group and this is a new era, so I'm resigning," but when the story broke of Jones buying the team and Johnson coaching it, it was too late for damage control.

As Jones put it, "Bum offered to fire Landry before I bought the team. He said, 'You should take my advice and come in with a clean slate.' I told him, 'This is my responsibility. I should make this change.' I was also advised that, 'Jerry, all the people and fans are going to know the change was made because of your ownership and if that is going to be the case, then you should visit with Coach Landry on a personal basis.' I'm not saying this to sound sanctimonious, but one of the reasons I bought the team was because of how much I did respect him. I never thought there would be any other way than to go down and face him and share with him that we were buying and making a change." Had Bright continued to own the Cowboys, there is little doubt he eventually would have exploded and forced Schramm to fire Landry. "I think he wanted to embarrass Landry," Roger Staubach said. "Jerry Jones did not want to embarrass Tom Landry."

After a loss to the lowly Falcons before the smallest crowd in Texas Stadium history seven weeks after the 1987 strike, which was the Cowboys 13th loss in their last 17 games (not including the 2–1 record of the replacement team), Bright finally voiced publicly his frustrations with Landry, which had been stewing inside him for years. He said he was "horrified" by the playcalling, and Bright knew about as much about playcalling as the Cowboys cheerleaders. He said if he had to do it over again, he would never have bought the team. He lambasted Landry with the worst criticism ever from inside the organization: "It doesn't seem like we've got anybody in charge that knows what they are doing, other than Tex," Bright said.

Bright had a blind spot for Schramm, who could be extremely charming. But Schramm ran the team as if he owned it. He ran it as a first-class operation, money be damned, because the checks were not coming out of his account. If Bright was insulted that Landry paid no attention to him at Cowboys parties before he made those comments, he had now lost any chance that the coach would ever suck up to him or, for that matter, even talk to him.

The Cowboys fans became attached to the replacement players during the three games the players were on strike. Many of the Cowboys crossed the picket line. Schramm, who had humiliated Tony Dorsett during a previous contract negotiation by leaking information about his financial problems, threatened Dorsett that he would jeopardize his annuity if he stayed on strike. "Tex was all about business," Dorsett said. "I was mad at him for exposing my tax problem at that time. Let's face it: People every day have tax problems. I'd already worked out an installment plan with the IRS."

Dorsett reluctantly crossed the line before the second game, but then said he would get on his hands and knees at midfield at Texas Stadium and beg Landry not to play him. He played and was booed. The fans also fell in love with Kevin Sweeney, the pint-size replacement quarterback from Fresno State, who had been cut in training camp. When Danny White crossed the picket line and Landry announced his intention to play him, fans held up signs proclaiming, WHITE'S A WEENIE. WE WANT SWEENEY.

After winning their first two strike games with Sweeney against the Jets and Eagles, many of the Cowboys veterans returned to play against Washington. Sweeney was benched. White, booed when he entered after halftime of the second replacement game, started against the Redskins. In one of the most humiliating games in Cowboys history, they lost to the Redskins, although Washington was one of the most solid union teams in the league and was going almost exclusively with the replacement players. The Cowboys finished 7–8 that year and that was followed by 3–13, the worst season since the first year in 1960, when Dallas was 0–11–1. By now, the fans wanted Landry gone. So did Schramm. But when Jones was the one who did it, he became a villain.

After he returned from firing Landry in Austin, there was a press conference at the Cowboys offices at Valley Ranch. Jones and his family were celebrating as though they had just won their own personal Super Bowl while the city of Dallas and Cowboys fans across America were in mourning. "This is like Lombardi's death," commissioner Pete Rozelle proclaimed.

It immediately became known as the Saturday Night Massacre. Jones alienated himself further by proclaiming, "History will show that one of the finest things that ever happened to the Cowboys is Jimmy Johnson." He turned out to be right, of course, but that night he was just plain insensitive.

Landry meticulously went through the drawers and closets in his huge office. He was wearing a flannel shirt and a pair of casual slacks, and unlike when he was seen on the sidelines, he was not wearing a hat. He took his personal belongings from the bathroom. He put trophies in boxes, took pictures off the walls. He made arrangements for removal of the custom-made wood-paneled door that had images of his two Lombardi Trophies carved in it. "Amazing how much you accumulate for that many years," Landry said. "You wonder why you never cleaned your files out before."

He knew he had not only beaten the odds, he had won the lottery. He lasted twenty-nine seasons with one team, and that will never happen again. During that time, Landry's old team, the New York Giants, had seven head coaches. He was fortunate to have an owner like Murchison for the first twenty-four seasons. Early in his Cowboys tenure, when Landry was labeled a coach who couldn't win the big game, another owner might have put him in a must-win pressure cooker to keep his job. But Murchison stayed in the background, gave him the ten-year extension, and let Schramm run the team—and Schramm was loyal to Landry. And when Bright, a Dallas businessman, put together a group and bought the Cowboys in 1984 from Murchison, a recluse who was in failing health and had a shrinking bank account brought on by tough times in the real-estate and oil business, not much changed in the way the team operated, except that Bright hated Landry but didn't have the nerve to fire him.

Bright never enjoyed owning the Cowboys. They never rewarded him with much success, and when his businesses in banking, oil, and real estate were hemorrhaging money as the Dallas economy sagged, he wanted out of football. He sold the team and the lease to Texas Stadium to Jones for $140 million, a nice return on his $86 million investment five years earlier, but that didn't help much, his net worth slipping from $600 million to $300 million the previous year.

NFL coaching jobs are not lifetime appointments, and eventually the losing caught up to Landry. And the roots of the demise of the Landry era go right back to January 10, 1982, at Candlestick Park. That game changed everything. The cap on Landry's Super Bowl appearances would be forever set at five.

"It was only because of one play—Dwight Clark's catch in 1981—that we didn't get back," Landry said. "Danny White was probably as fine a winner as we have had in football. He wasn't gifted as some quarterbacks were, but he knew how to win football games. I don't think anybody could have followed Roger and done as well as Danny. If we got to the Super Bowl in 1981, we might have won the Super Bowl a couple more times. I think Danny would have gotten us there again. Danny was a solid winner and nobody recognized that too much."

One play kept Landry from facing the Bengals in Super Bowl XVI. One game prevented the Cowboys from building on what could have been an easy victory over the Bengals and putting together a run of multiple Super Bowls. Instead, the 49ers became that team—the team of the eighties. Walsh was named the coach of the eighties by the Pro Football Hall of Fame. Landry? He got fired.

The Cowboys had suffered excruciating defeats in their history, like the back-to-back NFL championship losses to the Packers in the sixties. If the first one was agonizing, then the second one was a bitterly cold disappointment. The Cowboys first lost in Dallas to the Packers 34–27, missing a chance to send the game into overtime when Don Meredith was picked off in the end zone by Packers safety Tom Brown with 28 seconds remaining. Green Bay then beat the Chiefs in Super Bowl I. The Ice Bowl came the next year, with Bart Starr's quarterback sneak from the 1-yard line winning the game with 13 seconds left, 21–17. Green Bay then beat the Raiders in Super Bowl II. No doubt the Cowboys would have won those Super Bowls, too, if they had just gotten there. This was a team that became known not only as America's Team but Next Year's Champion as well.

The image of a frozen Landry on the sidelines for the Ice Bowl game as Starr dived across for the winning touchdown painted the perfect picture of the Cowboys' disappointment. "Lombardi put heaters under the field, and we were really looking forward to that game," Landry said. "It wasn't predicted to be that cold. It was twenty when we got there the day before. We stayed in a motel in Green Bay where the doors opened to the outside. I remember going to bed and getting up for breakfast in the morning, and I couldn't believe it. Everything was ice. It was like the North Pole. You can imagine the shock. [Minority owner] Toddie Lee Wynne had this big coat he gave me. I would have frozen to death if he didn't give it to me. Boy, it was freezing."

Landry did get the Cowboys to the Super Bowl five times in the 1970s, losing to the Colts on a last-second Jim O'Brien field goal, then beating the Dolphins the year before Miami's perfect season, losing to the Steelers, beating the Broncos, and then losing to the

Steelers again. Along the way, Landry put together his NFL-record twenty consecutive winning seasons.

Even with all those tough losses, Landry was always able to motivate the Cowboys to bounce back. They were so far ahead of the curve with the use of computers that they simply outsmarted everybody else on draft day. While some teams used Street and Smith's draft guide to help make their picks, Landry, Schramm, and Brandt were sitting in their draft war room with reams of computer printouts.

It's when they started to outsmart themselves, when they were convinced they were so much smarter than everybody else, that the Cowboys got into trouble. They were never able to recover from that 49ers loss. It suddenly was an aging team with a quarterback now 0–2 in championship games taking over for Roger Staubach, the most revered player in team history. If Dallas had won that game, if Clark hadn't jumped out of Candlestick when Montana let it go, then the Cowboys might have continued their streak of excellence. But Landry was helpless as the 1982 strike divided the team, and it was a tribute to his coaching greatness that he got them back into the conference title game that season, where they lost for the third straight year. He could not overcome a personnel department that had suddenly forgotten how to pick players.

"If we won that game, the psychology and the mentality of the team is drastically different when you come into the 1982 season as the Super Bowl champs as compared to you lost the championship game two years in a row," tight end Doug Cosbie said. "In the long run, I don't know. It was a veteran team that was getting older and some of the new players coming in weren't the same type of players as the guys going out. In the short term, it would have been a big difference for the team."

Many Cowboys still try to rationalize the significance of the loss to the 49ers by saying Dallas made it back to the NFC Championship Game in 1982, while the 49ers disappeared and didn't make the playoffs. But that season deserves an asterisk. It was destroyed by a fifty-seven-day strike that reduced the regular season to nine games. Dallas lost to Washington in the title game, while Walsh was trying to figure out how his team fell apart on him and finished 3–6.

"I think, for Dallas, the loss to us was the beginning of the end," Randy Cross said. "They lost the year before, but they lost to Philly. Losing to a cream puff on the West Coast was much more insulting. The NFL was very much like that old *New Yorker* magazine cover that when you crossed the Hudson River, not much existed. Once you got out of the NFC East, people didn't act like very much existed. I think for their team it was the turning point. It kind of proved, much to people's chagrin, and probably unfairly to him, that Danny White wasn't Roger. That as great as he was going to be, he wasn't going to have that unbelievable magic."

Landry was as driven and competitive as his good friend Vince Lombardi. When they were together on the Giants, they were the two best assistant coaches ever to work on one staff. But they couldn't have been more different. One look at Lombardi and there was never a question about what was going through his mind. He never hid his emotions. Other than the occasional grimace, it was nearly impossible to figure out what was going through Landry's mind. Sometimes he himself didn't know. He often came off as aloof, but that wasn't out of disrespect. He had a lot of the absent-minded professor in him.

As the Cowboys slipped in the late eighties, Landry's every move was questioned, and there were legitimate concerns that the game had passed him by. When he was challenged in his press conferences about some of his game-management decisions, his responses were often baffling. After a loss in Philadelphia, his answers left anybody who was listening with the unmistakable impression that Landry had lost track of the yard line and made a key decision based on bad information. That seemed to be happening more and more.

But the Cowboys were also standing still while the Giants with Bill Parcells, the Redskins with Joe Gibbs, and the Eagles with big-mouth Buddy Ryan were starting to run laps around them. Parcells and Gibbs held Landry in the highest regard and were always deferential to him. Ryan, on the other hand, hated Landry. He was incensed in a 1987 strike game when Landry put in his defensive veterans who had crossed the picket line to stop a late Eagles offensive drive by a bunch of nobodies in a game that the Cowboys easily won, 41–22. The Eagles and Cowboys played just two weeks later at Veterans Stadium in the first game back after the strike ended. There was less than one minute left and the Eagles had a 30–20 lead and a first down on the Dallas 29. On first and second down, Ryan ordered quarterback Randall Cunningham to take a knee. But then, following a plan he told his players about all week and had been dreaming about for two weeks, he wanted to stick it to Landry if he had the chance. The Cowboys' defense was expecting another kneel-down, but Cunningham instead threw into the end zone for Mike Quick. The Cowboys were called for pass interference, giving Philadelphia the ball at the Dallas 1. Keith Byars scored with no time left on the clock.

"Everybody has to live with themselves," Landry said.

Ryan promised to do it again the next year in Dallas if the situation was the same. "The can of worms was opened a couple of weeks ago," Ryan said. "We just put a lid on it for another year." What really had to incense Landry, if he ever gave it any thought, was what turned out to be the final game of his coaching career at the end of the 1988 season—a 23–7 loss to Ryan and the Eagles at Texas Stadium. Of course, Landry didn't know at the time it would be the last game he ever coached. He would have rather have gone through another Ice Bowl misery than give Ryan the satisfaction of beating him in his finale.

The feud with Ryan was an aberration for Landry. Everybody feuded with Ryan, who started picking on Jimmy Johnson the next year. The ugly ending to Landry's career was unfortunate. If anything, he deserved to take a victory tour around the league and go out on his own terms. But his firing did nothing to diminish his accomplishments in his twenty-nine years in Dallas. His two worst seasons were his first and last, when he had teams that didn't look capable of winning any games. He was 0–11–1 in the Cowboys' expansion year in 1960, the only nonloss being a 31–31 tie back at Landry's old home at Yankee Stadium against the Giants in the eleventh game of the season. Then in his final year, in 1988, the Cowboys managed to win only three games. His final victory came in the next-to-last game of the season against Gibbs, a man he admired and with whom he shared a similar commitment to faith and family. It was on the road at RFK Stadium, the scene of many of the most memorable games of Landry's career. Sadly, the Cowboys won only one home game that year, and Landry finished with a six-game losing streak at Texas Stadium.

But between the expansion follies of 1960 and the complete demise of his team in 1989, Landry had a Hall of Fame coaching career. The Cowboys were in the Super Bowl five times in the 1970s, the most appearances for any team in one decade. The Cowboys won two of those games. He was a defensive coach with the Giants, able to try out his latest innovations against Lombardi in practice. He invented the four-three defense with four down linemen and three linebackers. The middle linebacker was the key. Instead of lining up a fifth lineman over the center, Landry moved him back a couple of yards off the line. He had the perfect man to put in the middle and make it work: Sam Huff.

Of course, thanks to Landry, the four-three became the predominant defense in the NFL for the next forty years. When Landry was hired by Dallas, he refined it with a variation called the Flex defense. Two of his defensive linemen played right on the line of scrimmage and two of them lined up one yard off the line. The concept was designed to give the linemen better pursuit angles based on where Landry thought the play was going. The four-three caught on around the NFL. The Flex did not.

Defense was Landry's strength, but he allowed defensive coordinator Ernie Stautner to call the Cowboys' plays and determine the personnel groupings. Yet Landry called the Cowboys' offensive plays and was always tinkering with last-minute changes to the game plan after his assistants had worked with him on it all week. Landry revolutionized shifting and multiple formations to confuse the defense and had his big offensive linemen rise up and then get down in their stance just before the snap so as to hide the smaller running backs and receivers as they were going in motion or shifting in and out of the backfield. Until Walsh came along, Landry was the top offensive innovator in the game. There were lots of bells and whistles in his offense, but he still believed in two basic concepts to winning games: Play defense and run the ball.

Landry was a portrait in concentration as the game against the 49ers started to take shape in the second quarter. He was studying his play sheet, deciphering what Walsh was setting up for later in the game, trying to find a way for the Cowboys to take advantage of the turnovers the defense was providing. This was not going to be a smashmouth defensive struggle. It very well could come down to who had the ball last. Landry would communicate with his quarterback on the sideline, but you never saw him wandering too far onto the field shouting instructions to his players or questioning an official's call. That was not his style. But there were exceptions. When the 49ers were faced with a fourth and inches from the Cowboys

4-yard line on a third-quarter drive, Landry immediately knew the play Walsh was sending in to Montana.

In one of his most animated sideline moments, Landry shouted, "quarterback," then balled each of his hands into a fist and brought them together against his chest. "Quarterback sneak," he yelled. Montana took the snap and dove toward the first down. The officials didn't even need to measure. A flag was down and Randy White was penalized for being offside. Landry was thinking along with Walsh, although he was badly outcoached on the 49ers final drive, if only because he didn't overrule Stautner.

But it was hard to argue with his entire package of Xs and Os. Not many were better. "From a history standpoint, he was just a fantastic football coach," Roger Staubach said. "People respected him and he deserved it. He wasn't going to talk your arm off. He wasn't about small talk."

Staubach and Landry never sat down to drink beer and eat nachos and watch film. They watched film, just not with the alcoholic refreshments. Staubach never saw Landry drink anything that required a driver's license. Landry never let himself get too close to his players. One day he might have to cut them, and that would be tough enough. But he cared. He didn't have to be buddies with the players to show them that their life away from the field was important to him. "When I separated my shoulder, he sat through the operation. He was there the next day, visited me in the room. He cared about people," Staubach said. "We lost a child stillborn. He'd ask about Marianne. He was a good human being."

How could any coach, including Landry, overcome a draft like 1982, months after The Catch when the Cowboys selected Kentucky State cornerback Rod Hill in the first round and Yale linebacker Jeff Rohrer in the second round?

Hill was not only supposed to be a shutdown cornerback but a dynamic punt returner. It didn't take long for the veterans to nickname him Shrine, as in East-West Shrine. It was a clever way of chastising him for running east-west, sideline-to-sideline, on punt returns. Two years later, after Hill had been traded to the Bills, he was injured and didn't suit up for a game the Cowboys lost in Buffalo. The Bills had lost the first eleven games of the season until Dallas came to town. As the Cowboys players reached the tunnel after the humiliating loss, there was Hill screaming and pointing and making fun of them. He was a happy-go-lucky kid who just didn't get it. Surely it took self-restraint for one of the Cowboys not to deck him on the way to the locker room. And Hill would have gone down just as easily as he did on punt returns.

Rohrer was a great guy and very bright, but he was never much of a player. His biggest contribution might have been singing the *Beverly Hillbillies* theme song in the Cowboys locker room two days after Jerry Jones bought the team.

Brandt hit it big with Yale running back Calvin Hill in 1969, and he ventured many times into the small-college pool to get players with football backgrounds similar to Rod Hill's. But he overplayed his hand in 1982, not what the Cowboys needed coming off the loss to the 49ers. And just as they passed over Montana in the 1979 draft, when he fell deep into the third round, they failed to take advantage when Pittsburgh quarterback Dan Marino dropped all the way to the end of the first round in 1983. They had White and they liked unproven backup Gary Hogeboom, so they drafted Arizona State defensive end Jim Jeffcoat instead of Marino. Jeffcoat was a blue-collar player who stuck around twelve years and later was on their coaching staff, but in a span of five years, they passed on Montana and Marino, who then faced each other in the Super Bowl following the 1984 season. The only solace was, the Cowboys were not alone.

Brandt last worked his magic in 1977 when he traded up from

the back end of the first round to the number-two spot to draft Tony
Dorsett, a lightning-fast running back from Pitt. But he was unable
to repeat his sleight of hand in 1981 when he was desperate to get
North Carolina linebacker Lawrence Taylor. The Saints were picking first and wanted South Carolina running back George Rogers.
The Giants were next. The Cowboys were not bashful about trading
within the division. By 1974, Landry had ended the long-running
quarterback controversy by choosing Staubach over Craig Morton.
The Giants, deep into the post–Fran Tarkenton era, were very much
in need of a quarterback and wanted Morton. Brandt sent him to
New York during the 1974 season for the Giants first-round pick in
1975. Because everything seemed to be going the Cowboys' way in
those days, the Giants made the trade completely one-sided by finishing 2–12 and earning the second pick in the draft, which then
belonged to the Cowboys. Good thing there was a hole in the roof
at Texas Stadium because the laughter about the stupidity of the Giants might have blown the thing right off. The Falcons took quarterback Steve Bartkowski first and the Cowboys took defensive
tackle Randy White, who went on to have a Hall of Fame career.
They did pass on Walter Payton to take White but made the trade
for Dorsett two years later.

Brandt knew that Giants general manager George Young loved
LT. They were at the same game against Clemson, scouting him his
senior year. Young called it the most dominant individual performance he had ever seen. The Cowboys and Giants were playing the
next afternoon at the Meadowlands. Brandt and Young were seated
next to each other in first class on the flight from Greenville, South
Carolina, to LaGuardia. Young even gave Brandt a ride to the Cowboys' team hotel. But they never once discussed the Superman performance they had just witnessed. Young knew the Giants had to
have Taylor. Brandt knew he had to find a way to move up ahead of
the Giants to get him. There was no point in even asking Young if

he wanted to make a trade. Not only was Young much too smart to fall for whatever package Brandt would concoct, but after the Giants got burned on Morton five years before the Giants hired Young, there was no way he would let history repeat itself. Instead, when the draft order was established, with the Saints picking first and the Giants picking second, Brandt tried to jump over the Giants and steal the pick from New Orleans by offering the Cowboys' own number one, which was twenty-sixth overall, running back Ron Springs, defensive end Larry Bethea, and linebacker Guy Brown. A typical Dallas deal. Offering nothing they wanted themselves in return for a player they loved.

Unfortunately for Dallas and fortunately for the Giants, the coach of the Saints, Bum Phillips, looked at Rogers and saw the next Earl Campbell, who was his star in the Luv Ya Blues days with the Houston Oilers. Nobody else looked at Rogers that way. But it only took one, and Bum was the guy. He refused to take the Cowboys' package and drafted Rogers, which left Taylor for the Giants.

Despite a questionable draft, Landry took the Cowboys right back to the NFC Championship Game in 1982. They lost to the Redskins, the third straight season they dropped the conference title game on the road, after losses in Philadelphia and San Francisco. But they were overmatched in Washington. The strike reduced the season to just 9 games out of 16. The Cowboys finished 6–3 and were seeded second in the NFC to the Redskins, who were 8–1. In an attempt to overcome the lack of regular-season games and give the playoffs more meaning, the league elected to open up the post-season to eight teams from each conference instead of five. At the time, the Cowboys' appearance in the championship game hid the truth: Bad times and a vicious and divisive quarterback controversy were waiting for them. The Cowboys' second-round victory that year over the Packers turned out to be the last playoff victory for Landry. The Cowboys didn't win another playoff game until 1991,

the third year of Johnson's regime. Things really began to deteriorate in 1984, when the Cowboys' streak of nine consecutive playoff
seasons came to an end.

Emotionally, the Cowboys never got over that loss to the 49ers.
But Brandt didn't help Landry replenish the talent. You can't win
when only two number-one picks and two number-two picks from
the previous ten drafts are starting. And when you give up on a
second-round linebacker named Mike Walter after he played one
season in 1983, put him on waivers, watch Walsh pick him up for the
49ers, and see him play ten seasons for San Francisco, starting on
three Super Bowl championship teams—well, it's hard to keep making up for those kinds of mistakes.

"The draft!" Dennis Thurman, the Cowboys cornerback, says
with disgust as he sits having lunch in a restaurant by the harbor in
Baltimore, one year after he was not retained by John Harbaugh as
the Ravens defensive-back coach after Brian Billick was fired and
one year before Rex Ryan hired him for the same job with the Jets.
"You go back and look at it, the drafts kept getting worse and worse.
Instead of making Todd Christensen go play tight end, they ask him
to do it, he says no, so they cut him. Look at what he goes and does
for the Raiders as a tight end. 'Dude, you are going to play tight
end. We're not cutting you. We are going to convert you to tight
end and that's what you are going to do.' We drafted the Rod Hills
of the world, the Jeff Rohrers of the world. Man, you know what I'm
saying? You draft Mike Walter a year after Jeff Rohrer, and you keep
Rohrer, and Mike Walter goes on to be a better player than Jeff
Rohrer and plays in the Super Bowl."

What kind of guy was Landry? Was there another side to the man
people only saw on Sunday afternoons and Monday nights? He actually had a sharp sense of humor and was not afraid to poke fun at

himself. He did a thirty-second American Express commercial in 1983 dressed up like a cowboy from the Wild Wild West: Long trench coat and ten-gallon hat.

"Do you know me? I'm one of the best-known cowboys in Texas. But a lot of people don't recognize me in a cowboy hat. So I just carry the American Express card. It can help you out in plenty of tough situations."

He starts to exit through a swinging saloon door and says, ". . . Because you never know when you are going to be surrounded by Redskins," just as a group of players dressed in burgundy-and-gold football uniforms circle him.

"Howdy," Landry smiles.

As he walks out of the saloon, the swinging door hits the Redskins players following him. "The American Express card," he says. "Don't leave home without it."

Landry received rave reviews for his deadpan performance and dry sense of humor. Why didn't he show more of this side of himself to the public? His family knew the real Landry, and that's all that really mattered to him. But he could also stop his players in mid-sentence with one of his penetrating staredowns.

On the eve of the 1983 season, Landry cut safety Benny Barnes, who had played for the Cowboys for eleven seasons. He was a Landry favorite, a leader in the locker room and very popular among his teammates and fans. The players were crushed when Landry couldn't find a roster spot for him. The Cowboys were still practicing on Forest Lane, in that blue aluminum-sided dump with one practice field, a tiny locker room, and all the roaches. The lockers were arranged in rows with wooden benches in front of them. News that Barnes had been cut spread quickly throughout the locker room.

Ron Springs touched the ball just a handful of times per game, and his primary job was knocking down big bodies blocking for

Dorsett, but he was an All-Pro at keeping the fellows loose. He was the team comedian. Dorsett may have *looked* like Flip Wilson, but Springs had his sense of humor.

Springs decided to hold a revival meeting to protest Barnes's release. He stood up on the bench in front of his locker. He was in Ghetto Row, the name given by the black players to the section of the room where many of them lockered side by side. They nicknamed Springs Idi because he was a dead ringer for Idi Amin, the military dictator and president of Uganda from 1971 to 1979. But Springs patterned his preaching after Martin Luther King. Idi jumped up on the bench and began his sermon of the day. The subject: Barnes.

"How long are we going to take this!" he shouted.

"Not long, brother Ron!" the players answered.

"How long!" Springs shouted.

"Not long!"

Landry, ready for practice, had his game face on as he walked through the locker room. He glanced over at Springs up on the bench and all the players gathered around him and shot Springs a look that told Springs everything he needed to know: If he didn't knock it off, he could go hang out with Barnes.

"Meeting is over," Springs announced.

Landry never said a word. In ten minutes, the Cowboys were out on the field getting in their final practices before they would open the season with a thrilling 31–30 victory at RFK Stadium in Washington on a Monday night. The Cowboys began the season 7–0, finished 12–4, two games behind the Redskins, and then lost a wild-card playoff game at home to the Rams as the postseason misery continued.

The perception was always that the players were so intimidated by Landry that they couldn't be themselves in the locker room or speak their minds to the media. In reality, Landry was so consumed with the football part of his job that he rarely ventured into the locker room except passing through to get to the practice field.

The kidding around with the players was left to Dan Reeves and Mike Ditka, trusted Landry assistants. Landry listened to them. Reeves would go on to coach the Broncos, Giants, and Falcons and lose all four Super Bowls he coached. Ditka won the Super Bowl with the Bears, then had no success when he finished his coaching career with the Saints. But as assistants, they were the bridge from Landry to the players and had played recently enough that they could relate to them, understand their concerns, and know how to fix the problems. When Reeves was hired by the Broncos after the 1980 season and Ditka left for Chicago one year later, Landry lost not only his two best assistant coaches, he lost his main connection to the players.

"They would sit next to you at your locker and kind of play little games or tell stories," Thurman said. "You knew they were former players. They connected with the players, and the players saw them as easy to talk to. That was good. Coach Landry didn't come in the locker room. He might walk through. That wasn't his deal. To me, he was pretty much like this: 'As long as you're not breaking any of these nine-hundred rules I have here, you are fine.' I don't know how it was before I got there in 1978, but with Dorsett having got there the year before and with Tony Hill, Butch Johnson, and then me, and then Springs coming in the year after that, the dynamic of the guys they were drafting was changing."

Landry didn't feel the need to socialize, bond, or be friends with his players. He didn't police the locker room. He didn't work the room. He coached the team. He was oblivious to the growing drug problems on his team and around the league. He was beginning to lose touch with the players he needed to lead. Walsh would often go to postgame get-togethers with his players, and Bill Parcells worked the locker room better than anybody, sitting and drinking his coffee as he small-talked with them early in the morning, but the Cowboys only saw Landry in the meeting rooms and the practice field.

When Tennessee rookie Bill Bates made the team as a special-teams sensation in 1983, Landry marveled at how quickly the veteran players had taken to him and even had started to call him the Master, which Landry thought was a tremendous compliment. But the joke went right over his head. He failed to put Master together with Bill's last name. What was funnier: The nickname or Landry just not figuring out the joke?

As a result of Landry's growing detachment, the Cowboys of the eighties were easily the most outspoken team in the NFL. Regardless of which corner of the locker room the notepads and microphones ventured, somebody was always ready to say something outrageous. It was a team full of free spirits. Around the league, players felt sorry for the Cowboys, believing they were inhibited, restricted, and held back by Landry. If anything, he didn't have enough control of his players, because they had no misgivings or restraint about how they expressed themselves, whether it was about playing time, contracts or, quite frankly, one another. Butch Johnson was always upset about the way Landry used him. He thought he should be starting over Drew Pearson or Tony Hill. And he certainly never imagined Landry would pass him over for Doug Donley, whom the players nicknamed White Lightning. Hill was once hurt in a game and Landry put Donley in over Johnson. His reasoning was that Donley was Hill's backup at split end and Johnson was Pearson's backup at flanker. Johnson was incensed. The next day, he wasn't at the meetings or practice. It turned out Landry gave him the day off to cool off. Johnson took the short flight from Dallas to Cancun. Vince Lombardi, who grew up in the coaching business in New York with Landry and intimidated his players, surely would have questioned his friend about allowing an in-season vacation for a disgruntled player. Johnson wasn't any happier about his backup role when he returned, but at least he had a fun time in Mexico. Landry could be inflexible to the point where it hurt the team. As a player, Johnson was clearly superior to Donley, but Landry would not shift Johnson over to replace Hill, although he would have had no trouble adapting to split end from flanker.

Landry had his share of problems with players. There was Duane Thomas, of course. And Hollywood Henderson had such an extreme drug problem that he once claimed he was snorting cocaine on the sidelines of the Super Bowl. And when drugs became such an issue around the Cowboys in the mid eighties, they were nicknamed South America's Team, which didn't mean they had a large fan base in Buenos Aires. Landry didn't have a clue what was going on.

"If I have a weakness, it may be that I'm too compassionate," he said a few weeks after he was fired. "I give people a chance to see whether they can turn it around. It didn't work out for me too often. My disappointment in the case of Duane Thomas, is I had no idea what he was doing. At the end of the sixties, the drug culture came in, and everybody wanted to do their own thing. I knew something was different with Duane, but I didn't know what it was. Boy, it's a shame to see a guy's career being ruined. Thomas Henderson was such a showman, I couldn't tell whether or not he was serious. He was another great talent wasted. The most disappointing thing is, I just couldn't help them enough. I feel guilty that I couldn't get them back on the right track. Once you get on coke or crack, you're destined for trouble. Nobody is going to change you, either."

The players genuinely liked Landry and were distraught when he was fired. They were not disturbed by his aloofness and were amused by his absent-minded tendencies.

"Cliff Harris and Charlie Waters had a Christmas party at the Royal Oaks Country Club and threw Coach Landry in the pool,"

Pearson said. "He was pissed. I couldn't believe those guys did it. He had pants and a shirt on. No suit. It was one of those parties. It was just us. After a while, what do you do? You get rowdy as football players. Players started to throw each other in. Cliff and Charlie got the nerve to throw Coach Landry in. That was something."

Harris and Waters could get away with it, as sacrilegious as it sounds. But they had seniority and were among Landry's favorites.

Waters loved Landry. They thought as one. "He and I were probably as close as a player and coach could be," Waters said. "He was a quarterback in college, then moved to defensive back and played corner for his first years in the league and then moved to safety. Well, I was a quarterback in college that played corner for awhile when I first came into the league before I moved to safety."

One week Staubach was hurt, White was second team, and the third-string quarterback had a broken finger. "I was the fourth-team quarterback," Waters said. "Well, Danny goes all week and takes all the snaps. Roger never gets well." The third quarterback never takes a practice snap. "So the Friday before the Sunday game, we are riding over to the practice field," Waters said. "It was raining and we used to shift and bus over to an artificial turf field. I made it a point to go over and sit by Coach Landry on the way over there."

Waters starts a conversation. "Hey, Coach, let me ask you something. What's going to happen here? Roger is still hurt, right?" Waters said.

"Yeah," Landry said.

"Pete is not even going to dress out?" Waters said of quarterback number three.

"No," Landry said.

"What's going to happen if Danny goes down?"

"You're going to play quarterback," Landry said.

"Shit, don't you think I ought to take a snap or two?" Waters said.

Landry then told a funny story about himself. "He was like you and me telling war stories of a Thanksgiving game in your backyard with all your buddies," Waters said. "It was the greatest moment I ever had with him. You could see his little blue eyes. He tells me this story about coming off the bench as a defensive back to play quarterback. Two quarterbacks got hurt in a game. He started playing quarterback and then made up plays in the huddle and they won the game."

"And," Landry then told Waters, "the next week I had to play quarterback again, and we prepared for it and I took all the snaps and we got beat by fifty points."

"Well, what about me?" Waters said.

"The moral to that story is, I don't want you to be prepared," Landry laughed.

It was such an unusually light moment for Landry that all Waters could think was, *This guy is a real guy just telling a funny story.* "He was aloof. He was above it. But then he was just being a guy."

Staubach was Landry's favorite player. He admired everything about him. They became friends when Staubach retired. They played a lot of golf together. But when he was playing, Landry believed in Staubach because he knew how competitive he was. He wasn't in love with Staubach's style. He thought he ran too much. Even as Staubach was still running around in what turned out to be the final years of his career, Landry was telling him that some day he would learn. "I respected him and he was a great person, but we weren't always in sync," Staubach said.

It got to be a joke in the Staubach home on the Saturday night before home games. Roger would be sitting around with his wife, and the phone would ring, and Marianne would predict it was Landry before Staubach even picked it up. Landry wouldn't even say hello. He would just starting talking: "You know on that sixteen wing post?"

Landry would change plays the night before the game. On Friday afternoons, he would take the offensive film home and study it. Landry was a defensive coach, and each week would find flaws in the game plan. That's why he would call Staubach on Saturday night before home games, or if the Cowboys were on the road, they would get together in Landry's hotel room. Landry was a brilliant offensive mind, and it was a good thing Sunday came once a week, because once the game arrived, he couldn't tinker with the plan any longer. That was a big relief for his quarterbacks.

Landry's image as a coach his players feared may have been true earlier in his career, but when the eighties arrived, the Cowboys locker room was filled with guys who weren't afraid to speak out. Landry had no patience for distractions and simply ignored them.

Dorsett, a Hall of Famer and the NFL's seventh all-time leading rusher, always wanted the ball more than Landry would give it to him. "I still don't like it to this day," he said. Dorsett was just 183 pounds, but he was so adept at making the defense miss that he almost never took a big hit. He found ways to turn what would have been crunching hits into glancing blows. "But Tom was a real stickler about my size," he said. "I'm still frustrated to this day. Some of these guys probably will be passing me on the all-time rushing list."

Johnson couldn't believe he wasn't starting over Pearson or Hill. Hogeboom was frustrated that he wasn't playing, and he let everybody know about it. Harvey Martin never felt loved. Too Tall Jones dissed the 49ers. Randy White wanted more money. Dorsett wanted more money. They all wondered why Schramm gave all that money to Herschel Walker. Landry didn't care. He let Schramm worry about any discontent and Brandt worry about the contracts. Landry spent his time trying to outsmart Bill Walsh and Joe Gibbs and Bill Parcells.

"Including Tex, I knew him better than anybody," Brandt said. "The guy had vast knowledge of anything you wanted to talk about—banking, politics. He was pretty quick-witted. The reason we were so good with the computer is, he adapted to it. He didn't fight it."

Brandt lived a "pitching wedge" from Schramm and a half-mile from Landry, and although they worked together for an amazing twenty-nine years, they traveled in different social circles. Brandt and Landry used to ride to the home games together. Landry would leave his house on Rockbrook and in a minute or so be at Brandt's house on Myron. It was a routine they followed for decades, Landry driving, Brandt riding shotgun. "I saw a lot of sides of him," Brandt said. "It seemed that the easier the team we were about to play, the more ingrained he was. The harder the team, the more loose he was. There were days we were playing New Orleans when we were a 16-point favorite and he didn't even know I was in the car with him."

Landry believed that to make it through the season, his team could not get too high after a victory or too down after a loss. His goal for the first half of any season was for his team to be in position to make a run at the playoffs as they made the turn for home in the second half. This level-headed approach often wound up getting him criticized: His team needed to play with more emotion; not everything was related to a computer printout. How could his players come out fired up when the boss sometimes looked like he needed a couple of greenies?

The personality of the team often reflects the personality of the coach. But in the case of Landry's Cowboys in the early eighties, that was hardly true. They were a bunch of trash-talking, fun-loving guys who respected Landry but did not fear him. They never wanted him to call them out on his bullhorn at a training camp practice in Thousand Oaks with all the fans watching, but he would never intentionally embarrass a player publicly or criticize him in the media. A huge generation gap ultimately developed, and instead of trying to become more in tune with the changing attitudes and new problems his players presented to him, Landry retreated. In part, that led to their no longer being Landry's team. He wanted to make believe the drug problem didn't exist.

"We always had certain guys that dabbled," Thurman said. "Was it more than any other team? There were several guys who did their own thing. As long as they came ready to play, it didn't matter. We never really worried about it being an issue or a problem. The perception is, there were more guys doing it than there were. Once the media finds out about something, then it becomes magnified. Steroids have been around forever. Players were doing steroids back when I was in high school.

"We used to look at Pittsburgh, and we'd look at us, and we'd go, 'They're doing something different than what we're doing.' One of Dorsett's things is, he would say, 'Pittsburgh's offensive linemen come out and they lead with their biceps. Our offensive linemen come out and they lead with their gut.' That was one of his deals. He would say, 'Look at their offensive line and look at our offensive line. Whatever they're doing, we need to be doing.' We were different. There were a selected few guys on our team that got involved, but for the most, part, no."

Marijuana, cocaine, steroids? Landry was oblivious. "He was not the most worldly person," Thurman said. "Football was his world and religion was his world. Anything outside of those two things, I don't think he knew a whole lot about."

Jerry Jones will forever be ridiculed as the man who fired Tom Landry. But in reality, he did what most fans wanted for years in the Dallas–Fort Worth area. They wanted Landry out. They just didn't want an outsider from Arkansas coming in to sign the pink slip.

They wanted Schramm to do it, or even Bright. But Schramm would never fire Landry, and Bright offered to do it for Jerry Jones. Bright was an Aggie from Texas A&M, and Landry was a Longhorn from the University of Texas. It was a bad marriage from the moment Bright signed on.

Schramm hired Landry on the recommendation of Giants owner Wellington Mara, who had been very close to Landry as one of his players, then as a player-coach, and then just a coach on the staff of Jim Lee Howell. "I remember I signed for $6,000 with a $500 bonus, and the most I ever made was $15,000," Landry said. "When New York made me a player-coach in 1954, they raised me up to $12,000. I was playing left cornerback, I coached the whole defense by myself and made All-Pro. When I went into Wellington Mara's office to ask for a raise, he said, 'I don't know if you had a good enough year.' He's been picking up my lunches ever since."

Lombardi left Howell's staff after the 1958 season to coach the Packers. Landry left after 1959, deciding he wanted to move back to Texas and enter private business and raise a family. Howell retired after 1960. The Giants tried to get Lombardi, a native New Yorker, to return for what was once his dream job, but he elected to remain in Green Bay. The closest Lombardi ever came to returning to the Giants was having a rest stop on the New Jersey Turnpike near Giants Stadium named after him. With Lombardi and Landry both gone, the Giants promoted Allie Sherman instead. Lombardi and Landry are in the Hall of Fame. All Sherman is known for is trading Sam Huff and Giants fans serenading him with chants of "Goodbye, Allie."

Landry's retirement from football didn't last very long. The Houston Oilers and the Dallas Texans of the new league, the American Football League, were both interested in hiring him to be their head coach in 1960. Landry was one of the brightest young minds in the NFL, and the last thing Mara wanted was for him to go over to the rival league, even if no one from the NFL took the AFL seriously at first. Mara called Schramm and encouraged him to hire Landry, and Schramm sold him to Clint Murchison. Landry, Schramm, and Brandt were a team for nearly three decades. It was a simple relationship: Brandt scouted the players and signed them, Landry coached them, and Schramm, one of the great showmen in NFL history, promoted them and found a way to turn this expansion team from Texas into America's Team.

But in the final years of the Landry administration, Schramm was frustrated with his longtime coach. He felt he was trying to win in the eighties with the same philosophy that he'd used in the sixties and seventies. Time was marching on and Landry was not. After the 1985 season, Schramm was fed up. The Cowboys had just won the NFC East with a 10–6 record in a down year for the division but then were humiliated and shut out 20–0 in the divisional round of the playoffs by the Rams, whose quarterback, Dieter Brock, was in his first season after coming south from the CFL. But the Rams had running back Eric Dickerson, who played his college ball at SMU in Dallas, and he carved up the Cowboys defense for 248 yards. Once the season ended, Schramm got to work. Operating behind Landry's back, he hired 49ers offensive coordinator Paul Hackett to run the Cowboys passing game, which had been the sole domain of Landry. Hackett was an ambitious coach with eyes on Landry's job, and their relationship was frosty from the time Hackett arrived. Hackett had been in San Francisco with Walsh, who didn't do much to stop him from leaving. Hackett was Schramm's guy, and he immediately jumped to the front of the line as a potential Landry successor. If it had been up to Landry, Hackett never would have made it east of El Paso.

Hackett had fallen out of favor with Walsh in San Francisco, although he and Montana always shared a mutual admiration. One of the reasons Montana pushed for his trade to the Chiefs in 1993 was the presence of Hackett on Marty Schottenheimer's staff in Kansas City. It took a couple of years, but Landry neutered Hackett, stripping him of all responsibility. Schramm could force Landry to hire Hackett, but he was powerless to dictate how he deployed him. Landry had an ego far bigger than any of his players, and he viewed Hackett as threat to his power. So Hackett went from pass-offense coordinator to past-offense coordinator.

Schramm tried again during the 1988 season to make inroads on Landry's power, this time with more far-reaching intentions. After he heard the division rival Eagles were interested in Jimmy Johnson, who was dominating college football at Miami, Schramm had an idea: He would offer Johnson the opportunity to come to Dallas as Landry's defensive coordinator in 1989 and be designated the head coach–in–waiting. Johnson was Schramm's kind of guy: He was flashy, liked to have fun, and was the hottest name in coaching. But Johnson knew he didn't have to take an internship to become a head coach. He was ready to "shop for the groceries and do the cooking," as Bill Parcells would later say during his falling-out with Patriots owner Robert Kraft. Schramm didn't get very far with Johnson.

At the 49ers-Bengals Super Bowl in January of 1989, Johnson sat in the Cowboys' luxury box at the invitation of Brandt. Landry and Schramm were there too. Schramm, Brandt, and Landry had no idea that one month later, Johnson would have Landry's job and, in effect, have Schramm's and Brandt's jobs, too, because he was running the draft and making the key personnel decisions. Landry would be fired, Jones would pay off Schramm to leave, and Brandt would leave reluctantly. Brandt always considered himself the best friend of every college head coach in America, but that was not enough to save him with Johnson. There was no loyalty in the new Jones-Johnson administration.

Schramm did manage to get one last laugh on Jones. The NFL owners tabled the vote on Jones's purchase of the team at the league meeting in Palm Desert, California, in March 1989, ostensibly because they still had questions about Jones's financing plan. This was overshadowed by the shocking announcement at the meetings that Commissioner Pete Rozelle was retiring. But the word among the owners was that the vote was delayed because they wanted Jones to increase the golden parachute to Schramm before they would approve the sale and let him into their exclusive club. A couple of months later, Jones won approval at a league meeting in New York, and the sale was official.

"Tex had owned some shares of the team, and we agreed to buy his shares," Jones said. "But there was another area [in] which Tex felt he was due a settlement. As it turned out, at the end of the day, until we had all that resolved, then there was not going to be an approval."

Jones had already fired Landry and made major changes in the organization, but he still did not officially own the Cowboys. The league later instituted a rule that an owner could not start acting like the owner until he was the owner. "Bum Bright told me that he told Tex, 'I've just dealt with Jerry. You would have been better off handling it with him and saying, "tell me what you will settle for," than you would be hard trading. He will give you more than you will ever get out of him negotiating.'"

Landry was transformed into a martyr by Jones. Just a few months earlier, fans would have lined the streets to protest his return as coach. But when a bully like Jones came to town and fired the icon, almost a hundred thousand fans lined the streets of downtown Dallas for Hats Off to Tom Landry Day on April 22, 1989. Getting fired was the best thing to happen to Landry at that point in his life. The team was going nowhere, and the resentment toward him was just going to get worse. The longer he remained, the more damage he did to his legacy. In the end, Jones did him a favor. On the day of the parade, all was forgiven by the fans.

"You've made this day the most exciting and meaningful in my life," Landry told the crowd. "Not in my wildest imagination did I think this could happen. My family will never forget it."

It took him years to accept Jones's invitation to join the Ring of Honor at Texas Stadium that Schramm created. He was inducted in 1993. Nearly eleven years to the day after Landry lost his job, he lost his life at the age of seventy-five on February 13, 2000, after a lengthy battle with leukemia, the same illness that killed Walsh at the same age seven years later. Landry so desperately wanted one last trip to the Super Bowl. Joe Montana to Dwight Clark took that chance away from him.

4

MONTANA TO CLARK

WIGHT CLARK and Joe Montana became close friends right away. They enjoyed hanging out with each other, developed instant chemistry on the field, and had each other's back. Montana had faith in Clark, the most important part of any quarterback-receiver relationship. He always knew where he was going to be, and Clark knew Joe would always find a way to get him the ball.

Clark had good size and deceptive speed. He also had great hands. He had a breakout season in 1981 with 85 catches for 1,105 yards. Montana firmly established himself during the regular season as an elite quarterback who could win championships, by throwing for 3,565 yards and 19 touchdowns. But getting past the Cowboys right now was going to be a problem. Were these young 49ers ready for such a big moment? The Cowboys knew all about Clark. In the beatdown they took in October, he had four catches for 135 yards and somehow managed to take a Montana pass and turn it into a 78-yard touchdown. His yardage equaled the entire number put together by the eight Cowboys who caught the 12 passes Dallas completed.

Montana to Clark, of course, is synonymous with one of the greatest plays in NFL history, certainly the single greatest play of each of their careers. But before there was The Catch, there was the "triple move" by Clark that, surprisingly, didn't give Dennis Thurman vertigo.

It was just more than halfway through the second quarter of the championship game. The Niners trailed 10–7 but had the ball on the Dallas 20. The Cowboys dialed up a blitz. D. D. Lewis came through and was in perfect position to drill Montana. He left his feet anticipating a pass that he could swat into the third row, just as Bill Russell, the most famous shot blocker, had done all those years at the University of San Francisco. Lewis went up, but Montana held on to the ball. Lewis's left hand grazed Montana's left shoulder but did not bring him down. Clark, meanwhile, had split out to the left with Thurman assigned single coverage. Once he maneuvered Lewis out of the picture, Montana stepped up into the pocket. There he encountered Bon Breunig, a solid if unspectacular linebacker. He was Danny White's best friend on the team; sometimes it seemed as if he was Danny White's *only* friend on the team. They'd played together at Arizona State. Breunig was on the ground and had his arms wrapped around Montana's ankles. It looked like one of those cartoons when a dog sinks his teeth into the legs of the mailman.

Clark was a precise route runner, well known for being adept at the double move. He had done it to Walls earlier in the second quarter on a 38-yard reception. Forget about the double move this time. Clark pulled out the triple move.

"It was the best route I ever ran in all my nine years in the NFL," Clark said. He broke inside on Thurman, broke outside, and then cut in inside again. He ran for the post as Thurman was running for the sideline. Clark and Thurman were running in opposite directions. Clark wound up in the end zone. Landry might have been the closest Cowboy to Clark and he was standing on the sideline opposite the one from where the play started out. Montana didn't throw a classic pass, but it was a beauty under the circumstances. Clark went to the ground to secure it.

"What made it so great is, Joe found the time to stay alive," Clark said. "I'm not the fastest guy in the world, and to run a route takes a while. To run a triple move takes time. They were blitzing and Joe was bobbing and weaving. He found a way to get the ball out of his hand at the last second. He's lucky he could even throw a pass. It was a great pass. He had just enough on it with all those people all over him."

Clark spiked the ball, and it bounced high in the air. On the way down, it hit him in the head. "That's just God keeping me humble," he said.

He retrieved the ball. The 49ers led, 17–14.

Montana to Clark. They had great chemistry. There was more to come.

Clark was sitting at the counter at the restaurant of the Howard Johnson's in Redwood City, California, during a break in rookie minicamp. He had been drafted by the 49ers, and not even he could believe Bill Walsh used one of his ten picks to take him after he'd caught just 33 passes in four years at Clemson. This was the start of his professional career: dinner at HoJo's. For all Clark knew, it would be the highlight. He had to be careful how he spent his per diem.

He was cherishing every moment because there was no guarantee he was even going to make it to training camp. He could soon be back home in North Carolina trying to figure out what he was going to do with his life. He was selected in the tenth round, the 249th of 340 players taken in the 1979 draft. The rookies were staying at the HoJo's down the street from the 49ers' spartan training facility, and Clark was waiting for his meal when this frail white kid with skinny legs walks in and sits at the opposite side of the counter.

Who knew it was the future Joe Cool? Who knew this was the guy who was going to be his great friend, make him famous, but then blame him for trying to kiss up to management fourteen years later by interfering with his career and refuse to speak to him for two years? Who knew it was going to take his wife calling him with an invitation to his retirement celebration at Justin Herman Plaza in downtown San Francisco to end the cold war? There was a lot they didn't know about each other that day at the Howard Johnson's, including the way they would forever be linked in NFL history. Who could foresee that the kid quarterback from New Eagle—a dot on the map of western Pennsylvania, the part of the country that produced steel mills and coal mines and Johnny Unitas, Johnny Lujack, and Joe Namath, and later Dan Marino and Jim Kelly—would team up with the long-shot wideout from Charlotte, North Carolina, on one of the most memorable plays in sports history.

Clark had seen Joe Montana only once in person. It was November 12, 1977, Notre Dame's national championship season. The Irish traveled to South Carolina to take on Clemson, ranked number fifteen in the country. That day, Clark was about to learn what Joe Montana was going to be all about.

"We were ahead 17–7 and that son of a bitch brings them back and kicks our ass, 21–17," Clark said. "It was one of his miraculous comebacks."

Clark was thrilled just to be drafted. Montana was disappointed he lasted until the end of the third round because he said the Giants, Packers, and Chiefs told him they would take him in the first round. Montana came into the NFL motivated to prove he could win championships and be a Pro Bowl quarterback. Clark wanted to make it through the morning practice and be asked back in the afternoon. They would both eventually get their numbers retired by the 49ers, but on this day and at this minicamp, they were just trying to decipher Walsh's complicated West Coast offense while chowing down at HoJo's.

"He's got long blond hair and a Fu Manchu, and he's got on little running shorts and his legs are twigs. So he's walking in and I'm eating, and I can't decide if he's a player or not," Clark said. "In my mind, I'm thinking if he's a player, he's got to be a kicker because with that little scrawny body there is no way he can be a football player. I'm fairly outgoing, and I said hello to him."

"Are you with the 49ers?"

"Yeah."

"I'm Dwight Clark."

"I'm Joe Montana."

Clark nearly fell off his stool. "You got to be kidding me."

That's how their friendship began.

"He thought I was a kicker," Montana said.

"He actually had a car, so he was transportation and a really good guy," Clark said.

Montana knew about Clark, too, but not too much. "The kid on the other side at Clemson, Jerry Butler, at the time, he was very highly touted," he said. "The quarterback, Steve Fuller, also got a lot of play."

Butler was a first-round pick of the Bills that year, and Fuller was a first-round pick of the Chiefs. Both were picked way ahead of Clark and Montana. Fuller played so poorly that Kansas City drafted another quarterback, Todd Blackledge, in the first round four years later. Butler played in Buffalo for eight seasons. But if it wasn't for Fuller being considered one of the best players in the '79 draft, the San Francisco legend of Dwight Clark would never have happened.

NFL teams spend millions preparing for the draft. They have scouts all over the country trying to uncover talent. Back in 1979, in the days before the NFL started bringing in over three hundred players to Indianapolis to the scouting combine to work them out, interview them, get inside their heads, and examine them from head to toe, it was more an art than a science. There are no secrets anymore. Everybody is dealing with the same information, the same tapes, the same reports from the same doctors.

Luck was more of the equation in 1979. Sometimes, despite all the work a team puts into the draft, luck can be the great equalizer. The 49ers were lucky nobody saw in Montana what Walsh did when he had a private workout for him in Los Angeles.

"I didn't see Joe until the last three days before the draft," Walsh said. "We were totally enamored with Joe Montana."

He saw a quarterback whose skills would translate perfectly to the chess-game West Coast offense Walsh planned to install. Hit the receiver in stride. Give him an opportunity to make yards after the catch. Run a short-play action pass in the first quarter to set up a deep throw off the same formation in the third quarter. Run a sweep and later in the game run it again, only this time run a reverse to the wide receiver coming the other way. Montana had the perfect football IQ for Walsh.

In Clark's case, he lucked out when he picked up the phone. On a nice spring day in South Carolina, Clark was walking out the door with his golf bags on his shoulder to go hit and chase a few. The phone rang in the rented three-bedroom off-campus apartment he shared in his senior year with Fuller and tight end Cliff Bray. The phone call was supposed to change Fuller's life. But it changed Clark's instead. He stared at the phone. The tee time would have to have to wait one minute. He picked it up.

The voice on the other end was authoritative but unfamiliar. "This is Bill Walsh and I'm here to work out Steve Fuller."

"Well, hold on, and I'll get him," Clark said.

"Wait a minute, who is this?" Walsh asked.

"Dwight Clark."

"Did you play wide receiver?" Walsh asked.

Walsh went on to explain that he was in a bind. He needed somebody to catch passes for Fuller so Walsh wouldn't have to do it himself. He wanted to concentrate on Fuller and not worry about stumbling or catching one that would leave a mark in his gut. And he surely didn't want to pull a hamstring.

"If you don't mind, could you come and run routes?" Walsh asked.

"Of course," Clark said.

He had only worked out for two teams. The Steelers had come to Clemson to check out the seniors. And Clark worked out for the Chiefs receivers coach. He was not expecting to be drafted. Having Walsh invite him to Fuller's workout was like skipping the *American Idol* auditions and making it right into the finals. But Walsh was a lot tougher than Simon Cowell. He was meticulous in choosing all the pieces for his state-of-the-art offense. This was Clark's opportunity to make an impression even if Walsh's intention for him was just to give Fuller a target. He was just a body. This was not intended to be anything resembling a tryout for Clark. But there is only one chance to make a first impression, and Clark knew this was it. He was excited.

"I went and ran routes for Coach Walsh and just had one of those really lucky days," Clark said. "I caught every pass. A couple of circus catches. It was just a very fortunate day."

When they were done, Walsh spoke with Fuller for a couple of minutes on the field. But then the scene shifted, as in one of those clichéd chick flicks where the guy goes to the dance with one girl and goes home with another. Walsh liked Fuller, but he loved Clark. The 49ers didn't have a first-round pick, and Fuller was projected to go in the middle of the first round. Walsh was not about to trade up to get him. He would think about him if he slipped into the second round. Instead, he turned his attention to Clark.

"Can we go watch some tape of you playing?" Walsh asked.

"Coach, I only caught eleven passes this year. There's just not that much to watch," Clark responded.

"Is there any game where you caught two passes?" Walsh wanted to know.

"Yeah, against North Carolina," Clark said.

They went off to the film room and went into the archives looking for the so-called highlight reel.

Clark was recruited to Clemson as a quarterback, but Tigers coach Red Parker signed four other quarterbacks in his recruiting class, including Fuller, one of the last players to commit. So Parker brought Clark into his office his freshman year. This wasn't the NFL, so Clark was not getting cut or traded. He hadn't done anything wrong, so he wasn't losing his scholarship. Parker explained that the defense was in need of athletes and that if he could play on the other side of the ball, he would make the traveling team. That was a big deal for a freshman. Clark was switched to strong safety. He was such a good athlete, he could play anywhere. "I tried it," Clark said. "I played defense one year."

But this wasn't what he'd signed up for, and he was miserable. He hated it so much that two weeks before returning to school for his sophomore year, he was sitting at the dinner table with his family and told his father, Gene, he wasn't going back to Clemson. Clark had a connection to Bobby Cremins, the basketball coach at Appalachian State, who would later go on to national prominence at Georgia Tech. Clark decided he was switching sports and started working on his jump shot. "Well, that's interesting," his dad said. "Let's think about this for a little bit."

Gene Clark, without telling his son, called Clyde Wren, who had recruited Dwight to Clemson. The next day a contingent of Clemson coaches showed up at the Clark house. "It's tough to turn down eight coaches," Clark said. "I had my jaw locked and all that. But Clyde Wren was a great salesperson, and he sold me on coming back and playing wide receiver. So I did."

He didn't play much his sophomore year—caught five balls. But at least he was playing offense. His junior year, he alternated as the messenger bringing in the plays to Fuller. "We had Jerry Butler on the other side," Clark said. "When we were going to throw, we threw to Jerry Butler."

He caught 17 passes as a junior and slipped to 11 as a senior. About the only thing that popped out was his 17.3 yards per catch. He was good once he had the ball in his hands, a prerequisite for any receiver in Walsh's offense.

"I watched film with Bill," Clark said. "One of the passes I caught was over the middle. I had to go up for it and I got hit pretty hard. When you don't have a lot to watch, if there is one good play, you watch it over and over. So he probably watched that play ten times. The rest of the game I caught one other pass. At Clemson, if you didn't block on the back side of a run play during practice, you had to bear-crawl back to the huddle. So we were definitely blockers. That bear-crawling got old."

Clark, at six four, 215, was built. He blocked like a tight end and ran like a wide receiver, with a 4.5 in the 40. He was a big possession receiver with good enough deep speed to get down the field. "I ran pretty fast for 215," he said. "I'm a foot taller than most of the DBs, so I'm annihilating them. Bill thought that was alright."

Picking up that phone changed everything. Clark is convinced that, if not for Walsh, he would have signed as a free agent with the Chiefs, where his quarterback would have been Fuller. Maybe in the

NFL he would throw him the ball. After Clark ran a 4.5 for the Chiefs, the assistant coach started talking real quiet to him even though nobody else was around.

"You just ran a 4.5. Can you do that every time?" he whispered.

"Don't know," Clark responded.

Bad answer.

"It was like he was trying to keep it to himself," Clark said. "That was kind of funny. That's where I would have ended up. Kansas City."

Walsh went back to San Francisco knowing he'd found a receiver, an important part in his construction project to transform one of the NFL's losers into Super Bowl champions. "Dwight looked good to me. I knew he didn't look necessarily good to many other scouts," Walsh once told NFL Films. "As the draft progressed, many of our scouts said, 'Coach, you can get him in the free-agent market a month from now.' I said, 'No, that man is going to be here, you watch.' And so we drafted him."

Here's how Clark viewed his workout for Walsh: He would be able to tell his kids about it one day. That's about it. He was still just dreaming he would get drafted. The reality was, he felt his name would not be called. Then something positive happened. Archie Reese, a former Clemson player, had come back to visit. He was now playing on the 49ers defensive line.

"Coach Walsh really liked that workout," Reese said. "I wouldn't be surprised if they drafted you."

For the first time, Clark thought there was a chance he would be selected. By the fifth round, Walsh was trying to get the scouts to second his desire to take Clark. Walsh could assert his autonomy; he did have final say and could take Clark any time he wanted, but that was no way to build a franchise. One voice disregarding ten others so early in the draft usually means a bad team. All Walsh kept hearing back was, "Hey, Coach, this kid is a free agent. Don't waste one of our picks on him. He'll be there after the draft. You can get him; we'll sign him then."

Walsh backed down until the sixth round. "How about that Clark kid?" he said.

"Not yet," they said.

But Walsh didn't wait so long to be a head coach to be completely talked out of taking a player he really wanted. By the time the ninth round ended, Walsh wasn't listening to anything but his football instincts.

"He just took my card. He didn't ask anybody, took my name off the board, and turned it in," Clark said. The pick was called in to draft headquarters in New York. It didn't create much interest except perhaps for the Clark family.

There was a big party at Clark's apartment on draft weekend. But it was for Fuller, a lock to go in the first round. It was one year before ESPN started televising the draft, so there was a big crowd around the telephone waiting for it to ring. Fuller went twenty-third overall to the Chiefs. Everybody celebrated. The party was over. Then Clark waited for the phone to ring again. He kept waiting.

On day two of the draft, he was sitting in the apartment by himself. The Fuller party had dispersed. There was no Clark party waiting to happen. It was just him and the phone. It's like watching water boil. The more you watch, the longer it takes. He still didn't truly believe he would be drafted, so he tried to figure out how the free-agent market worked. The Chiefs told him if he didn't get picked, they would offer him a contract. That sounded good. He would be with Fuller, not that his buddy had thrown him a lot of passes when they played together. If he had, maybe Clark wouldn't still be waiting. Would any other team call with a free-agent offer? Would he actually have a choice? He was just hanging out when the phone finally made some noise.

"Hi, this is Sam Wyche." Wyche was a passing-game assistant for

Walsh. "I'm with the 49ers, and we just drafted you in the tenth round," Wyche said. "How do you think you'll like the Bay Area?"

Clark grew up in Charlotte. The nickname for the University of North Carolina–Charlotte teams is the 49ers. Clark was confused. He wasn't expecting a call, not even from the 49ers, not even after his workout with Walsh and after Reese giving him the heads-up that Walsh wanted to draft him. Why was UNCC calling?

"49ers? Where is the Bay Area?" Clark said.

"San Francisco 49ers," Wyche emphasized. "We just drafted you in the tenth round."

Clark wanted to scream. He thought to himself, *I just got drafted by the 49ers!*

His first phone call went to his dad, who wouldn't let him quit playing football after his freshman year. Now he had a chance to play for Bill Walsh and with Joe Montana.

"Holy shit," Clark said.

Bill Ring's first-quarter fumble, which set up Danny White's touchdown pass to Tony Hill only 50 seconds later, was the first of six turnovers for the 49ers. Six turnovers won't win many championship games. Coaches preach every week, not only in the playoffs, that whoever wins the turnover battle wins the game. "They blamed our defense for losing the game," safety Charlie Waters said. "When you get six turnovers you usually win the game."

The Cowboys withstood the 49ers' early surge. The Niners scored just 4:19 into the game, and while nobody expected them to beat Dallas 45–14 as they had in the regular season, allowing Montana to take his team down the field so easily on the first possession was not an indication that Landry's defense had learned anything from the first meeting. But the 49ers only picked up 11 yards the rest of the first quarter. They opened the second quarter at their own 20 and developed some rhythm in the offense. Montana moved the 49ers to a third and 5 from the Cowboys 22. He tried to get it all on a pass to Mike Wilson along the right sideline, but Walls picked it off. His momentum carried him into the end zone, but the officials placed the ball down at the 2.

That put the Dallas offense in a hole, backed up to its own goal line. The 'Boys went three and out, and White punted from his own 10, allowing the 49ers to start their next drive from the Cowboys 47. It didn't take long for Montana to turn that into points. Earl Cooper went up the middle for 11 yards, Montana hit Solomon for 12, Elliott ran 4 yards, and then with Breunig wrapped around his ankles and Larry Bethea about to hit him, Montana threw to a wide-open Clark in the end zone. Now the 49ers led 14–10.

But it would not last very long. After the kickoff, the Cowboys moved from their 20 to the San Francisco 47. It was going to take a lot of points to win this game, so opportunities could not be wasted. Danny White went deep down the right sideline, a pass intended for Pearson that sailed over the receiver's head, Lott intercepted it at the 49ers 12-yard line. He returned it to the San Francisco 37, and it seemed the momentum of the game has switched back to the 49ers. But Lott was called for pass interference by side judge Dean Look, a questionable penalty. If anything, Lott may have cut off Pearson, but it didn't appear it merited a flag. It gave the Cowboys a first down at the 12. Lott was upset, the 49ers fans were booing loudly, and Dallas was about to take the lead again. Three plays later, Dorsett, back in the game after shaking off Hicks's inadvertent kick to his eye, made one of his patented quick bursts around the left corner, picked up a nice block from Ron Springs on Carlton Williamson, and sprinted untouched into the end zone from the 5 to give the Cowboys a 17–14 lead. It stayed that way the rest of the half despite two more turnovers, one by Dallas's James Jones on a punt and one by Montana after he was hit by Harvey Martin with Bethea recovering.

The Cowboys had to feel good going into the locker room with a three-point lead. The 49ers had come out with a lot of emotion. They were beating the Cowboys to the punch, if only by inches, just as Walsh implored them to do, but the Cowboys were still standing. They were the team with the championship experience, and it was beginning to show.

Montana went to training camp his rookie year not worrying about making the team. And considering the 49ers were coming off a season in which they had won only two games and had a new coach intent on turning over the roster as quickly as possible, all his new buddy Clark really had to do was show he could catch the ball and then run with it and he was going to stick, too. Walsh was looking to find as many new players as possible to get the rebuilding process started, so the more rookies who made the team, the quicker he could get his program established.

But Clark was a nervous wreck. Every day he woke up hoping to avoid Max McCarthy, an area scout during the football season, but the Turk in training camp. He was the man with the cruel job of telling players their services were no longer required and to turn in their playbooks. Some kid's dream was about to end when McCarthy approached, so players went running for cover. It happens in every training camp. But if the Turk wants to find you, he will eventually track you down. It was a waste of time hiding under the bed sheets or avoiding the dining hall or wearing another number at practice. The Turk gets what he wants. Clark was convinced he wanted him.

At first, Clark didn't try to avoid him. "I didn't know who he was," he said. "Then you kind of realize he is the guy grabbing the guy right beside you saying, 'Can you get your playbook and see John McVay?' "

It didn't take long into camp before Walsh sent McCarthy into action. The veterans joked how Walsh was not wasting anybody's time and that some players wouldn't even make it to lunch. "Holy shit, guys were getting cut already," Clark said.

Montana was throwing the ball to Clark in practice. But not enough. Montana would go back and watch the practice film and realize he should have been going to him more. That would have eased some of Clark's nervousness about McCarthy coming to visit. But Montana knew Clark would make the team. Freddie Solomon was the 49ers' only established wide receiver.

"He was always concerned every day," Montana said. "I don't think he unpacked his bags. He always thought he was going to get cut. I said, 'You're crazy, man. All you have to do is look around. There is nobody there that has the size you have, the speed you have, and the ability to catch the ball.' Once it started to get to the point where people were getting cut, then it really got out of hand. Every day it's like, 'Here he comes, the hatchet guy, here he comes. I know he's coming to get me.' Almost every day, poor guy."

Montana thought it was pretty funny. "Will you shut up?"

Walsh ran players through training camp so frequently he was keeping the airlines in business by himself. Clark, of course, made the team. Not that he was able to relax. The 49ers played the opening game of the 1979 season in Minnesota, and Gene Clark made the trip from North Carolina to see his son make his NFL debut. They were sitting across from each other the day before the game in the team hotel. Clark was in shock. He told his father he couldn't believe he'd made an NFL team. Three years earlier, he'd been ready to quit football and play basketball at Appalachian State.

Clark didn't catch a pass against the Vikings. "So after the game, we fly home, and the next day I go in for treatment with the trainers," Clark said. "There's twelve receivers in there trying out." He called his father and told him his employment was week-to-week. "It's not a season thing," he said.

He didn't catch a pass as a backup in his first eight games. He was playing special teams, which was the NFL equivalent of hazing for rookies. Clark broke the ice in game nine with one reception for 6 yards on a quick-out against the Bears. His streak of consecutive games with a catch ended at one when he was shut out the following week at Oakland. But with the 49ers having injury problems at wide receiver the next week at New Orleans, Clark was able to play more than just special teams. He caught 5 passes for 50 yards. He felt like a player again. "Holy shit, this is lots of fun," he said.

He caught 18 passes as a rookie, 82 his second year, and 85 in the magical year of 1981, when he made the Pro Bowl. The next year he made first-team All-Pro.

After getting blanked in the first half of his rookie year, Clark would go on to catch 506 passes in his nine-year career with the 49ers, most of them from Montana. He would play in one more Super Bowl following the 1984 season, which might have been the 49ers' best team of their five Super Bowl champions. Clark caught 52 passes with 6 touchdowns that season. The next year the 49ers moved up in the draft and selected Jerry Rice, who went on to become the best receiver in the history of the NFL.

Montana outplayed Dan Marino in Super Bowl XIX and by then was clearly the best quarterback in the NFL. But the Niners lost in the wild-card round to the Giants in 1985, and then after the season opener in Tampa in '86 came distressing news: Montana needed back surgery to repair a herniated disc. Incredibly, he returned two months later and threw three touchdown passes in a

43–17 victory against the Cardinals, but the 49ers were humiliated by the Giants 49–3 in the divisional round of the playoffs, and Montana took such a huge hit from future teammate Jim Burt that he looked dead. He was nearly traded to the Chargers following the '87 season after a disappointing playoff loss. By 1988, Walsh had a new interest: Steve Young.

Montana and Clark were not only linked by The Catch in football history, but off the field they were close friends. In their early years with the 49ers, they ran around together at night and were inseparable at training camp. In the summer, Clark would go back to the Carolinas and run up and down Myrtle Beach, where he owned a summer house. Six months after The Catch, in the summer of '82, he met a woman on the beach who had no idea who he was. "I thought she looked awesome," he said. "I went and talked to her, and a year later we got married."

When she moved to San Francisco in 1983, she soon became pregnant with the first of their three children. Clark said Montana lived with them during the '83 season while he was going through a divorce and before he would meet his third wife, Jennifer. "There I am, married, and he's going out with all these models," Clark said.

After he finished playing in 1987, Clark took some time away from football and then began a new career, working in the front office of the 49ers for ten years and then with the Browns until he left after the 2001 season, following Butch Davis's first season in Cleveland. Clark moved back to Charlotte to work in real estate and the custom home-developing business. But by 2009, he was finalizing a costly divorce and had moved back to the Bay Area, living in Los Gatos and working for a resort in the wine country.

Clark's first post-football venture was in the restaurant business. He opened Clark's By The Bay near the port in Redwood City. Once the management staff was in place, he accepted an offer from the 49ers in late 1988 to work in the front office. He started off in marketing and public relations on his way to the top. In the 49ers media guide, he read that Eddie DeBartolo's father had done the same thing with him when he got him started in the family business. Clark would show up in his jacket and tie at eight in the morning and work until eight at night. He spent some time in sales, did some coaching in training camp, and worked to set up George Seifert's training camp schedule. He did everything to make himself invaluable. Carmen Policy, an attorney and a longtime friend of DeBartolo's from Youngstown, joined the 49ers a few years later as team president. Policy became Clark's mentor, and he was in position to make sure Clark had a clear path to a position of power.

The Niners had a disappointing end to Clark's final season in 1987, losing to the Vikings in the divisional round of the playoffs. They had been 13–2 during the regular season, which included three games played by replacement players and veterans who crossed the picket line during a twenty-four-day strike. Walsh benched Joe Cool during the game against the Vikings and put in Young, whom he had acquired before the season from the Bucs for second- and fourth-round picks.

Walsh was mesmerized by Young's freaky athletic ability and strong arm. He began his career with the Los Angeles Express of the USFL with a ten-year contract that was advertised at $40 million with a majority of the money tied to an annuity. Young would have been the first overall pick of the Bengals in the 1984 NFL draft had he not signed with the USFL, which had made a big splash the previous year by signing Heisman Trophy winner Herschel Walker. The NFL held a separate supplemental draft of USFL players and the Bucs selected Young in the first round.

Young went to Tampa following two seasons in Los Angeles and ran for his life for two seasons before his career was saved by the trade to San Francisco. Meanwhile, Walsh was having a midlife crisis with Montana. He suddenly discovered somebody younger and more vibrant, a player who could redefine his West Coast offense with the skills to escape the pass rush and buy more time in the pocket or take off and run to salvage a busted play. Montana had great feet and was elusive in the pocket and with sprint-outs, as the Cowboys found out, but Young was like a new toy for Walsh, and he couldn't wait to play with it. Walsh never pulled the trigger on trading Montana—how could he?—and after declaring the quarterback job open during the summer of 1988, he stuck with Montana. Once the season began, however, he used any excuse to insert Young into the game. Montana injured his elbow in the first game of the season. Walsh started Young the next week, but he fumbled on the 49ers first three possessions. Still Walsh kept looking for reasons to play Young.

Too hot? He didn't want Montana to wear down. Too cold? He didn't think his old bones could handle it. It got to the point where Montana would start but Walsh had almost gone to a rotation, although not as severe as when Tom Landry used Roger Staubach and Craig Morton as his play messengers in a 1971 game in Chicago. They actually alternated plays. After that game, Landry settled on Staubach, and Dallas went on to beat Miami for its first Super Bowl title. The two-quarterback system has never worked in the NFL. The 49ers were only 10–6 using Walsh's Montana-Young rotation.

"I don't mind competing for the job, but he made it into a quarterback controversy," Montana said. "To a certain degree, you always just hope you at least get the benefit of the doubt, especially after what you've been through and what you have done. It wasn't like I was playing bad. I might have a bad game or two where he would make those changes. There are a lot of guys who come in a game or two and play well. To do it consistently is a whole other story."

By the time the '88 playoffs arrived, Montana was entrenched once again as Walsh's guy, and the 49ers went on to win the Super Bowl in what turned out to be Walsh's final season. Landry learned during the 1971 season that if you have two quarterbacks who think they are the starter, you actually have none. Walsh wound up the season with the same result as Landry. They won the Super Bowl. The 49ers won it again the next year in George Seifert's first season, giving the 49ers four titles in the eighties, matching what the Steelers did in the seventies.

Montana reacted to the rumors that Walsh was going to trade him by winning back-to-back Super Bowls in 1988 and 1989. He also won his only two MVP awards in 1989 and 1990 and led the 49ers to eighteen straight road wins, an NFL record. He had five of his greatest achievements after Walsh was prepared to trade him. And in 1990, Montana and the Niners were going for an unprecedented three-peat. Walsh was already deep into regretting his decision to leave after the 1988 season, especially because the team he left Seifert was loaded with talent. The 49ers came as close to a three-peat as any team in the Super Bowl era. They were 14–2 in 1990. They beat the Redskins in the divisional round of the playoffs and were hosting the Giants, who were 13–3 during the regular season, at Candlestick Park in the NFC Championship Game. The 49ers had defeated the Giants 7–3 at home during the regular season in an emotional game that ended with Phil Simms and Ronnie Lott getting in each other's face.

In the rematch, the game was even more intense. Once again, the Giants could not get into the end zone. Simms had broken his foot late in the season and was replaced by career backup Jeff Hostetler, whose mobility helped neutralize the 49ers' fierce pass rush. The 49ers knew they were going to have to reload after the season, with twelve players on the roster thirty or older and another six who were twenty-nine.

But with 9:41 left in the game, Montana's career with the 49ers

Joe Montana was completely drained following the 1981 NFC Championship Game. He threw the winning touchdown pass to Dwight Clark with less than one minute remaining and played the entire game knowing some kook had phoned in a death threat right before kickoff. © *Michael Zagaris*

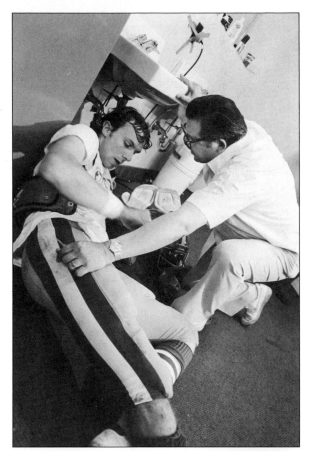

Joe Montana and Dwight Clark were inseparable in the early years of their friendship. And at halftime of The Catch game, they were side by side trying to figure out how to beat the Cowboys. Neither envisioned the wild ending. © *Michael Zagaris*

Bill Walsh traded for Jack "Hacksaw" Reynolds in 1981, and he brought experience, leadership, and personality to the 49ers, who needed every bit of what he had to offer. Reynolds set the tone for the 49ers' intensity against the Cowboys by showing up for the team breakfast before the title game in full uniform. © *Michael Zagaris*

Lenvil Elliott was a journeyman running back Bill Walsh knew from his days in Cincinnati. He gashed the Dallas defense on the last drive, including this 7-yard run on 19 Bob—a sweep to the left—that brought the 49ers to the Cowboys' 6-yard line, setting up The Catch. © *Michael Zagaris*

Ronnie Lott, a future Hall of Famer, joined rookies Eric Wright and Carlton Williamson as starters in the 49ers' "Dwight Hicks and the Hot Licks" secondary in 1981. © *Michael Zagaris*

The calm after The Catch. Joe Montana talks it over with Dwight Clark and Mike Shumann moments after his touchdown pass to Clark sent the 49ers to the Super Bowl. © *Michael Zagaris*

Ed DeBartolo Jr. (left) embraces his father Ed Sr. in the locker room after the 49ers beat the Cowboys. Eddie is probably thanking his dad for buying him the team. © *Michael Zagaris*

Joe Montana and Steve Young, studying pictures of the Rams' defense at halftime of a game in 1988 with offensive coordinator Mike Holmgren, were never friends. It was the most explosive quarterback controversy in NFL history, but Montana raised his game fighting off Young, leading the 49ers to two more Super Bowls. © *Michael Zagaris*

Bill Walsh was always one step ahead of the opposition. The Hall of Fame coach won three Super Bowls in his ten seasons coaching the 49ers and always regretted leaving too soon. George Seifert won two more in his first six seasons. © *Michael Zagaris*

Cowboys fans and Danny White looked up to Roger Staubach (shown here on the left standing next to Don Meredith) after he won two Super Bowls and became an American sports icon. It was an impossible act for White to follow. *Courtesy of the Dallas Cowboys*

Danny White took the Cowboys to three NFC Championship Games in his first three years as the starting quarterback. Unfortunately for White and his legacy, he lost all three. *Dallas Cowboys Star Magazine*

Drew Pearson came so close to breaking a 75-yard touchdown on the play after The Catch, which would have made Dwight Clark just a footnote in NFL history. Sadly, two years later his career was over. Here Pearson is facing the press for the first time since he was the driver in a horrific car accident that killed his younger brother. © *Dallas Morning News*

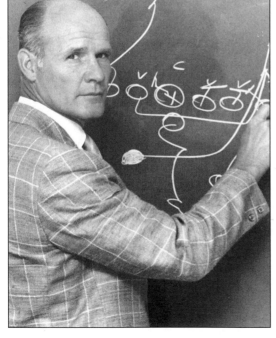

Tom Landry was as innovative on defense as Bill Walsh was on offense, but he left his stamp on NFL offenses with multiple sets and creative formations that helped produce five Super Bowl appearances. *Dallas Cowboys Star Magazine*

Ed Jones was one of the most feared defensive ends in the NFL but not so much as a heavyweight boxer. He took a leave from the Cowboys during the 1979 season to pursue his love of the sweet science, but Dallas was happy to have him back when it became clear he was no threat to Larry Holmes. *New York Times*

Everson Walls made the Cowboys as a rookie free agent from Grambling in 1981; he led the NFL and set a team record that season with eleven interceptions. But he will forever be remembered for trailing Dwight Clark on The Catch and reaching in vain to knock down Joe Montana's pass. *Dallas Cowboys Star Magazine*

Charlie Waters's career concluded at Candlestick Park on January 10, 1982, with him facedown in the painted grass of the end zone after Dwight Clark caught the winning touchdown pass. Nearly fourteen years later, he was devastated by the unexpected death of his oldest son. *Dallas Cowboys Star Magazine*

Tony Dorsett wasn't big, but he was fast and was fearless running the ball. His biggest complaint during his Hall of Fame career was that Tom Landry never thought he could hold up to twenty-five carries a game and paced him in his eleven seasons with the team. *Dallas Cowboys Star Magazine*

Tom Landry cleans out his office on February 26, 1989, the day after the Saturday Night Massacre at Valley Ranch where new owner Jerry Jones announced that he had fired the coaching legend. *AP Photo/Ron Heflin* all but came to an end. He was buried in the Candlestick turf, crushed on a ferocious hit by Giants defensive end Leonard Marshall. The impact not only bruised Montana's sternum, but also broke the little finger on his throwing hand. If the 49ers were able to make it to Super Bowl XXV the following Sunday against the Bills and their fast-paced, no-huddle K-gun offense led by Jim Kelly, they were going to have to do it without Montana. He would not have been able to play in the Super Bowl. Young would have started.

Young came in to try to finish off the Giants. The Niners had trouble running the ball all season and that inability would be their demise. The Giants cut the 49ers lead to 13–12 on Matt Bahr's 38-yard field goal with 5:47 remaining. Now all the 49ers had to do was run out the clock, and they were on their way to Tampa. Young moved them to a first down at the Giants 40. But with 2:46 remaining, Erik Howard knocked the ball loose from Roger Craig, and the great Lawrence Taylor recovered. The Giants then drove into position for Bahr's 42-yard game-winner with no time left on the clock. The fans were stunned. Craig, one of the team's warriors, the first player with a season of 1,000 yards rushing and 1,000 yards receiving, had left the ball on the ground and blown the three-peat.

The next summer, Montana played in the 49ers preseason game against the Bears in Berlin, but a few days later, back in training camp in Rocklin, he suffered a slightly torn tendon near his elbow when he was attempting to throw a 40-yard pass. He'd had elbow problems going back to 1981. The 49ers shut him down. He held out hope that he would be able to play at some point during the 1991 season, but after throwing four times in a week in October, the pain was too much, and he underwent surgery to reattach the tendon. He missed the rest of the season. Young managed only ten starts due to a knee injury and was only 5–5. He returned for the final game of the season. The Niners nearly rallied to make the playoffs, with Steve Bono playing well when Young was out, but despite finishing 10–6, the same record they had in their '88 Super Bowl year, they lost out to the Falcons for the NFC's last wild-card spot.

The 49ers chose to go very slowly with Montana the following summer, and he started the season on the four-week injured reserve list. He underwent another procedure in September to clean up scar tissue in his elbow—the second time he needed that—but was convinced Seifert had no intention or desire to let him play. Young was the starter, and Seifert was distancing himself from the Montana era. Montana met twice with Policy. He was itchy to get back on the field and saw his job slipping away forever. Montana was supposedly Walsh's guy. Seifert had no such allegiance. Seifert wanted to carve out his own identity and was anxious to transition to Young. But Montana wanted back in.

He had already accomplished so much. He and Terry Bradshaw were the only quarterbacks to win four Super Bowls. It would have been easy to walk away and not have anybody question why. His right elbow was barking. It's hard to play quarterback in the NFL when that's happening. But just like Brett Favre years later, Montana couldn't pull himself away.

"I love this game," he said at training camp in 1992. "I've played it since I was eight years old, and pretty soon there is going to be a definite end to it. I'm still going to be relatively young. It's not like other careers that if you miss it, you can go back to the office. Players want to make it last as long as they can. When it's over, that's it, it's over. The excitement—there's nothing like it. That's what it's all about more than I want to come back and show people I'm not done yet."

By now, Clark had taken the fast track up the corporate ladder. He was Policy's right-hand man. His buddy Montana was beside himself with frustration. Clark was making progress in his new career and knew if he kept working hard, DeBartolo and Policy would take care of him. Montana wanted to play, but the 49ers were on the way to hosting the 1992 NFC Championship Game, and Young was about to win the first of his two MVP awards. He had emerged as one of the best quarterbacks in the league. This was exactly Montana's fear. Even the legends worry about their job security. Young was the flavor of the month, maybe the flavor of the decade, and Montana was turning into yesterday's news.

So he did what any normal mid thirties man would do to pass the time. He found a new hobby. "I went and took flying lessons," Montana said. "I would leave the facility and go right to the San Jose airport."

The thrill of flying did not replace the thrill of playing. He remained on injured reserve. The 49ers were a powerhouse, and Seifert was not about to start working Montana into games. He was the most important player in the history of what had been a sad-sack franchise, but this was Young's team now. The transition was complete. Seifert finally activated Montana for the next-to-last game of the 1992 season against the Bucs, but he did not play. Finally, twenty-three months after Marshall laid him out in the championship game, Montana was back on the field the next week in the meaningless final game of the regular season against the Detroit Lions.

It was a Monday night game and the buildup for the return of Montana captivated fans. Seifert announced before the game that Young would start but Montana would play either the second and fourth quarters or the entire second half. It was his farewell to San Francisco.

WELCOME BACK, JOE.

JOE: JUST DO IT.

The Montana signs were all over Candlestick Park. When he came out with Young and Steve Bono for pregame warm-ups, he got a standing ovation. Then he nearly brought the place down when he started the second half. Everybody knew this was the last they would see of Joe Cool in a 49ers uniform, his encore performance. He completed his first pass, a 4-yard toss to running back Marc Logan. It put Montana over 35,000 yards for his career. He was rusty but still showed signs of vintage Montana, completing 15 of 21 for 126 yards with two touchdowns.

"I didn't think I'd be so nervous," Montana said. "I was being too cautious. Once I settled down, I got a lot more confident."

After the game, the concern was not Montana's elbow but Young's fragile psyche. He had lived in the shadow of Montana for all these years. Now the team was his, so what happens? Montana comes back, and the place goes wild.

"I understand," Young said after the game. "And I hope the people understand that I understand."

Montana knew he could have come back a lot earlier, but he was not oblivious to the politics around him. He was on his way out. The issue was where he would finish up his career. He had been asking Roger Craig, now with the Vikings, about Minnesota. Paul Hackett, his old quarterback coach with the Niners, was the offensive coordinator in Kansas City, working for Marty Schottenheimer. The Cardinals, who had taken away the NFL's number-one expansion market when Bill Bidwill moved the team from St. Louis to Phoenix in 1988, needed a quarterback, but even more than that, needed the credibility and identity Montana could bring the franchise. And the Bucs, Young's former team, was a potential and logical landing spot.

Whatever was going to happen, Montana believed he could count on Clark to protect his interests. Clark had been promoted to the 49ers coordinator of football operations and player personnel on his way to VP of football operations. Clark and Montana had each come a long way from HoJo's back in the spring of 1979. Montana helped turn Clark from an obscure wide receiver from Clemson into a man who had his number 87 retired and doesn't go a day without hearing about The Catch. Montana would have been great without Clark, but that '81 championship game is when Montana became a star. And it wouldn't have happened without Clark.

"I'm still making appearances and doing autograph shows from a play that happened in 1982," Clark said. "To me, that's pretty remarkable."

Montana would be thirty-seven by the time the 1993 season started. He had no plans to retire. He had taken a physical beating in his career: the back surgery, knee surgeries. The *New York Times* reported he needed to take cortisone shots in his elbow eleven weeks in a row during the 1987 season. He still wanted to be the 49ers quarterback but knew that was not going to happen. So he wanted out.

If Clark wasn't the ultimate decision maker, he was at least in the loop. That should have worked to Montana's advantage, as the organization had an obligation—moral if not legal—to do the right thing. It's called loyalty. They could cut Montana and let him sign wherever he wanted. That was not likely, because he was sure to have value on the trade market. Or they could let him pick a new team and then work out the trade.

Montana wanted to play, but he also had had enough of Young. To say he had no use for him might be putting it mildly. He hated him. Until Montana was injured at the end of that 1990 championship game, Young had sat on the bench for nearly four years, except for the stretch when Walsh was using the tag-team approach. Montana simply had something Young wanted, and Young was watching the best years of his career slip right by. Montana felt Young was being a little too aggressive in his approach to winning his job, and those feelings never subsided.

"Ronnie said to me, 'Why don't you two just bury the

hatchet?' " Montana said. "Ronnie's favorite thing was, 'You don't have to like the guy, you just have to be able to play with him.' "

Montana started to explain to Lott why he hated Young. "Never mind," Montana said Lott told him. "I understand."

From a football standpoint, it made sense for the 49ers to keep the younger and healthier player. They told Montana in January that Young would be the starter in 1993, and on March 9 they gave Montana permission to look for a new team.

It was clear: Joe must go.

But the fan backlash was overwhelming. Montana was still the most popular athlete in town. He visited Kansas City, then Phoenix, then back to Kansas City. He wanted the Chiefs. They were further along than the Cardinals and had a much better offensive line, which was crucial for a mid thirties quarterback trying to squeeze another year or two out of his career. But there were two problems. Chiefs president Carl Peterson was a stubborn and sometimes un-reasonable negotiator. And the Cardinals were offering a better deal to the 49ers.

Policy put Clark right in the middle. Policy wanted to trade Montana to the Cardinals, DeBartolo didn't want to trade him at all, Seifert wanted Young to play, and Montana wanted to be traded to the Chiefs.

Here's how Clark and Montana remember what happened:

Clark: "George Seifert decided we should trade Joe and keep Steve Young, which was a logical assumption. As a guy on the team with Joe, I was not in favor of that. I think Steve Young is a fabulous player, Hall of Famer, all that, but I had a bond with Joe. My thing is, Joe Montana is magical. They thought about trading him after the 1987 season, and he wins back-to-back Super Bowls. That's the kind of guy he is. For George Seifert to think that was the right move, it was totally understandable, but yet isn't there some way to figure out how to keep them both? There wasn't. Too much money."

Montana: "It wasn't that Dwight could have stepped in. Carmen was trying to test him. So he put him on to telling me what the 49ers wanted, and I wasn't going wherever I wanted. They wanted me to go to Phoenix. They had a better deal worked out. Dwight said, 'They won't let you go to Kansas City.' Our friendship was tested only because he went to that side of the table—to the extreme. Not that it was 'this is what they want.' It wasn't a conversation. It was to the point where he was saying, 'It doesn't matter, you're not going to get what you want.' He was so adamantly on that side. I know exactly what is going on. Carmen is saying he's going to see how loyal Dwight is going to be in the upper office. So what better way to test him than to put him against me. He's thinking, *This is a good opportunity to show him I'm not a player anymore. Yeah, he's my friend, but I can make that distinction when I have to.* And I totally understood that. But when it came time to cut the line one way or the other, he became more adamant, and that's when I think they sent him to tell me that I was not going to Kansas City."

Clark: "I'm in management and I'm part of the team that traded him. That made it a little bit tough. What made it a little tougher was, Arizona was offering a certain package that was better than what Kansas City was offering. Joe wanted to go to Kansas City. Carmen Policy asked me to go to Joe about going to Arizona. So I did, and from that point on, that kind of put a wedge between us. That took a long time to get over."

Montana: "Hell, I would have been better off in Phoenix. When I left there, I thought I was coming back. I was going to make three times the money, but the issue was, they didn't have an offensive line. And my agent [Peter Johnson] kept saying, 'You can't go back there. I understand the difference financially, but they don't have an offensive line that can support you. And they went through three or four quarterbacks this year.' I'm telling you, if it wasn't for my agent, I would have gone to Phoenix. But if they traded me there, I wouldn't have gone. That's what I told Dwight. 'If they trade me, I'm not going. I'll sit out a year.' "

Policy knew he was putting Clark in a tough spot: "It was his friend, it was history, it was Joe Montana. He was the 49ers. How could we trade Joe DiMaggio?" he said.

Clark had to make the break toward the management side, and Policy was indeed testing him. Montana's perception and instincts were right. "Truth of the matter, Dwight was part of the organization. He was working for us," Policy said. "I wanted to make sure the message got through loud and clear. I thought Dwight would be an excellent person to pass the message on. He was the messenger delivering the message I wanted delivered."

DeBartolo didn't want to trade Montana at all. In April, he flew Montana to the DeBartolo family compound in Youngstown and tried to convince him to stay. "I was going to give him an opportunity to play," DeBartolo said. "He decided he wanted to go. He spent a couple of days with me. We reminisced and talked about things."

Because the boss wanted his football people to keep Montana, the 49ers scrambled to come up with ways to entice him to stay. They had been criticized as a cold organization when they cut ties with Ronnie Lott and Craig, and it would later happen with Rice. As a result, Seifert came up with the bizarre proclamation that Montana was going to be his "designated starter" going into training camp. Nobody was sure exactly what that meant, but Montana knew Seifert wanted Young, and it wasn't going to be a fair fight.

"Joe was like, 'Fuck that,' " Clark said.

"I still don't understand the whole process that took place," Montana said. "My point is, if they wanted me to stay, I'll stay, if I can at least lose my job or at least have a chance to win it. But I wanted to play. And to me, [Young] wasn't better than I was. . . . Put two salaries on the table, I'll take what comes my way. I never heard of designated starter. Are they going to put me in and, the first series, pull me out? I don't know. I said, 'Thanks, that's OK.'"

Bill Walsh picked up the philosophy from his years with Paul Brown in Cincinnati that it's better that players leave too early than too late. He passed that on to Seifert. "We were told Joe wasn't going to play much longer, maybe one year," Seifert said. "My instincts were, we had come to that time. The feeling was, Steve would be the starter, and then all hell breaks loose. Eddie had his own emotions on this. He was tremendously loyal and had a great feeling for Joe. As I saw the organization tearing itself apart, I knew this can't be an open competition. Everybody's nerves were on edge. Joe was upset with me. It was an ugly, horrible time. Joe had a wonderful career. Steve had a great career. In the end, it worked out."

Montana flew back to the Bay Area from Youngstown with DeBartolo, an emotional man who was broken up over it. Policy said that Montana and DeBartolo got off the plane with "tears flowing."

Policy says Montana could not bring himself to tell DeBartolo that he had his mind made up, that he wanted out. He says at one point Montana even told DeBartolo he would stay. "Joe, you got to tell him now," Policy said.

Policy did it for him. He told DeBartolo that Montana really wanted to leave and finish his career where he could be the starter. "The ultimate realist in the whole drama was Joe Montana," Policy said. "He would come into my office privately and say, 'Look, I understand, believe me. I know what's going on, and you're doing the right thing.'"

Policy, Seifert, and DeBartolo then went to Montana's house to see him and his wife, Jennifer. "With us around him, Joe told Eddie that it was the best thing," Policy said.

Just a few days later, the 49ers did what at one time would have seemed incomprehensible and unconscionable. They traded Joe Cool. "It tore my heart out," DeBartolo said. "I didn't want to be involved with it."

The Niners didn't get as much from Kansas City as they would have from the Cardinals. They picked up the Chiefs' first-round pick in 1993 in exchange for Montana, safety David Whitmore, and a third-round pick in 1994. The Cardinals were offering their first-round pick in 1993 straight-up for Montana. But Policy told Montana that as long as Kansas City's deal was in the same neighborhood as the Cardinals, he would send him where he wanted to go.

"Carl Peterson was trying to basically steal him and use Joe's relationship with Eddie and him saying, 'OK, you can go.' I wouldn't stand for it," Policy said. "Finally, we didn't get what Arizona offered. We did get a pretty decent package, but in the process, things got heated in the building."

Montana's relationship with his onetime best friend, Dwight Clark, was fractured. He was livid that Clark had attempted to prove himself to Policy at his expense.

Policy saw it another way. "Dwight was trying very hard to keep Joe," he said. "His enthusiasm to keep Joe painted him into a role as an obstructionist. Words were exchanged between Dwight and Jennifer. That caused hard feelings on both sides."

On the day Montana was traded, he was in the 49ers' offices, which were now located in Santa Clara, across the street from the Great American Amusement Park. He bumped into Clark in the hallway. "We were having one of those moments where I was telling him I wasn't for any of this and I didn't want him to go," Clark said. "But still, I was part of the management team that traded him."

What did Montana say to him?

"Nothing," Clark said. "It was just more what he didn't say."

Montana was off to Kansas City. Clark remained in San

Francisco, and it would be two years before they spoke again. Montana felt betrayed. He believed Clark sold him out. "I was that upset," Montana said. "It was hard. I really liked him as a friend."

Montana played two years in Kansas City and beat Young and the 49ers in a game in Kansas City in his second season. The Chiefs made it to the AFC Championship Game in Buffalo in 1993 and might have gotten to the Super Bowl if Montana hadn't suffered a concussion in the first half. The Chiefs lost in Miami in the wild-card game in his second season, another Montana-Marino postseason matchup. The 49ers won the Super Bowl that year, beating San Diego, and Montana angered the 49ers by saying he was now an AFC man and was rooting for the Chargers. Young finally escaped the Montana shadow. He had been playing as much against the past as against the opponent. Around Thanksgiving in 1994, the *New York Daily News* and HBO's *Inside the NFL* broke the story that Montana was going to retire at the end of the season. Naturally, he denied it. He did not want to become the story during the season as the Chiefs were positioning themselves to make a playoff run. He retired, of course, with the announcement made in a big ceremony with 20,000 people showing up in the streets of San Francisco in the spring.

But Young was the victim of a hoax when somebody placed a phone call to him saying Montana wanted him to be at the ceremony. Young was dubious, found out it was a prank, and didn't attend, but in a way he was probably hoping that the years had put the animosity to rest. They never did. But one relationship was repaired. Jennifer Montana called Clark and told him that Joe wanted him there. Clark believes it was Jennifer's idea, and he really appreciated it. He accepted the invitation.

"I always wanted him there," Montana said. "He was my friend. Even though that was the toughest time of my life—well, I won't say of my life—but it was frustrating, because here's a guy I loved from the day I met him and to be in the position where you are not even speaking, it was ridiculous to me, and it was time to put everything behind us. I was glad."

The friendship took a couple more years to completely heal. "The whole situation with the 49ers really hurt Joe," Clark said. "He was really bitter about that. You know, I can't blame him. I guess, in the NFL now, you can get rid of anybody."

They talk seven or eight times a year. Before Clark moved back to the Bay Area from Charlotte and Montana moved to southern California, Montana would lean on Clark for real-estate investment advice in North Carolina. They indeed had come a long way from HoJo's.

5

THE GREAT WHITE HOPE

Danny White's problem was that he wasn't Roger Staubach, the most popular player in Cowboys history. Tom Landry always said nobody could have done a better job than White taking over for Staubach, and he might have been right. He stepped in for an icon and guided the Cowboys to three straight NFC Championship Games in his first three years as the starter, but Dallas lost all three games. Nobody's career was hurt more by that loss to the 49ers. So many things would have been different if he could have been Staubach just that one time.

His teammates were never quite sure how to feel about Danny White. In one corner of the locker room, he was viewed as being in an impossible spot, following a legend, and they felt sorry for him. He was in a no-win situation unless he won the Super Bowl, which was not an unrealistic expectation, because the Cowboys were loaded with talent. In another corner, he was viewed as a management suck-up, especially after he twice met privately with Cowboys president Tex Schramm in the first nine days of the 1982 players strike and endorsed taking management's offer. Teammates and players around the league perceived he was going behind their backs and trying to settle the dispute on his own. Schramm was the main advisor to his good friend Pete Rozelle, the NFL commissioner, and he was viewed as the real power broker in the league. Whatever White was trying to accomplish didn't work. The strike lasted fifty-seven days, and the disconnect from his teammates lasted much longer.

Even worse, a few months later, Dexter Manley's vicious hit in the NFC Championship game in Washington ended White's day and began a quarterback controversy with a young gunslinger named Gary Hogeboom from which White never recovered. He would never win another playoff game in his career.

White didn't have the locker-room power base that is essential for any quarterback to succeed. He needed all his teammates to support him, and it was never that way. Instead, they were talking behind his back. He waited such a long time for Staubach to retire so he could get on the field and start making some money and a name for himself. White was the loyal backup, and knew better than to lobby for playing time when an icon was still at the top of his game. But when concussions forced Staubach's retirement after the 1979 season, White had his chance to be a Cowboys hero, to elevate himself to elite status, but he always fell short.

White could have made The Catch nothing more than a footnote to a great game if he had been able to emulate Staubach's comeback magic after Montana and Clark pulled off their miracle. There are defining moments in all players' careers, moments when they either rise to the occasion and distinguish themselves or fail and become forever grouped with those who come up small when the moment is biggest. Danny came up very small in San Francisco, and that shocked a lot of his teammates.

Three years earlier, he replaced Staubach in the second half of a playoff game in Atlanta after Staubach suffered a concussion. The Cowboys trailed 20–13, but White led them to a pair of touchdowns to win the game. And then two years later, in the first playoff start of his career, White brought the Cowboys from behind, once again in Atlanta in the divisional round of the playoffs. The Cowboys were trailing 27–17 when White hit Drew Pearson with a 14-yard touchdown pass with just 3:04 remaining. After the Doomsday Defense forced a punt, White took the Cowboys on a 70-yard drive and hit Pearson for another touchdown from 23 yards, this time with 47 seconds left, to send Dallas to the NFC title game in Philadelphia, where they were dominated by the Eagles. But nobody blamed White. He won a playoff game in his first year, more than Staubach did in his final one. And he showed he did have some Staubach in him.

The Cowboys went into the locker room at halftime in San Francisco knowing that 30 good minutes would put away the 49ers and reestablish their superiority in the NFC. The 49ers felt the Cowboys scored their second touchdown on a gift from the officials on the Lott pass interference call and if they had not turned the ball over three times they would be ahead. But was this the sign of a young team cracking under the pressure of playing for the Super Bowl?

"We were real upbeat at halftime," 49ers guard Randy Cross said. "We were getting the ball to start the third quarter. We are going to score. There was no lack of confidence, that's for sure. Bill's halftime speech? His memorable halftime speeches you could squeeze into a head of a thimble. He wasn't a big speech guy."

The 49ers locker room at Candlestick was two-tiered. The defense was downstairs, the offense upstairs. The quarterbacks huddled, going over adjustments. Offensive-line coach Bobb McKittrick was at the board diagramming protections for his guys.

"We were not concerned about being behind," Cross said. "We knew we could score 28 points in 11 minutes. We didn't care about the Cowboys. They were yesterday's news to us. That's how we prepared all week long."

Landry wasn't big into halftime speeches either. Or postgame speeches. Probably the best speech he ever gave to his team came on the Monday after he was fired, at the start of the off-season conditioning program. In the big team meeting room at Valley Ranch, he said good-bye. He choked up, stopping and starting his speech several times, and had to cut it short when he could no longer speak. "It was one of the most difficult things I had to do," Landry said. "I tried to tell them that this crisis will pass, that you have to keep moving forward."

He told his players he loved them, and they responded with a standing ovation. "He told us that we'll forget him in about two weeks," Everson Walls said. "No way. It's the end of an era, but we'll remember him for the rest of our lives."

There was no emotion or ovation at halftime in the Dallas locker room. The position coaches made their adjustments. The players hit the bathroom, relaxed for a few minutes, and were back on the field. "Coach Landry was exactly the same no matter what game was played," safety Charlie Waters said. "He was so precise. He never felt like we didn't have that game under control. He just said they were doing some things and we can stop it."

Tony Dorsett had come to the Cowboys in 1977 after winning the Heisman Trophy at Pitt, and Dallas won the Super Bowl in his rookie year and lost in his second year. The Cowboys made it to the Super Bowl five times in the seventies, and playoff money and Super Bowl shares were something taken for granted. The trade for Dorsett, when the Cowboys jumped all the way up to the second spot in the draft in a trade with Seattle, was contingent on the Bucs, who were picking first, not taking him. The Seahawks and Bucs were coming off their expansion seasons. Tampa selected Southern Cal running back Ricky Bell instead, a favorite of Bucs coach John McKay, the former Southern Cal coach. The only people in Dallas who knew the Cowboys were about to trade up for Dorsett were

Landry, Schramm, Brandt, and the sporting goods store owner the team commissioned to make up a Cowboys jersey with Dorsett's name and number 33 on it.

"I was completely taken off guard," Dorsett said. "I was probably the happiest football player on earth. I realized that running behind an expansion line was not going to be very healthy."

Just a couple of weeks before the draft, Dorsett and his agent ran into Brandt at a banquet in Pittsburgh. Dorsett told him he would play in Canada rather than play in Seattle. Brandt told him not to worry, that he would end up with a good team. Dorsett was hoping he would end up playing for the Steelers, his favorite team while he was growing up in Aliquippa, Pennsylvania. He was more than happy to be with the Cowboys, but still he always dreamed of finishing his career wearing the black and gold of the Steelers.

The Cowboys were one of the most successful organizations, but they were not among the highest paying. Management let the players know it was a privilege to play for them and when it came to money, they should be thankful Coach Landry wanted them. And Brandt used to tell the agents of players holding out that their clients, "can wear the star on the helmet or the star on the chest." Translation: Play for the Cowboys or go pump gas at Texaco.

Danny White had proven he was a big-game player twice in Atlanta, which is why the Cowboys were not panicking after Clark's acrobatic catch. There were still 51 seconds on the clock, and Dallas had two time-outs remaining and trailed by just one point. The Cowboys had complete faith that White was about to upstage Montana and get Rafael Septien into position to kick the Cowboys right into Super Bowl XVI against the Bengals, a game they would have won. Plenty of time. Plenty of time-outs. Plenty of weapons.

"I just knew we were going to get in field-goal range," Dorsett said at his office on Preston Road in North Dallas more than twenty-five years later. "I just knew it. There were no ifs, ands, or buts in my mind. We were moving the ball. It was going to happen."

It was a tough situation the team was facing after Clark's catch—a hostile environment in San Francisco with less than a minute remaining—but they were the Dallas freakin' Cowboys. Tom Landry, one of the best of all time, in his twenty-second year with Dallas, versus Bill Walsh, the man who looked as though he should be teaching chem lab at Stanford, in just his third season as an NFL head coach. The Cowboys looked up in the stands, and it was a madhouse. The Niners fans were drinking their white wine and munching on their cheese a little early.

It took a second for the shock of Clark's touchdown to wear off on the Dallas sideline. The 49ers sideline was chaotic. They thought they had the game won. Had they not paid attention to the Cowboys history? Were they all too young to remember the Hail Mary? Did they have any idea what Staubach had done to the 49ers not even ten years earlier with a frantic playoff comeback? Ronnie Lott had not been watching the 49ers offense as it moved down the field. He was already thinking one step ahead. "I really don't remember that much at all about our drive, to be quite honest with you," he said. "I wasn't really paying that much attention to it. I had a feeling in my mind that if we did score, we still had to go out and play defense. And if we didn't score, we still had to go out and play defense. A lot of my focus was figuring out a way to see how we were going to stop them. The one thing growing up and watching the game of foot-ball, everybody, at least in San Francisco, was saying, 'They're going to find a way to lose it.' There were a lot of people that would say the Cowboys always had a way of figuring out how to come back and win. They were Captain Comeback."

If there was any doubt among the 49ers defensive players, there was good reason. The Cowboys knew they would come back and win. They had done it so many times. But there was one huge difference now. Staubach was on the Cowboys sideline watching. Danny White was the quarterback.

"When the 49ers scored the touchdown, the air kind of let out of us for an instant," Cowboys tight end Doug Cosbie said. "Then you realize there was plenty of time to get a field goal. We didn't have to go ninety-five yards in twenty seconds. You definitely had a chance to win the game. You had a bunch of guys on the field who had done it before. There was still a lot of confidence."

Danny White was in this position only because Roger Staubach wasn't. Not that Roger the Dodger wanted to be a full-time real-estate mogul at this point in his life, but he was tired of getting his brains scrambled every time he took a big hit. In the 1979 divisional round of the playoffs against the Rams at Texas Stadium, Staubach threw a two-yard touchdown pass to Jay Saldi that put the Cowboys ahead 19–14 in the fourth quarter.

"Jack Reynolds grabbed me and I hit my head on the turf," Staubach said. "The one with Reynolds bothered me. Man, is this going to happen all the time? It wasn't like my normal bad concussion, but it definitely screwed me up. I wasn't myself. So afterwards, I was really thinking about retiring."

By his count, that was either the tenth or twelfth concussion of his career and his second of the season (the Steelers registered the first one on October 28). That is way too many trips to la-la land. Staubach consulted with several doctors after the season. He went to New York for a CT scan. Dr. Ted Plumb of the Cornell Medical School told him he should retire. Dr. Phil Williams of Dallas told him he didn't have any brain damage, but he was worried about what havoc the next concussion could bring. When Staubach suffered a concussion, it wasn't minor; he was knocked out.

His competitive instinct was driving him back to the field. His doctors, his wife Marianne, and his common sense were all saying he had had enough. Staubach made the right decision—to walk away—and he knows it.

Nearly thirty years after he retired, he is looking out a large glass window in the conference room of the Dallas headquarters of the Staubach Company, his worldwide commercial real-estate firm. Down below, cars are zooming up and down Dallas Parkway. Staubach looks pained as he describes the head trauma he survived against some of the fiercest pass rushers in NFL history: the Steel Curtain, the Fearsome Foursome, the Purple People Eaters. If he'd stuck around a couple more years, he would have had to deal with Lawrence Taylor, too.

"Usually the next day I would have a little headache and I would feel fine again. Things get bounced around there, they can affect you in different ways," he said. "The trouble is, like Dr. Plumb said, 'Roger, I see a reflex difference in your right and left side. That's the only thing. Nothing neurological, but something is causing it.' He said it's almost not noticeable, but the next one could be the beginning of problems because you've had that many of them. He talked about the scar-tissue syndrome. Dr. Williams, who is really great, said he didn't see anything physical but said, 'Hey, you've had a lot of them.' "

A couple of months went by, and Staubach made up his mind. He was done. He had served five years in the Navy after graduating from the Naval Academy, had won two Super Bowls with the Cowboys, and had become one of the last true American sports heroes. No drugs. No steroids. No cheating on his wife. No physical abuse.

But he worried about postconcussion syndrome. He worried about life after football. He wanted his wife to have a husband with all his wits about him. He wanted his kids to have a father who wasn't suffering from early Alzheimer's.

"I went in and told Landry, and he understood. Tom understood Danny White was ready to go," Staubach said. "Tex tried to talk me into playing. He offered me a two-year contract that would match the highest contract in the NFL, which was Archie Manning at the time. Archie had just signed a big contract—750,000 bucks a year for two years. It was a big deal. Tex definitely wanted me to still play. Tom probably couldn't have talked me out of it, but he didn't try to talk me into it. If we didn't have Danny White, I wouldn't have let the team down."

As much as Staubach wanted to keep going, he knew he was playing Russian roulette with his brain by risking another head injury. Reluctantly, he walked away knowing he still had plenty left to give to his team.

White was one of the first Staubach informed of his decision to retire. They had a mentor-student relationship, and Staubach truly liked him. He never considered him a threat to take his job, even though he was aware how much White wanted to play. Staubach felt the Cowboys had Super Bowl potential in 1980, and he wanted to erase the bitter way the 1979 season ended. They wound up losing that game to the Rams 21–19 when wide receiver Billy Waddy grabbed a Vince Ferragamo pass tipped by Dallas linebacker Mike Hegman and ran for a 50-yard touchdown with 2:06 remaining. It was a disappointing ending to a disappointing season. But it had been a great career.

"Everything that could have gone wrong went wrong as far as the potential of the team," Staubach said. "Charlie Waters tore up his knee and Ed Jones boxed. Thomas Henderson pulled his hijinks and got kicked off the team. We went into the playoffs with Dorsett having a partially separated shoulder. Drew messed his knee up trying to spike the ball in the end zone."

On March 31, 1980, Staubach announced his retirement at a press conference at Texas Stadium. He held all the major team passing records and was the NFL's all-time leader in the quarterback ratings. He played eleven years after the Cowboys drafted him in the tenth round in 1964, and then they waited five years for him to serve his Navy commitment. He was thirty-eight years old when he retired and had bigger plans than football. He started in the real-estate business while he was still playing and later branched out to commercial real estate and founded the Staubach Company, which grew to sixty-eight offices with 6,800 employees, as well as international partnerships.

Eight years after he finished playing, Schramm came to him with a business proposal. Bum Bright, who had purchased the Cowboys from original owner Clint Murchison in 1984, was bleeding money in the banking business and was selling the team. "Tex wanted me to look at finding a buyer with the idea there would be a transition in a few years where Tex would retire and I would take over," Staubach said. "I told Tex that I was building my real-estate company and I can't look like I'm not happy with what I am doing."

Schramm had selfish motives in addition to admiring Staubach. He hoped Staubach would bring in an owner who would continue to run things the Schramm way. That meant not worrying so much about the bottom line but rather operating the Cowboys as an entertainment company. It also meant finding an owner who would stay in the background and let Schramm run the show as he had since the Cowboys' inception in 1960. Dallas businessman Richard Rainwater would have been the money man in the deal, with Staubach becoming the face of the franchise.

Jim Francis, who was Bright's right-hand man, introduced

Staubach to Jerry Jones at a game at Texas Stadium early in the 1988 season. Staubach immediately knew the oilman from Arkansas was intent on making the best bid. Schramm had no desire for Jones to buy the team, because he knew he would be out. He was desperately looking to protect his turf and steer Bright away from Jones. Rainwater never became a big player in the negotiations.

"Tex knew right away that Jones was a buyer. And he was an active owner," Staubach said. "Tex knew the handwriting was on the wall if he got Jones. So he was looking for somebody else."

The irony was that if Staubach had agreed to be part of a group with Rainwater, he could have saved Landry's job. Bright hated Landry, feeling Landry had ignored him when Bright owned the team. "I think Bum Bright was very unhappy with the four years he had," Staubach said. "If Richard had done the deal and brought me into it, I would have considered looking at it. But I didn't want to be in the forefront of it."

Staubach would have given the Cowboys a much different personality. Schramm was a showman and an innovator. The Dallas Cowboys Cheerleaders? Schramm's creation. Staubach was conservative, the opposite of his risk-taking personality on the field. He was also a Dallas institution, a man admired for his service to his country and to America's Team. Following Schramm was going to be tough for Staubach, but not as tough as following Staubach was for White or following Montana was for Young. Ultimately, Jones bought the team, fired Landry, and hired Jimmy Johnson, who declined to pick up White's option in 1989, precipitating his retirement. But in 1980, Staubach passed the torch to White and wished him luck.

"I think Danny was excited about taking over," Staubach said. "He's a good guy, and we had a good relationship. I think the only thing that started to develop was, Danny probably didn't have the chemistry with the entire team."

The Cowboys had gone from Meredith to Morton to Staubach and now White. This team was full of expectations and talent.

"I thought Danny was ready, there was no question about it," Dorsett said. "I'd seen all the athleticism of Danny White. Hell, when I was a freshman at Pitt, we played in one of the first Fiesta Bowls out there against Arizona State. He was the quarterback and punter when they had all those great players. I had a lot of respect for him from his college days."

Taking over for Staubach was a tough job but not impossible. "The core of that team was still together," cornerback Dennis Thurman said. "The playmakers were still there. It wasn't like Drew, Thrill [Tony Hill], Butch Johnson, Billy Joe DuPree, Doug Cosbie all left. You got Dorsett, Newhouse, and Springs."

He was given the keys to a Cadillac. "So drive it," Thurman said. "For the most part, he did."

White embraced the challenge, and early on, he had the support of his teammates. "It's a whole different ballgame when you are backing up," Dorsett said. "I thought Danny was old enough, mature enough, and would be the guy who could really step in the shoes of Staubach, and the beat would continue to go on. Which it did, except for the fact that we could not get back to another Super Bowl. Some of that you might want to point towards that position, but you can't totally point it all towards him."

Danny White had his chance to become part of Cowboys history even after Montana to Clark put the 49ers ahead with less than a minute remaining. All he had to do was be Staubach. Timmy Newsome was called Tippin' Timmy by his teammates because of his propensity for tiptoeing his way through the line despite being six one, 232. After Clark's catch, Newsome took Ray Wersching's line drive kickoff on one hop at the Cowboys 11 and returned it to the

25. White brought the offense onto the field with 47 seconds left. Septien had already hit field goals of 44 and 22 yards, so if White could get the Cowboys to the San Francisco 28, he would be setting Septien up with a 45-yard attempt to win the game. He was money from that distance. "This was not a time for a letdown," White told NFL Films. "I'm sure everybody was probably very discouraged over the fact they had just scored and taken the lead when we thought we had the game in the bag. So my point in the huddle: 'Alright, here we go. Let's get it done.'"

On first down, Landry did not put White in the shotgun. He took a straight snap from center Tom Rafferty and dropped back and threw what might have been the greatest pass of his Cowboys career. It was a laser to Pearson, who was running a deep slant from left to right. White had a good arm, but certainly not the kind of rocket John Elway or Brett Favre would later show off during their Hall of Fame careers. But that pass to Pearson looked like it was shot out of one of the Jugs machines that fire fastballs at receivers from short distances to save quarterbacks' arms in training camp. Pearson was dragged down by rookie corner Eric Wright, who made a desperate game-saving tackle at the San Francisco 44-yard line. It was a 31-yard gain.

No matter, White was in great shape. The Cowboys were inside San Francisco territory, there were 38 seconds left, and they used their second time-out. Another 16 yards and it would have been time for Septien. The 49ers were nervous. Clark was on the sidelines holding his head in his hands. Montana was standing next to Walsh. It was hard for them to watch.

Johnson and Pearson were split to White's right this time, Hill to the left. Landry once again did not have White in the shotgun, which would have bought him more time. Lawrence Pillers was lined up as the 49ers right defensive tackle with Jim Stuckey to his left. When the ball was snapped, Pillers and Stuckey ran a stunt, with Pillers looping around. On the previous play, the 49ers ran a stunt with Dwaine Board, and he didn't get close to White. But now, Pillers ran over Cowboys right guard Kurt Petersen and crashed into White, who was looking to throw to Hill. The ball came out. Cowboys left tackle Pat Donovan was on the ground desperately trying to reach for it. But Stuckey pounced on it. White immediately began arguing with referee Jim Tunney that his arm was going forward and it should have been an incomplete pass. But even if the NFL had had instant replay on that day, the play would not have been reversed. It was a fumble.

"My arm was going forward. I was throwing the ball," White said in the locker room after the game. "I told Jim, but he said no. He said my arm was coming up rather than throwing. Tony was open on the sidelines. I knew the rush was closing in, but I didn't feel any guy in particular. I didn't want to take a sack. I was in the middle of throwing when I got hit."

Eleven years later, when the Cowboys played the 49ers for the first of three consecutive years in the NFC title game, Schramm reminisced about White's fumble in a story in the *Dallas Morning News*. "I think Danny made a mistake because there was so much noise he went up under center," he said. "I thought he should have stayed back in the shotgun. He went back and got rushed and lost his footing and went down and fumbled the ball. We had Tony Hill open. I think it's funny how something happens to some people and it doesn't happen for everybody.

"If Roger had thrown that ball, that guy probably never would have gotten Drew Pearson. But we had a chance to win it, and probably those two plays were the biggest factor in the downward spiral Danny White's career took after that and started the decline of the Cowboys in the 1980s. It seems like we were never the same after that."

The Cowboys locker room was a morgue. The Vince Lombardi Trophy was waiting for them to pick up two weeks later, but White had left the Cowboys ticket lying in the dirt in Candlestick Park.

"Why bring it up? I almost forgot about it," Dorsett said. "God damn it. You're talking about all the air going out of the sail. Oh my God."

Steve Young eventually got the Joe Montana monkey off his back when he won the Super Bowl following the 1994 season in the Niners' 49–26 rout of the Chargers. Young threw a Super Bowl record six touchdown passes. Danny White never had another moment. His came in San Francisco and ended with the ball on the ground.

"Contrary to popular belief and opinion, my recollections of the game are very positive," White told the *Morning News* in 1993. "Most people think it was a negative turning point. It was the two best teams in the league playing the most important game of the year, and I think it was one of the three or four best games I ever played. The play I remember more than Dwight Clark in the end zone was Eric Wright dragging Drew Pearson down by his jersey. There were a lot of big plays and turning points. It was a typical great game."

Still, right after the game, White left little doubt how much the loss hurt. "It is just a frustrating feeling to come up one point short," he said. "There are high points and low points in professional football and you have to learn to live with those. But this is the lowest of the lows. I would rather have been beaten by four touchdowns." Unfortunately for White and the Cowboys, they experienced that feeling as well at Candlestick just a few months earlier.

In an NFL Films interview, White was later in denial about how Clark's catch and that game fit into the context of the Cowboys' demise. "I've heard everybody credit the rise of the 49ers and the fall of the Cowboys to that play in that one game," he said. "And I totally disagree with that."

As was the case with many issues during his playing career, White often stood nearly alone when he expressed an opinion. He spent his entire starting career with the Cowboys defending himself. It was just his nature. And not surprisingly, he is in a tiny minority downplaying the significance of the game in the history of the Cowboys. Even Landry and Schramm never stopped talking about it. Of course, if the Cowboys had won, White would have been the first to be shouting about how it was the turning point for that era of the Cowboys. That game prevented him from convincing fans the Cowboys were in good hands in the post-Staubach era. Staubach never would have fumbled less than 20 yards from getting the Cowboys into the Super Bowl.

"It's frustrating to listen to people talk about it as the beginning of the demise of the Cowboys," White told the *Morning News.* "I think that happened the next year because of all the negative internal conflicts with the strike. That game was a great football game and, shoot, I was happy to play in it. We outplayed the 49ers and felt we should have won the game. But I don't think you can complain about the situation. And all you can ask for is to get in that situation and play well. Personally, I think I did."

White was 16 of 24 for only 173 yards. He threw two touchdowns, one interception, and lost 38 yards on four sacks. His longest completion was his last throw, the 31-yard pass to Pearson. He dropped the ball when his legacy was on the line. The Cowboys were stunned on the sideline. They were used to Staubach rescuing them. This was the kind of mistake the Cowboys always forced the other quarterback to make. They stood in shock as they watched White lose the ball.

"It's insane, but it happened," Thurman said. "You got to be kidding me. If we won that game, we would have won the Super Bowl. Then we might have won two more."

In the end, White will be remembered as the bridge, although built on a shaky foundation, between Staubach and Troy Aikman. Aikman went on to win three Super Bowls.

"If he wins one, you can't say he can't," Thurman said. "He's not Brett Favre, but at the same time, he's not a bust. Now when you mention Danny White, you can't mention him in the same breath as Staubach and Aikman. All of a sudden, you become a guy who can't get it done in the playoffs."

White's warts in the locker room are even more glaring when framed against the administrations of Staubach and Aikman, who were each revered by their teammates. White was very political, always looking to present a boy-scout image but failing too many times in clutch games. "I think it's obvious anytime you are a starting quarterback on a Super Bowl championship team you are elevated to a different level whether or not you deserve it," tight end Doug Cosbie said. "Eli Manning is a different guy today than before he won the Super Bowl. He's the same quarterback, but everyone thinks he's a different guy. It would have been the same for Danny."

When the 1981 season ended with the 49ers winning the championship, players were upset with White for fumbling. They felt he cost them the Super Bowl, but they were not campaigning for Landry to give backups Glenn Carano or Gary Hogeboom an opportunity to compete for the starting job. Once things settled down after the disappointing loss, Landry was back in his office the next morning, declaring he would be returning to coach the Cowboys in 1982, which would be his twenty-third season. One of the annual exercises in Dallas once the season ended was to check in with Landry to see if he would return the next year. He really had not given any indication he was ready to step aside, but he would never commit to the next year until the current season ended.

White lost a lot of respect in his own locker room and around the league with his private strike-settlement meetings with Schramm in 1982. He claimed the owners' offer was sufficient and he wanted to go back to work. What further infuriated his team-mates was the fact White was not even the team's player rep. That job belonged to Robert Newhouse. "I'm sure that pissed a lot of people off," Cosbie said.

The next strike, in 1987, presented players with the option of crossing the line and getting paid. It did not tear the Cowboys apart when White and so many others returned to work, just as it didn't destroy the 49ers when Montana and Clark came in. "In 1987, I was the player rep, and all those guys crossed the picket line," Cosbie said. "Danny was one of the first ones. Everybody makes their own decisions. I told the guys that all of our situations are different. Most of it was based on finances. I just felt the cause was greater than sac-rificing some money for a year. A lot of people didn't. Joe Montana crossed the picket line in '87. Half their team did."

But the 1982 strike had been different. White isolated himself. "Everybody wants to get this thing settled, but at the expense of look-ing like a traitor? It wasn't good," Thurman said. Thurman was one of the most popular players on the team and the leader of the defensive backs. He was also tight with Dorsett. Their votes counted. White solidly supported the union before his first meeting with Schramm. After their first get-together, he began to side with the owners. After the second meeting, he was for an immediate settlement.

"I'm making $250,000 playing football, and I challenge any guy on our team to make more than that outside football," White said. "The owners own the football team. They don't have to pay us a penny. I guess that's a thought from the old school, but I'm a bit old-fashioned. If what I felt mattered, we would be playing football."

Less and less what White said mattered in the Cowboys' world. But in 1982, he tried to circumvent the union and take over for

1,400 players. "There was a lot of dissension," Dorsett said. "There was a lot of dislike towards Danny White because of what players were thinking he was doing. There is no question if guys had a chance during that strike to string him up and give him a hundred lashes, they would have been more than happy to dish out those lashes.

"We kind of thought he was working both sides of the fence. He was trying to give information about the players. He was spending too much time with Tex. He shouldn't have been doing that."

White was able to get the Cowboys back in the NFC Championship Game in the strike season while the 49ers had a dreadful time and missed the playoffs. The combination of getting a bit too full of themselves and the tumultuous strike was too much for Walsh's young team to overcome. But after Dallas beat the Bucs and Packers in the first two rounds of the playoffs, they went to RFK Stadium to play the Redskins with a trip to Pasadena for Super Bowl XVII at stake. This was an opportunity for White to vindicate himself, but instead he further lost his hold on the job.

Dexter Manley took White out with a big hit late in the second quarter, and Landry put in Hogeboom, who, coming out of training camp, had jumped ahead of Carano on the depth chart. Hogeboom was a fifth-round pick in 1980 from Central Michigan. All anybody knew about him was he had a big arm and the offensive linemen loved him. He was one of the guys, while White came off as an extension of Landry. Besides, in the NFL, everybody loves the backup quarterback, especially when the starter is not producing Super Bowls. Hogey eventually would gain more attention for his appearance on the television reality show *Survivor,* 20 years after his career ended, than for anything he ever accomplished on the field.

Hogeboom did some impressive things against the Redskins, however, with touchdown passes to Pearson and Butch Johnson, but he threw two interceptions in the fourth quarter, one leading to a field goal, and the other tipped by Manley and returned 10 yards for a touchdown by defensive tackle Darryl Grant, turning a 21–17 lead for the Redskins after three quarters into a 31–17 rout. Hogeboom did display his rocket arm, a commodity White lacked. Thus there was a Boomer Bandwagon that started to load up after the season—but not to the point where he was a serious threat to White in 1983, especially after Dallas opened the season with a wild 31–30 victory in Washington on its way to a 7–0 start, its best since 1977.

But White completely lost whatever support remained in the locker room when he defied Landry in a crucial late-season loss to the Redskins, running a play on fourth and short rather than following through on Landry's order to try to draw the Washington defense offside. Instead of taking the five-yard delay-of-game penalty or calling time out, White decided he knew better than the coach and ran a play that failed. The NFC East title was at stake that day with the Cowboys and Redskins tied at 12–2.

"No, no, no, Danny, no," Landry screamed.

Well, for him, he was screaming. Landry rarely showed emotion, other than an occasional pained look on his face. This was a breakthrough. He was pissed off. At the time, the Redskins were up 14–10 in the third quarter. Dallas faced a fourth and 1 at its own 48. During an injury time-out, Landry gave White strict instructions what to do. He ordered him not to run a play. The quarterback audibled. White went to a long snap count, and with the play clock down to 4 seconds, he handed off to Springs, who was thrown for a 2-yard loss.

"This is what killed Danny," Thurman said. "That's where guys were done with him. To me, that was the pressure of not having accomplished in 1980, '81 and '82. Now it's 1983, after four seasons of being the starting quarterback of the Dallas Cowboys, even though you've been in three championship games, you've lost them all.

People are saying you can't win the big one. And now you are in the biggest regular-season game, and you feel like you got to make something happen."

That was the competitor in White, although his decision defied logic. In the game, the Cowboys rushed 20 times for a mere 33 yards, but at a crucial moment, White basically told his Hall of Fame coach to mind his own business and tried to beat the Redskins with a running play by the fullback. Although the Redskins didn't immediately capitalize, it changed field position. The Redskins won 31–10 and made it to the Super Bowl as the NFC East champs. Then the Cowboys, with nothing at stake, lost 42–17 on the road to the 49ers in the final game of the regular season, giving them no momentum going into the playoffs.

The Cowboys were stuck playing in the wild-card round against the Rams. And when severe cold weather hit Dallas in the week before the game, Landry and Schramm decided to move practice indoors to the Astrodome in Houston. It didn't matter. For the second time in five seasons, the Rams came into Texas Stadium and eliminated the Cowboys.

The last time, it turned out to be the last game of Staubach's career. White wasn't retiring, but the loss to the Rams, which followed three straight losses in the NFC Championship Game, finally and completely eroded his hold on the job.

Players were now openly talking about Hogeboom's potential. They saw him throw every day in practice and were excited about what he could bring. He was one of the reasons the Cowboys passed on Dan Marino when he slipped in the 1983 draft. White was astonished and hurt that so many of his teammates were lobbying so hard for him to get benched.

When the Cowboys reconvened for their off-season workouts in March, there was a buzz around the team. For the first time since Staubach vs. Morton, it was clear a quarterback controversy was developing with the potential to tear the team apart. It had been thirteen years since Landry alternated Staubach and Morton in that game in Chicago. He had great affinity for both players, even though he once had chosen Don Meredith over Morton. He felt bad that he was always choosing somebody else over Morton. He knew the team would function better with Staubach and made the move. Landry loved White, even if he felt frustrated with him at times. He wasn't particularly close to Hogeboom. But Landry often relied on his "feel" of the team, so he was going to pay close attention in training camp that summer to see how the players were responding to White. It was going to take an awful lot for him to make the change, especially because he could not even pronounce Hogeboom's name.

Landry was unintentionally funny the way he fumbled over the pronunciation of any players' names more complicated than White or Smith. He always told them if he pronounced their name wrong to let him know. He called Hogeboom Hogenboom or Hogenbloom, so in his second year with the team in 1981, Hogeboom attempted to correct the coach. Landry's response: "Gary, when you become a starter, I'll learn how to pronounce your name."

It was one of the few fibs Landry ever told. He never learned how to say Hogeboom. He settled for Hogey.

The White-Hogeboom situation dominated the Cowboys off-season going into training camp in 1984. Many players were telling the *Dallas Morning News* off the record that they preferred Hogeboom, but they never thought Landry would have the courage to make the change. It would be an interesting conflict for Landry: If the players truly wanted Hogeboom and he had a good camp, could Landry sit down the player who was considered the teacher's pet?

Most of the Cowboys spent their off-season in Dallas to get a head start on conditioning. It was very rare in the mid eighties for players to live year-round in the town where they played—or to even come back in March to work out. Once the season was over, the players would scatter, and other than for an occasional three-day minicamp, they'd be invisible until camp opened in mid-July. Not only did the Cowboys choose to live in Dallas, but many NFL players from Texas came back to spend the off-season there as well. And with the locker room full of activity every day, the *Dallas Morning News* contacted thirty-four Cowboys for a quarterback poll. Two questions were posed:

1. Whom did they want as their starting quarterback? Result: Hogeboom, 20; White, 4; no comment, 10.
2. Whom did they think Landry would choose? Result: White, 23; Hogeboom, 5; no comment, 6.

Clearly, this was a pro-Hogeboom team run by a pro-White coach. The story, published in May 1984, brought the national spotlight to an explosive controversy.

None of this would have happened if Montana's pass on Sprint Right Option had been swatted down by Jones or if the ball had sailed through Clark's hands. And surely it would have been a moot point if Pearson had broken free of Wright or if White had not fumbled after making that great pass to Pearson.

Hogeboom and White each played well that summer at Cal Lutheran University in Thousand Oaks, California, the Cowboys training-camp home, but Landry had not given any indication who was going to start the Monday night season opener against the Rams in Anaheim. He would reveal his decision at the team's welcome-home luncheon before the start of the season. Landry stepped up to the podium at a downtown hotel and was going through depth-chart changes when he finally came to quarterback. The few strands of hair he had remaining on the top of his head were out of place. He looked as though he had not slept. It had the drama of the Heisman announcement or the crowning of Miss America. Landry was visibly nervous.

Then he made his quarterback announcement: Phil Pozderac.

Huh? It might have been the only time Landry lost his composure in public. He was a bit of a mad scientist anyway, prone to comments that made you wonder what was happening deep inside his fertile mind. Pozderac was a young offensive tackle from Notre Dame. Landry had decided to start him—but not at quarterback. He quickly caught himself, but the audience was stunned by his screwup. Then, in a surprise almost as startling, he made the correction and said Hogeboom would start. In explaining his decision, he made reference to the *Morning News* poll, which opened his eyes to how White had lost any of his remaining power in the locker room.

"That was a big mistake by Coach Landry," Staubach said. "He got swayed into that deal. Hogeboom was a good athlete, but he wasn't the proven commodity like Danny. Tom is thinking, 'I'm getting back into this "We can't win the big game"–type thing.'"

Of course, the Hogeboom era was a bust and didn't last the season. He completed a team record 33 passes in 47 attempts for 343 yards, and the Cowboys beat the Rams in the opener, but they scored only 20 points. That many completions and yards should produce more than 20 points. But Hogeboom had an interception and a fumble in the first quarter, and Dorsett fumbled four times, losing three of them.

Landry was able to relax after the game. The White-Hogeboom controversy had been exhausting. "Obviously, Gary was outstanding," he said.

Not so much the next week, though: Lawrence Taylor of the Giants forced him into two fumbles, one of them returned 81 yards for a touchdown by linebacker Andy Headen. The Cowboys lost 28–7.

After that 1–1 start, Hogeboom had the Cowboys at 5–3 halfway through the season, in position to extend their streak of nine consecutive years in the playoffs. But White came off the bench to relieve an injured Hogeboom in the eighth game and rallied them to a victory over the Saints. Landry started White the next week, but injuries made it a back-and-forth revolving door at quarterback the rest of the year. The low point was a 14–3 loss in Buffalo when the Bills were 0–11.

Hogeboom started that game, but Landry went back to White the next week. White won his first two starts but lost the last two, and Dallas finished 9–7 and out of the playoffs. White retained his starting job in 1985, and the Cowboys won the NFC East but again lost to the Rams in their first playoff game. Hogeboom was traded to the Colts following the '85 season, and the next time anybody heard about him he was trying to survive on a television reality show.

A few months after he was fired, Landry tried to explain why he'd benched White, considering how strongly he felt about him. "That was two years after the strike, which was a bad year for the Cowboys, a year of dissension," he said. "It took a long time to get over that. My feeling at that time was that Danny could not lead the team at that point because of what was said during the strike and the way the players felt. I decided to make a change and give Danny a chance to recover. And he did. He worked himself back and got the confidence of the team."

White went on to have a successful career as a coach in the Arena Football League. Pearson, who ran the New Jersey franchise in the short-lived XFL, tried to hire him as his head coach, but White was not interested. "A lot of people tend to forget that quarterback between Roger and Troy," Pearson said. "Danny was a damn good quarterback."

The Cowboys history book would be much kinder to White if he had beaten the 49ers. "It's a whole different deal," Staubach said.

"They wouldn't have screwed around with that whole thing with Hogeboom. That was the end of Danny's career with Dallas. He came back and played some more, but things were never the same. After those three championship games, it was never the same again."

White did accomplish one thing Staubach did not. He became the first Cowboy ever to appear on the cover of a national cereal box when Kellogg's made him the cover boy for Corn Flakes. But it was Wheaties that was the breakfast of champions.

6

THE DRIVE AFTER
THE GAME

DREW PEARSON is in the lobby of the Dallas/Plano Marriott at Legacy Town Center staring intently into the screen of a portable DVD player. The disc is cued up to 47 seconds remaining in the 1981 NFC Championship Game, Cowboys on the San Francisco 25-yard line, Pearson split wide to Danny White's left with Butch Johnson in the slot to Pearson's right. Tony Hill was lined up split to the right of White.

Pearson is watching the actual game broadcast that aired on CBS with Vin Scully doing the play-by-play and former Chiefs and Saints coach Hank Stram providing the analysis. On the radio side, Jack Buck and Pat Summerall called the game. But Pearson doesn't need to hear anybody describing the plays, even though more than twenty-five years have passed, and he certainly knows he's not about to get a surprise ending, despite all the twisting and turning he's about to do on the couch.

Pearson hits the play button. He sees himself running free through the 49ers secondary. He never had great speed except when the ball was in the air and he was chasing it. He had separation speed. White throws a bullet and hits Pearson in stride at the Cowboys 47. He's still bitter that it was only his first catch of the game. Pearson couldn't have thrown it better himself, not even in his days at South River High School in New Jersey, where he played quarterback after Joe Theismann went to Notre Dame. Pearson sees rookie defensive backs Ronnie Lott and Carlton Williamson converging on him but taking each other out of the play after he caught the ball. His eyes light up as thoughts of Hail Mary II enter his head, a reprise of that signature moment in the 1975 divisional playoffs in Minnesota, when he did or did not push off Vikings defensive back Nate Wright to grab Roger Staubach's long pass and turn it into a touchdown. The Cowboys trailed the Vikings 14–10 when they took over at their own 15 with just 1:51 remaining. Fran Tarkenton had just led the Vikings to the go-ahead score. Staubach worked the Cowboys to midfield with 24 seconds left. He lined up in the shotgun, looked to his left, and then fired the ball deep down the right sideline. Pearson came down with it at the Vikings 5, pinned it against his right hip to gain control, and scored the winning touchdown. The old Metropolitan Stadium in Minneapolis just about crumbled.

Pearson never stopped hearing that it should have been called offensive pass interference. He has never stopped resenting it, either. "I didn't push him," Pearson says, as he hits the pause button for a moment. "There was contact. I was going for the ball. But there was no deliberate push. You can't see any kind of extension of the arm or anything. It seems like other plays in NFL history have had controversies, but people forget and move on and eventually say it was a great play and let it rest in the annals of great plays like the Immaculate Reception. Did it hit the ground? Did two players on the same team hit the ball? There is a lot more controversy involved in that play than in the Hail Mary, but they don't look at it that way."

It is clear there is a lot of hostility built up. Maybe it stems from Pearson being an undrafted free agent out of Tulsa and always feeling he had to prove himself. The Hail Mary was an athletic play that has been given an asterisk because of the debate as to whether a flag should have been thrown. So what if there was contact? It happens on just about every play. If Pearson was skilled enough to get away with it, more power to him.

"It was a clean catch," Pearson said. "Franco Harris made a great catch on the Immaculate Reception. He did his job. Way to go, Franco. But there ain't nobody who ever said, 'Way to go Drew, you did your job.' But they said, 'Did you push?' They say, 'You pushed him, didn't you?' What that does is water down the two plays I made before the Hail Mary. On fourth and 18, we hit for 22 yards. I made four catches for 91 yards in that drive. I had no catches leading up to that point in that game. One third down got us a first down. Then fourth down got us a first down. And then the Hail Mary. Because of the controversy with the Hail Mary, nobody even brings up fourth and 18. What a great play. What a great catch. Did I push him then? Give me a break with the Hail Mary.

"Everybody, of course, they don't recognize the effort, the route to get downfield. How did I get even with Nate Wright in a prevent situation to even be in a position to push? How did I come around to make a play on an underthrown ball to catch it and still get in the end zone? But, no, it's all about the controversy."

An orange went flying by Pearson's head in the end zone. He was hit by a beer can as he left the field. Vikings safety Paul Krause and defensive tackle Alan Page voiced loud complaints to the officials about the lack of a flag. Head linesman Jerry Bergman was the official responsible for that side of the field. Field judge Armen Terzian, from 15 yards away, confirmed that no flag should be thrown.

"Both men were going for the ball," Terzian said. "It was just one of those plays."

After the game, Staubach gave that catch a nickname that would stick. "I just threw the ball as far as I could and said a Hail Mary," he said. A fan hurled a whiskey bottle out of the stands that hit Terzian in the head and briefly knocked him unconscious. He later needed eleven stitches. The Cowboys went on to beat the Rams in Los Angeles in the NFC Championship but lost the Super Bowl to the Steelers. Still, the Hail Mary is remembered more than the Super Bowl loss.

"It was the single most exciting play I ever saw," Landry said. "Interference? No, I never saw Drew push off. I looked back on that play and slowed the film down and all you could see is the ball sitting on Drew's hip and nobody holding on to it. It's incredible that the ball didn't bounce. I never lost faith that we could pull that game out. Roger Staubach was not at his best in that game. But he just believed so hard, it was contagious."

Now, six years after the Hail Mary, Pearson sees a clear path to the end zone in San Francisco. He is about to turn White's pass into a 75-yard touchdown and cement his place as one of the all-time clutch receivers in NFL history. If Pearson is able to score, then the White fumble never happens. Pearson makes another amazing play to win a playoff game and White throws a 75-yard touchdown pass to send Dallas to the Super Bowl. If only Pearson could have hit the erase button instead of the play button. He would have been better off fast-forwarding.

Pearson watches Williamson diving in a failed attempt to get a hand on the ball and thus causing Lott to stumble over him, making it impossible for Lott to get back into the play. For a few steps, it looks as though Pearson is about to break it. Eric Wright, one of the fastest 49ers, enters the picture. Then Pearson lets out a scream that gets heads turning in what had been a quiet hotel lobby on a Tuesday morning. They turn to see a bald man, a contrast from his early days with the wild Afro, staring and cursing at a DVD player sitting on a coffee table in front of him. The scene was funny, unlike what Pearson was watching. Wright, the 49ers rookie corner, shoots across the screen and reaches out with his left hand across Pearson's left shoulder. It is not enough to bring him down, but it does slow him down enough for Wright to extend his right hand and grab Pearson under his right shoulder pad. It's a borderline horse-collar tackle, which was not against the rules in 1975, but is now a 15-yard penalty. Pearson picked up nine yards after he made the catch.

If Pearson had had one more step on Wright or if Pete Rozelle had authorized tear-away jerseys, he could have been gone. Dwight Hicks had an angle on Pearson, but it's not likely he would have caught him before Tony Hill would have blocked him.

"I wanted to be the hero," Pearson now said solemnly. Instead of Hail Mary II, it was Heartbreak I.

After watching the tape of the last possession more than twenty-five years later, he sounded the way he did back in the day when the Cowboys would lose and he didn't get the ball enough. In this case, he was right. His only catch of the game was that 31-yarder on the next-to-last play, and it pained him to watch how close he came to breaking the play. But he was just as angry about the next play when White was attempting to throw to Tony Hill.

"I was upset, not that Danny fumbled, but that he didn't come back to me," Pearson said. "I'm the hot guy right now. Ride it. I've proven it. You rode it in 1980 with the Falcons with two touchdowns in the final four minutes. You know what the deal is. Bring it here. Don't even go nowhere else. Don't even listen to Coach Landry. With all due respect, he ain't got the feel. It's a feel thing now. That's what Roger relied on. You're a quarterback. It's a feel thing. They know I'm not going to tell them I'm open if I can't get open."

Pearson pleaded with White in the huddle to look his way. "Come back," he said. "I'm going to fake it in and break it out. That's another twenty yards right there, and you're in field-goal range."

Instead, White fumbled.

Unfortunately, there would be more heartache for Pearson. Much too much.

The 49ers regained control of the game in the third quarter, but not immediately. They drove to the Cowboys 16 on their second possession of the second half. Montana was trying to pick up a few yards on a short throw to Elliott coming out of the backfield on a delay route, but the ball bounced off his hands and floated to defensive tackle Randy White, who was not exactly a ball hawk. He did play some linebacker after the Cowboys drafted him in 1974, a questionable experiment by Landry, but this was the first interception of his career. The Manster, half man, half monster, was one of the best interior linemen in the NFL, and this was a gift from Elliott. The Cowboys started from their own 13, the second time in the game they took over deep in their own end after forcing a turnover. This was turnover number four. The Cowboys converted the three they had in the first half into only seven points. The Cowboys offense had to start taking advantage, even if they were deep in their own end.

Danny White's first-down pass was too far for Springs in the right flat. The next throw to Springs bounced off his left hand and was intercepted by linebacker Bobby Leopold, who was right behind Springs at the Cowboys 18. He returned it five yards, placing Montana in immediate range of putting the 49ers back on top. This was a championship game, but nobody could hold on to the ball. Walsh kept the ball on the ground for three straight plays and then sent in short yardage specialist Johnny Davis to take it in from the 2 to put San Francisco back on top, 21–17.

The game was starting to take on the look of a classic. Throughout the stadium, you could sense the anticipation that a dramatic ending of some sort was coming up. But who was going to make the play? Or better put, the way this game was unfolding, who was going to make the big mistake?

On the Cowboys next possession after the kickoff, they moved from their 31 to the San Francisco 40. Once again, Lott became a major player for the wrong reason. White was going for Butch Johnson down the right side and Lott was badly beaten by Johnson. He had his back to the play and put his hands up in a feeble attempt to prevent a long completion. He had no idea where the ball was. The flag went down. Pass interference. This time it was legitimate. It was a 28-yard penalty that put the Cowboys at the 12.

But as the third quarter turned over into the fourth, the 49ers defense held tough. Landry sent in a three-tight-end alignment with Doug Cosbie, Billy Joe DuPree, and Jay Saldi on a third and 3 from the San Francisco 5. White went for Cosbie in the end zone. The ball was swatted away by Wright, who made a very nice play. Cosbie was screaming for pass interference, but the contact he felt came from Springs, who bumped him from behind. Septien then kicked a 22-yard field goal.

San Francisco 21, Dallas 20.

Drew Pearson was named after a famed Washington newspaper columnist. His father, Sam, loved the writer, read him all the time in the *Newark Star-Ledger.* "One time we played in D.C., and I got a note from his secretary," Pearson said. "She wanted to meet me. We arranged to meet in the lobby, and she brought me some mementos of his, a St. Christopher medal with his name on it that had a little saying, a stopwatch with his name on the back that he used to time radio reports."

Sam Pearson died in 1980 when the Cowboys were playing the Redskins in the week before Thanksgiving. "I found out at halftime," Pearson said.

He went back home to New Jersey for the funeral and returned to Dallas on Wednesday, the day before the Cowboys were playing the Seahawks in the annual holiday day game at Texas Stadium. "Landry wouldn't start me. I was so pissed," he said. "But I understood. I had been gone after the game on Sunday."

He was at practice running laps when Landry called him into his office. First thing, he was surprised to see him back in Dallas so soon. Then he told him Butch Johnson was starting in his place at flanker. "I knew I had to play," he said. "My dad wanted me to play. We killed Seattle 51–7, and I played the second half. I caught one pass over the middle and as I was laying on the turf, I held the ball up. The crowd went wild. I said, 'That's for you, Dad.'"

Losing his father was difficult, but having to deal with the losses of those close to Pearson was something he would have to get used to over the next two decades. It became more than he could handle. After his father died, at least Pearson still had football. Unfortunately for him and for the Cowboys, however, it would not be that way much longer. He was certainly not ready to retire in the spring of 1984. He was just thirty-three years old. Life after football started way too soon. He played eleven years with the Cowboys, still had plenty left, and had carved out a borderline Hall of Fame career. Besides, he was one of the all-time good guys.

But life forever changed for him on March 22, 1984, the night Pearson was driving and his younger brother, Carey, was the passenger and was killed. The accident began a series of tragic events over the next seventeen years, leading to a life of isolation and depression until he finally sought some help from a Cowboys team doctor, the only doctor he knew in Dallas. Pearson's day-to-day existence had become such a struggle that he had transitioned from an outgoing, trash-talking All-Pro wide receiver to a man who spent the day sleeping and doing yard work.

He could not face the world. When he managed the courage

and energy to go outside, the only solace he found was in gardening around his house. He used to love to go to clubs. Now he would drive up to an upscale Dallas nightspot and find a place to park, but anxiety would overcome him and he would go home without even getting out of his car. His dates were now arranged through text-messaging, and the typical get-together was, his friend would come over and they would hang out at his home. Eating out was a problem, too. He would drive up to a fast-food joint, order his meal at the drive-through window, and then just keep on driving past the pick-up window. Pearson couldn't bear the thought of facing another human being, so he left.

"I've done that a million times," he said. "I've been divorced a long time. I used to hang out and go look for some women. I would get dressed, get clean, and go to the club, drive up there and drive back home. I would never go in. It was the same thing going into a grocery store."

He sat and cried in the locker room after the loss to the 49ers. Just over two years later, he suffered a much greater loss that brought more tears. Pearson was the coach and traveling secretary of the Cowboys off-season basketball team, which barnstormed throughout the Southwest playing against schoolteachers, cops, firemen, and anybody else who wanted to arrange a game against a bunch of Cowboys players who were out for a good time, a little exercise, and even less money. There was the occasional road trip to Washington to take on the Redskins. On this night in March 1984, the Hoopsters were playing in Coalgate, Oklahoma. Pearson's younger brother Carey, who was called Moose for no apparent reason—certainly not for his size, because he wasn't a big guy—had moved down from New Jersey to live with Drew in Dallas. Moose was having a tough time up in Jersey, so his brother put him to work at Pearson's Super Shine, off Midway, right across from the Addison Airport, where Landry would land his own plane after his weekend trips to Austin. Pearson put just about his whole family to work at the car wash, including his sister and her boyfriend. It seemed that one or another of his relatives was always either living with him or being supported by him.

Pearson picked eight of his teammates to take on the trip to Coalgate, paid them $200–$250 for the night, and provided transportation on a nice coach bus. Carey earned his way as the equipment manager. "Moose was excited about going to the game," Pearson said. "All the guys liked him, and he loved being around that stuff."

After the game, win or lose, there was always beer for the bus ride home. There was beer that night on the three-hour trip back to Dallas. "I might have had two," Pearson said. "I knew I had to get up in the morning. We were going to D.C. the next day. I was taking eighteen players, so I knew I had stuff to do."

Pearson arranged two different flights to Washington. Just in case of a tragedy, he didn't want all the players on the same plane. "I couldn't do that to the Cowboys," he said.

The young guys were on the early flight. The veterans, like Pearson, Tony Hill, Tony Dorsett, Doug Cosbie, Ron Springs, Billy Joe DuPree, and Harvey Martin, were on the later flight. "Harvey couldn't play worth a lick," Pearson said. "But he was an attraction. The fans loved him. He would get fired up for a little basketball game like it was a football game."

Everson Walls, Michael Downs, Angelo King, and Dexter Clinkscale were also making the trip to Washington. "Three games," Pearson said. "My big problem was, how was I going to play them?"

He wasn't going to worry about it on the bus ride back from Coalgate. It was time to relax. And it was a perfect time for team bonding. "I had gotten so hot playing cards, and I never play cards," Pearson said. "I got a whupping from my father when I was a kid and was caught stealing cards from the Sav-on Drugs in Edison in the ninth grade. My dad whipped me so bad, I didn't want to *see* a deck of cards. To this day, I don't gamble or play cards. I don't even play solitaire on the computer."

He was playing with Doug Donley on the bus, and he just couldn't lose. He won back Donley's basketball paycheck. "I had a couple of beers," he said. "I wasn't drunk by any means."

The bus arrived back at the Cowboys facility on Forest Lane in North Dallas at one A.M. Pearson asked his teammates to help him unload the bus, but by the time he turned around, they were off into the night. "So it's just me and my brother, and we helped the bus driver clean out the bus, and we loaded the uniforms," he said. "I had to go home and put those uniforms in a washing machine and get them ready. It was an all-nighter for me."

Pearson had just gotten divorced one month earlier. He was living in an apartment at the Prestonwood Country Club. But because he was going on a three-day road trip and Moose was not coming, he was taking him to his brother Andre's house over in Garland. He planned to drop off Moose, head home, wash the clothes, and call the players to remind them of their flight times the next morning. The first flight was at nine. "You had to babysit those guys," he said.

Drew and Moose crammed the uniforms into the back of the Dodge Daytona he had on loan from a local dealer. "I was in a little sports car. It was a stick shift, and I never drive a stick shift," he said. "It was so sweet. The general manager was saying, 'That ain't you, that ain't you.' Normally I get the Chrysler Fifth Avenue, a big stylish car."

He only had the car a couple of days. Drew and Moose got in for the relatively short ride to Garland, on the interstate in the direction opposite to that toward Pearson's home.

The next thing he knew, Moose was dead and the cops were

telling Drew he was going to have to take a Breathalyzer. He still has no idea how the Dodge Daytona slammed into a stalled eighteen-wheeler on the shoulder of I-635 East in the middle of the night. "I just remember getting on the ramp of the freeway, going up the ramp. That was it," he said. "I don't remember what happened. I do remember waking up and seeing that parked truck there, seeing all the lights and sirens. There was one lady who called and said she saw what happened. She said I was weaving and tried to weave back to avoid the parked truck. In doing that, I hit the truck. They thought I was dead. When you look at the car, it was like, 'How can anybody survive?'"

Pearson doesn't know if he fell asleep at the wheel. He was never found to be drunk. He just knows that he doesn't know what happened. He never heard any screeching. Never felt any impact. "I woke up and I was laying on the steering wheel. My brother was laying on my shoulder," he said. "I tried to shake him."

C'mon Moose, wake up. Don't die, little brother.

"I could tell he was limp," he said. "I got out, and they couldn't believe it. I'm walking around the car looking and wondering what happened. Then I asked if my brother is dead. Next thing you know, I'm in an ambulance. A day later, I wake up, I was hemorrhaging. I had a lacerated liver, which was the main problem. I was bleeding internally. Had a broken clavicle."

Forget about football, Tony Dorsett worried what impact the accident would have on the rest of Pearson's life. "To see your brother, one of your loved ones like that, it would be like, 'Lord, take me. Why let me survive this?'" Dorsett said. "This was towards the tail end of Drew's career. Coming back would have been great therapy for him, to be around the guys. It would take his mind off things. To me, he seemed to weather the storm as well or better than anybody I know of."

Doctors had to drain his liver, and in order to insert tubes, they cracked two ribs. Pearson was surviving on Demerol. "You got to give me everything," he told the docs. "They couldn't put me to sleep to do it. They're pushing, pushing, and I heard the crack. Boy, that is the most excruciating pain I ever felt in my life."

He has no idea how he survived the crash. "It was like my soul was taken out and put back," he said.

Once reality set in, Pearson was looking for reassurance from his family that nobody was holding him responsible for his brother's death, for somebody to say, "Drew, we know you loved Carey and would never do anything to put him at risk." He desperately needed to feel love from his family. From his mother.

Those words never came then and never came later. "I never got any feeling from my family that it was OK, that we don't blame you. No one ever came up to me, my brother or sister or mom, and said, 'It wasn't your fault.' Nobody," Pearson said. "You're just looking for something. As it turned out, that was the root of the depression I was going through. Something that was building inside me that ended up being a problem later. To this day, it bothers me. Always in the back of my mind."

The funeral for Carey Pearson was in New Jersey, but Drew Pearson was unable to attend; he was still in Presbyterian Hospital in Dallas. His family came to Dallas after the funeral to comfort him through his physical ailments, but the words he wanted to hear were never spoken. He had helped out all his family members financially at one point or another, but when he was hurt inside, when guilt was a constant companion, the only people who could have made it just a little bit better failed him.

One person who *was* there for him was Tom Landry. "I loved Coach Landry," Pearson said.

He knew that Harvey Martin, his best friend, and Roger Staubach, his close friend, would be by his side in the hospital. But every time Pearson would look up, Landry was standing there.

Landry was in a cold, bottom-line business with a premium on winning, and he didn't have the personality of Bill Walsh or Bill Parcells, but his players knew he cared. He had an ability to separate personal feelings from football decisions that he felt were crucial to the team's success, and that was one of the reasons the Cowboys were so successful. He was not afraid to make the tough decision, letting go a longtime popular player if it was in the best interests of the team. If that led to more victories but an unflattering image, Landry accepted the trade-off. He was loyal to his players as long as they were producing, but he was not running a benefit designed to give them paychecks for an extra couple of seasons if younger, more athletic players were ready to replace them. Nevertheless, it would hurt him to say good-bye, and he didn't turn his back on them. He was a spiritual man and was always willing to help.

Pearson was still playing for Landry at the time of his accident. He doesn't remember anything about the crash, but he remembers Landry's support. "He was awesome," he said. "That kind of let me see or let me and other teammates who were coming around to see a human side of Coach Landry. He was there the whole time. He was not only trying to comfort *me,* but he was comforting my family. I was laying in the hospital and the funeral was going on; he was the one that was there with me. Every time I rolled over, the three people I remember seeing initially when I woke up were Staubach, Landry, and Harvey Martin."

Pearson's injuries forced him to retire from football. He was in no condition to play, and the lacerated liver would have made him a walking time bomb if he got hit in that area. That's not to say he didn't get the itch again. He was working toward a comeback in 1985 after getting medical clearance, but after coming early to camp in 1985 to help with the Cowboys' rookie receivers Karl Powe and Leon Gonzalez, he realized his career was over. Landry asked him to stick around that season to work with the young wideouts.

"It was hard on him," Thurman said. "He coached for us for awhile, but he wasn't the same guy. You could tell it affected him. But he's such a proud guy, he wasn't going to let you do too much for him, even though you say, 'Hey, man, I'm here for you.' You knew he was going to work his way through it on his own. But you could see the pain in his face."

Pearson wouldn't let anybody in. The physical pain subsided, but the mental pain never did. That accident stayed with Pearson all these years: The guilt. Not knowing exactly what happened. His brother dying. His football career ending. That was overwhelming. He found comfort in being around Landry.

"I loved Coach Landry even more after I got done playing for him. I was now in a position where I could see why he was doing some things," Pearson said. "Sitting in those staff meetings, showering with the son of a gun. That was weird. I'd try and wait for all the coaches to get out of the shower. The next thing, here comes Coach Landry. I said, *Oh my God, I don't want to see this. I'm out of here.* He was a great coach, no doubt about it. We were good because of him. And a lot of us were able to prosper as NFL players because of the system. It was a system that just didn't depend on talent and ability. You had to have intelligence, character, and all those kinds of things. But I tell you, I just felt we could have done so much more."

The hours were too long and the pay wasn't enough for Pearson to make coaching his next career. He was gone after the 1985 season. Tex Schramm helped set him up in the sports-apparel business by cutting through some red tape to get him an NFL licensing agreement to manufacture hats. But life away from football was hard. Pearson was revered by the fans in Dallas and respected by his teammates. Cosbie, Donley, and safety Cliff Harris all named their sons Drew. "For a name I hated growing up, for three teammates to name their kids after me, made me feel real good," he said.

Pearson was more than a decade removed from the loss of his

father and younger brother when not just the roof caved in on his life, the entire house came down. Harvey Martin was his closest friend on the team, maybe the closest friend Pearson had in the world. They both came to the Cowboys in 1973, Pearson as a long-shot free-agent wide receiver from Tulsa and Martin as a third-round defensive end from little East Texas State. They became very tight. Martin was there for Pearson when his brother was killed. Pearson was there for Martin when he was having drug problems that became public knowledge when the Cowboys sent him to Hazelden in Minnesota in 1983 for treatment. The Cowboys and Martin tried to cover it up once the news was broken by the *Dallas Morning News*. Landry put out the word that Martin was merely sent to Hazelden to determine whether it would be a proper place to send Cowboys players if they were having a drug problem. And because Landry never lied, people believed him. Martin retired after the 1983 season. Pearson's final season was also 1983. Martin continued to have drug problems and was sent to jail in 1996 on domestic-violence and cocaine charges. He received probation on each charge and was sent to the Dallas County Judicial Treatment Center for eight months. He was also having financial trouble.

Too Mean Martin was the bookend to Too Tall Jones. He was a ferocious pass rusher and registered 23 sacks in 1977, before sacks became an official statistic. It would be the NFL single-season record if it were recognized. In the locker room, his teammates looked at him as a big, playful teddy bear. By 1998, he had turned his life around. John Niland, a former offensive lineman and Cowboys teammate, hired Martin to work for Arrow Magnolia International, a chemical-products company based in Dallas. It sold materials for the cleaning and maintenance of buildings, and three times Martin was selected the company's salesman of the year. He was also giving antidrug speeches to children and recovering addicts. He was making something of his life. He was always very likable. He just made some bad choices along the way.

On Christmas Eve, 2001, he was dead. Martin battled pancreatic cancer, among the deadliest diseases, and he died at Baylor Medical Center. It was just another tragedy for Pearson to try to find a way to accept. He didn't realize that the problem he was having functioning on a day-to-day basis was actually depression. "It was something that was building inside of me, but didn't come to the forefront until Harvey got sick and passed," he said. "I was supposed to go see my mom on Christmas Eve and surprise her. That's when Harvey was in the hospital. Harvey's mother called me on Christmas Eve.

"Drew, you got to come to the hospital. He ain't going to make it," she said.

Martin died that day. "I was there," Pearson said. "So I didn't go to Jersey to see my mom. Then a month later, she dies of a heart attack. Then six months later, my baby sister dies of breast cancer. Then after that, my older sister, who ended up living with me for five years, was diagnosed with breast cancer. Around the time Harvey died, my older brother Sam died of a heart attack. Coach Landry died about two years earlier. So there is all these things compounded. That's when it really hit me."

Pearson became so depressed he could not leave his house. His sister was living with him, but to him, suffering from all these losses, he was living alone. He would be in his bedroom all day. "I didn't know I was going through depression until I read an article they did on depression with professional athletes. It was a cover story in *Sports Illustrated*," he said. "The two athletes they focused on were Ricky Williams and Terry Bradshaw. I'm saying, *Ricky, I might understand. But Terry Bradshaw is depressed? He looks like the happiest guy in the world.* All the things I was doing, these guys talked about."

The 2003 piece in *SI* detailed Williams's social-anxiety disorder and Bradshaw's depression, as well as the issues of other athletes. "I thought I was getting past that after the accident," Pearson said. "Maybe some depression was setting in when my father passed. After I read that article, I got really concerned. I didn't know any doctors except Dr. Zamorano. He could see it."

"What's wrong with you?" Pearson said Dr. Z asked. "You look so sad. I can see it in your face. You don't look like Drew."

He told Zamorano, a Cowboys doctor whom the players called Pepe, about all that was going on in his life since the car accident ended his career. Pearson said Dr. Z told him he was clinically depressed and prescribed antidepressant medication.

Pearson said he didn't realize it was depression that he'd been suffering from during all those years through the eighties and nineties. Not as much was known about it then, and there was a stigma attached to it. "Depression? Get the fuck out of here," Pearson said. "Depressed? I'm depressed every day. Get over it. That's how depression was looked upon then."

Pearson was also fighting high blood pressure and high cholesterol. "I'll take stuff for that. I want to live," he said. "Something like depression, it's not life or death. I think I can work through it with herbs or something."

He took the pills the doctor prescribed, but not for very long. He called and told him, "This shit has got me going crazy."

The doctor urged him to give it time. His body needed time to adjust. Pearson elected to deal with it on his own. "He still prescribes it. But I don't take it," he said. "I still have times I'm up and down. I'm not healed, by any means. At least I know what it is. I was never the typical athlete. I'd get hurt, but I didn't want to go in there and deal with the treatment. I'd rather try and take care of myself."

He knows he is being stubborn and perhaps a bit foolish, but just as he wanted a sprained ankle to heal on its own, he is hoping the same thing happens with the mental issues that have plagued him. "It is a disease," he said. "Sometimes you have it and don't realize it. You have to recognize it and hopefully do something about it, and that it is not that deep-rooted. Mine is deep-rooted. It will always be there. I have learned to accept it. I just try not to let it control me."

Life can be a game of what ifs. What if the Cowboys hadn't played in Coalgate that night? What if Carey had stayed back in New Jersey? What if Drew had decided to take him to his house instead of his brother's house? It makes *What if Eric Wright hadn't been able to bring him down with a desperation lunge?* seem so damn insignificant.

7

THE TACKLE

EORGE SEIFERT, the 49ers secondary coach in his second year on the staff in 1981, was holding his breath in the coaches' booth. If the room had been big enough, he would have been pacing. Nine months earlier, Bill Walsh had drafted Ronnie Lott, Eric Wright, and Carlton Williamson and gave Seifert a simple mandate: Make it work. Right away.

"I didn't have much time to feel anything other than *I better get it done,*" he said.

Butch Johnson was in the slot, and Drew Pearson was split wide to his left. Lott was in front of Johnson. Wright was in front of Pearson. Lott was one of the elite players in the draft, taken eighth overall from Southern Cal. Walsh had two second-round picks and used them on defensive tackle John Harty from Iowa and Wright from Missouri. In the third round he selected Williamson from Pitt, and in the fifth round he took cornerback Lynn Thomas from Pittsburgh. Walsh had rebuilt the secondary in a couple of hours.

Seifert studied the defense Marion Campbell put in for Dick Vermeil with the Eagles, which helped them get to the Super Bowl the previous season. He felt it was a defense suited for young players. "The rookies were all very, very competitive," Seifert said. "They bought into the whole deal. We didn't think about what would happen if we failed. We didn't have time to think about that."

Seifert grew up in San Francisco and was an usher at the 49ers games. He went to high school right across the street from the old Kezar Stadium. He was there to see Y. A. Tittle, Hugh McElhenny, Joe Perry, John Henry Johnson, all future Hall of Famers. High school and college games were also played at Kezar, meaning by early in the season, there was no grass in the middle of the field. The 49ers entered the NFL in 1950 after the All America Football Conference folded. San Francisco beat the New York Yanks in the league's final playoff game. The 49ers' rivalry with the downstate Los Angeles Rams was the reason they were invited to join the NFL. The Niners had some very good teams in the fifties, with six winning seasons, but they won only one playoff game. When they had McElhenny, Perry, and Johnson together, they had three future Hall of Fame running backs. Johnson was traded to Detroit after the 1956 season, breaking up the backfield.

John Brodie, the 49ers' first-round pick, from nearby Stanford, in 1957, took over at quarterback when Tittle was traded to the Giants in 1961. Red Hickey was the coach by then, and he introduced the shotgun formation to the NFL. It would spread out the defenses. But the Niners didn't make the playoffs at all in the sixties, and then in the early seventies, they lost to the Cowboys in the playoffs three years in a row, including back-to-back NFC Championship Games. Brodie was gone after the 1973 season, and by the time Montana and Walsh arrived in 1979, the 49ers had gone through nine quarterbacks and five head coaches in between.

Walsh didn't know Seifert very well when he hired him after his first year with the 49ers, but Walsh had given him four highly rated defensive backs from the draft, and Seifert's job was to get them up to speed by the time the season opened. Lott, Wright, and Williamson would all be starting. By 1984, Lott, Wright, Williamson, and safety Dwight Hicks, a Walsh reclamation project, all made the Pro Bowl. That was the first and only time one team's entire defensive backfield has been selected. "Bill was pretty complex," Seifert said. "Obviously, he's a very bright football mind. He could be as hard as nails and pressure you. He either brought the best out of you, or you would crumble and not survive."

The 49ers, who were picking eighth, liked Lott and UCLA safety Kenny Easley in the first round. The 49ers had Easley rated higher, but after Walsh sent Seifert to scout them at the Hula Bowl, he felt Lott could play corner, and that's where the Niners needed the most help. They never had to make the choice, because the Seahawks drafted Easley with the fourth pick. The Niners wound up signing fullback Walt Easley, Kenny's cousin, who had a big fumble in the fourth quarter against Dallas. The 49ers staff coached Wright in the Senior Bowl, so they had a good feel for him. "He had been a safety at Missouri, but we felt he could play corner after working directly with him at the Senior Bowl," Seifert said.

Williamson was a pure safety, and having already taken Lott and Wright, Walsh wanted someone to pair with Hicks, the young safety. No matter how good these rookies were going to be, it looked like a long year for Seifert and the 49ers secondary. Cornerbacks are often out there all alone, and it's one of the toughest positions for a rookie to come in and excel at. But the 49ers were only 6–10 in 1980, and nobody was expecting a playoff season. The Super Bowl was never mentioned.

Lott struggled early in making the transition to the corner. His mentor at Southern Cal was Dennis Thurman, a senior when Lott was a freshman. Thurman was drafted by Dallas in 1978 and made the same move from safety to corner. He and Lott spoke every other week during Lott's rookie season. In the third week, the 49ers were playing in Atlanta. The Cowboys had a Monday night game in New England, so after practice on Sunday, Thurman went home and watched some of the 49ers-Falcons game before heading to the airport for the team flight to New England.

"Ronnie wasn't playing well on the corner," Thurman said. "He was doing what I had to do. You got to learn how to play in the fucking NFL. So he wasn't comfortable. I probably watched the first half of that game, then had to dress and go. I remember calling him during the next week and telling him, 'It looks like you are giving people too much respect. Just go out and play. Do your studying. Do your preparing. It's no different. Football is football.' He fucking took off. He got an interception in the regular-season game they played against us and ran it back for a touchdown. He got two interceptions in that game."

Lott would have been NFL defensive rookie of the year if not for a guy named Lawrence Taylor. Thurman's talk helped get Lott straightened out, but neither one of them played well in the championship game. Thurman gave up two touchdowns, and Lott was called for two pass-interference penalties. "It was like me playing against my brother," Lott said.

The four 49ers rookies became close friends right away. They went out to eat the day before road games. When you saw one of them, you saw all four of them. They would watch *Monday Night Football* together. In fact, they were all looking forward to making the halftime highlights the day after they beat the Cowboys 45–14 during the regular season. It would help make up for not being selected by the NFL to play on Monday night that season. But the 49ers were left out of the highlights, and the players were deprived of hearing Howard Cosell narrate their destruction of Dallas. That slight provided motivation the rest of the season.

"That was a unique group of guys and I don't know if it will ever happen again," Lott said. "We came from winning programs, and we had a great coach. George Seifert was the secondary coach, and Ray Rhodes was the assistant secondary coach. Ray had a lot of experience playing in the NFL. And George was a very technical, smart coach. The one thing about George is, he was very thorough. He prepared you for all situations."

Lott also developed a close relationship with Montana. They competed against each other in college and were drafted two years apart by the 49ers. They later went into business together. "We just had that SC–Notre Dame competition," Montana said. "Like oil and water. We played against each other in college, and you gain that respect. Then when you get there and see each other working, it just kind of happened naturally. He's obviously a great guy."

In Montana's senior season, Notre Dame trailed USC 24–6 late in the second half. The Irish were ranked number eight and the Trojans number three for the late-season game at the Los Angeles Coliseum. Mounting an incredible comeback, Montana's two-yard touchdown pass to Pete Holohan with 46 seconds remaining had put Notre Dame ahead 25–24. But Trojans quarterback Paul McDonald drove USC into position for Frank Jordan's game-winning 37-yard field goal with just 2 seconds remaining. Lott, playing safety for SC, became a believer in Montana that day.

"He had a special quality," Lott said.

Joe and Jennifer had two girls and then two sons, both quarterbacks. Ronnie Lott is godfather to their second son, Nicholas. "It made me nervous a little bit because I think Ronnie's influence had Nicholas wanting to play defense for awhile," Montana said.

It was a special day in Canton in the summer of 2000 when Montana and Lott were inducted together into the Pro Football Hall of Fame. "He's probably one of the greatest competitors," Lott said. "He's one of those guys who doesn't wear it on his sleeve, but before you know it, he's probably cut you three or four times. He'd be a great poker player."

But knowing that Montana had become such a great comeback quarterback, seeing firsthand how he led that comeback against Southern Cal, still didn't make Lott believe Montana would drive the 49ers 89 yards in the final minutes for the winning touchdown to beat the Cowboys. "I've always been somewhat of a pessimistic person," Lott said. "That's just how I'm wired."

Now it was up to Seifert's rookies. He wouldn't start calling the defenses until Walsh promoted him to defensive coordinator in 1983, but he had come an awfully long way from walking up and down the sideline as the head coach of Cornell in the Ivy League.

The 49ers were protecting a 28–27 lead. Dallas had the ball on its 25-yard line when Danny White connected with Drew Pearson. Up in the press box, Seifert was one missed tackle away from getting fired. Wright saved Seifert's job with his desperation swipe at the back of Pearson's jersey, bringing him down at the San Francisco 44.

"They always talk about The Catch," Seifert said. "Supposedly Tex Schramm commented, 'The heck with The Catch, it was the tackle' that cost Dallas the game. The Catch was a big play, but Drew Pearson was going to score a touchdown. My career would have ended about that same time."

Clark scored with 51 seconds remaining. Wright brought down Pearson with 38 seconds left. Those 13 seconds changed everything about that game and everything about two franchises. Wright had a nice career with the 49ers. He played ten years, made two Pro Bowls and was voted first-team All-Pro once. But the biggest play of his career came in his rookie season.

"The thought went in my mind: Somebody has to make a tackle," Wright said. "Why is this guy running so open? I just knew he was going to score if I hadn't made the tackle and grabbed him by the jersey like that. It wasn't panic, just something had to be done or we were going to lose the game."

Back in the summer that year, the Niners were playing the Chargers in a preseason game at Candlestick Park. San Diego rookie receiver Bobby Duckworth caught a pass near the end of the game, Wright ran him down and lunged at him, trying to bring him down by the back of his shoulder pads. Duckworth broke the tackle and scored.

"The next week in practice, Bill was just beside himself," Seifert said.

Walsh's anger was directed at his defensive backfield coach. "How could you ever let Eric Wright try to tackle somebody like that?" Walsh screamed.

Walsh then demonstrated to Seifert and the defensive backs the proper technique. "It kind of became an issue," Seifert said.

Now Pearson is running free. Hicks is behind him and had an angle on Pearson, but would not have been able to cut him off in time to prevent him from scoring. "Eric Wright dove and tackled Drew Pearson by the shoulder pads in the back," Seifert said. "Just as he missed the tackle and we all got in deep doo-doo in the pre-season, we were in a two-deep zone and Eric came out of nowhere to make that play. I've been indebted to him ever since. There was The Catch and there was The Tackle."

Wright has watched that play over and over. "If I don't get him, he's going to score," he said. "I just turned the jets on and tried to make the play. Right place, right time."

He also saved Lott, who made multiple mistakes on the play. "They kind of ran a slant, a square-in, and I just remember taking the wrong angle," Lott said. "[Williamson] and myself collided. I was playing the slot position. It was one of those deals where I turned to go get him, [Williamson] was turning to make the tackle, and we ran into each other. I remember thinking to myself, *Here we are saying we have to stop them, and the first play, they get a long pass.* For a moment there, you could see they had a chance to win it. When Eric got him, that really calmed everybody down. Had he not gotten him, or they got further down the field, the dynamics would have changed."

Twenty years later, Wright, Lott, and some of the other defensive backs were with Eddie DeBartolo at a function, talking about the game. "Somebody said to Eric, 'You saved the game,'" DeBartolo said. "Keena Turner turned to him and said, 'Saved the game? The guy never should have caught the pass.'"

Turner was on the opposite side of the field when Pearson grabbed White's pass and took off. "Uh oh," Turner said. "Almost out of nowhere, Eric Wright reaches and grabs him at the collar."

On the next play, White fumbled, and the 49ers were going to their first Super Bowl. "Look at how the career of Joe Montana skyrocketed. And look at Danny White from that point," Seifert said. "Obviously, Danny was a fine quarterback, but his career never took off. Coaches talk about this being a game of inches. In fact, look at how a play or two can affect a ball game and history."

Montana has always heard from Cowboys fans how he broke their hearts with that pass to Clark. They even tell him they hate him. Montana responds that their hate is misdirected. They should hate the Cowboys for not scoring after The Catch.

"Thank God for Eric Wright," Montana said.

The 49ers had the ball, they had the 21–20 lead, it was early in the fourth quarter, and now it was time to put a little distance between themselves and the Cowboys. After Septien's field goal cut the lead to one point, the 49ers had moved to a second down at their own 44 two plays after Montana burned Everson Walls with a 21-yard pass to Freddie Solomon. Walt Easley picked up 4 yards in the middle of the Dallas defense, but he fumbled when he was hit by middle linebacker Bob Breunig. Walls, who was either making big plays or giving up big plays, was there to recover for the Cowboys. Incredibly, this was the fifth turnover by the 49ers. This time, they had also given up great position, the Cowboys took over at midfield.

Dorsett ran for 11, then White passed to Springs for 12, and

Dorsett ran for another 6. Dallas had a second down at the San Francisco 21. Landry called a play action fake to Dorsett and White rolled out to his left. Willie Harper's blitz was picked up at the line. White threw to Cosbie, the Bay Area native, who was all alone at the 1. Linebacker Jack Reynolds was in a zone, and he didn't follow Cosbie, who caught the ball and walked into the end zone. Dwight Hicks was too late coming over. Cosbie pointed up in the stands, where he had plenty of friends and family at the game. There was 10:41 remaining, the Cowboys were on top 27–21, and the 49ers had turned the ball over five times.

But the Cowboys were not thinking they had the game won. Not yet. "I really didn't think anything other than it gave us the lead," Cosbie said. "There was still a lot of time left."

It was the fifth lead change. Thirty-four seconds later, the 49ers imploded again with turnover number six. There were just 10 minutes left, and they were 6 behind, their largest deficit. For the first time, the game was slipping away from the 49ers. This nice story of a team coming from nowhere to the NFC Championship Game was in serious danger of being short-circuited by their own mistakes and a team that more often than not knew how to handle itself in big moments. Now was the time for the 49ers to step up.

Instead, turnover number six. Are you kidding? How could this be happening?

After throwing incomplete to Cooper on first down, Montana hit Clark down the left sideline for 18 yards. The Niners were at their own 35. Now it was time for Montana to pick on Walls for what seemed like the fortieth time of the game but in reality was just the seventh. Walls already had one interception. Now he had two. Montana went down the right sideline for Solomon, the same play Walls picked off earlier in the game when Montana was trying to hit Wilson. Walls established excellent position on Solomon and had another pick at the Dallas 27.

The clock was down to 10:07, and the Cowboys' goal was simple: Drain the clock and get at least three points. That would make it a two-score lead and truly test the comeback ability of Joe Cool.

Landry mixed up the run and the pass trying to accomplish both goals. Eight plays into a time-consuming drive, the Cowboys were at the San Francisco 47. The 49ers fans were nervous. Just over five minutes remained, and another first down would force the Niners to start using their time-outs. The Cowboys were faced with a third and five. They needed a first down to keep the drive going and another 20 yards to put Septien in position to stretch the lead to nine. White went back to pass and threw the ball to Donley, who was wide open at the 41-yard line. The poor guy had a history of shoulder problems, and White's pass twisted him around. Keena Turner was trailing Donley, and Eric Wright was closing in. The ball was too high and behind White Lightning, and he wasn't able to bring it down. Pearson, Hill, and Johnson were also on the field. Any of them could have made the catch. Instead, the pass went to a rookie. On such a huge play, White made a poor throw and a poor choice of receivers.

"It was behind him, but Doug should've caught it," Pearson said. "Now if Doug had a good shoulder—anybody else could've went up and got that. Doug had very limited movement. That's why he didn't play that much."

Instead of a first down, the Cowboys had to punt. If Donley had made the catch, or if White had thrown the ball to a receiver with more flexibility, the Cowboys could have taken more time off the clock and moved closer to field-goal range. White stayed in the game to punt, and he got off a nice one. Solomon called for a fair catch at the San Francisco 11-yard line.

Montana got his instructions from Walsh on the sideline and came onto the field. There was 4:54 left and a long way to go.

.   .   .

Seifert was promoted after one more season to run the 49ers defense, a natural progression on his way to becoming a head coach. He was the hottest assistant in the NFL by the time the 1988 season ended. The 49ers won the Super Bowl in 1984 and again in 1988, and when Walsh did not immediately announce his retirement after Montana led a superb game-winning drive to beat the Bengals in Super Bowl XXII, Seifert was officially on the market.

The speculation was that Walsh was going to quit after the Super Bowl, and he did get emotional in the locker room after Montana hit John Taylor with the game winning 10-yard touchdown pass with 34 seconds remaining. But he did not announce that he was leaving. The 49ers returned to San Francisco from Miami, and within days Seifert was on a flight to Cleveland to interview for the Browns head-coaching job. He was scheduled to change planes in Dallas, and while his flight was in the air, Walsh quit and the Niners started searching for Seifert, who was the natural in-house candidate to succeed Walsh. They were also considering University of Miami coach Jimmy Johnson, who one month later would be hired by the Cowboys to replace Tom Landry. When Seifert, who was endorsed by Walsh to succeed him, landed at DFW airport, he called home. His wife told him the 49ers needed to speak with him. He called back, was told Walsh had quit and Seifert was the choice to replace him. He boarded the next plane back to San Francisco.

The tackle Wright made seven years earlier helped Seifert become an NFL head coach. He won the Super Bowl in his first year and barely missed making it back in his second year, which could have given the 49ers an unprecedented three-peat. "I feel I was the right guy for the job," Seifert said. "I don't know if we would have won the Super Bowl in 1989 if anybody but me was the head coach. I could keep it going. There were no other complications. Another coach would have come in, and things would have changed. It was a tough, grueling job. The time was right for Bill to make the move he did at that time. I know he regretted it later. At the time, it was the right thing for him to have done. I loved working for him and with him."

By the time Seifert took over for Walsh, he was ready to be a head coach. Nine years trying to please Walsh was a lot more pressure than being in charge. "It was easy compared to being the defensive-backs coach or the coordinator," Seifert said. "The expectations and pressure to get the job done were extraordinary as an assistant. When I became the head coach, I was used to that lifestyle. It wasn't as stressful as it would have been for other coaches. Bill taught me how to win."

Montana to Clark won the game. Wright pulling down Pearson helped George Seifert have a very successful coaching career.

8

TEAMMATES

ALL OF us would consider ourselves fortunate to have a friend like Everson Walls. The shirt off his back? That's nothing. How about a kidney?

Walls is in a hotel room in Manhattan in the summer of 2007 explaining what compelled him—and what gave him the courage—to donate one of his kidneys months earlier to former teammate Ron Springs, whose body had been ravaged by diabetes. Springs already had been forced to have his right foot amputated; his hands were curled up in balls, and he required dialysis four hours a day, three days per week. He needed a kidney transplant to survive, and after several relatives were unavailable or were just not a match, the clock was ticking on his life. He had been on the national transplant waiting list since 2004. Walls, forty-seven at the time, three years younger than his friend, refused to watch Springs deteriorate, so he had himself tested, found out he was a perfect donor match, and told Springs he would give him one of his kidneys. He just couldn't let him die.

Walls had played thirteen years in the NFL with the Cowboys, Giants, and Browns and never once needed surgery. They wheeled him into the operating room at Medical City Dallas Hospital on February 28, 2007, and other than a little soreness and a scar as a souvenir, he was fine and went home two days later. He had given

Springs the gift of life. The transplant went smoothly, and his kidney was functioning perfectly in Springs's body.

"Walls, I appreciate this kidney," Springs said. "This kidney is a motherfucker. I'm pissing all over the place."

He was always a comedian, but he never actually thanked Walls. But being off dialysis, being able to have normal body functions, being able to walk, bragging about his ability to urinate, Walls says, "That's his way of saying thank you. I don't need much. That is enough right there. He hadn't been able to pee on his own for I don't know how long."

It was the first time one former professional athlete had donated an organ to another. It was supposed to be *Brian's Song,* but with a happy ending—the love Gale Sayers had for his Bears teammate Brian Piccolo, who died from cancer in 1970 at the age of twenty-six.

"It tells you that a person truly cares for me," Springs said months before the surgery. "It tells me that he is truly a good, giving man. A lot of people talk about it but are scared to do it. I'm so grateful, it's unbelievable. This gratitude has to last a lifetime."

Less than eight months after the transplant, however, Springs was back in Medical City for what was supposed to be a routine procedure—the removal of a cyst from his arm, which would help him regain the use of the arm and hand. But something went terribly wrong that October 12. After the anesthesia was administered, Springs slipped into a coma and never came out. Although it is believed he could live a long time, the prognosis for snapping out of it is grim.

After going through the complicated transplant, it wasn't fair that a simple procedure left Springs alive but without a life. "I just refuse to believe that this is the end," Walls told HBO's *Real Sports,* which had prepared a heartwarming piece on Walls and Springs, but had to update it before it aired after Springs went into the coma.

Walls became a national name again nearly fifteen years after his playing days ended. He was always known for being in the picture when Dwight Clark got a rush of adrenaline, channeled his inner Michael Jordan, and jumped higher than he ever had or ever would again to snare Joe Montana's pass to win the '81 NFC Championship Game. He looked ten feet tall next to Walls.

The Catch wasn't necessarily all Walls's fault. Clark pivoted in the back of the end zone and headed to his right near the end line while the Dallas pass rush was generously giving Montana enough time chasing him to the sideline to count to "seven Mississippi." Walls couldn't believe how long he had to stick with Clark, and when he took his eye off him for one millisecond to check out Montana's location, that's when he lost Clark and the ball.

Walls was just a rookie free agent that season. He grew up in the Hamilton Park section of Dallas, not far from the Cowboys' practice facility, and went to Grambling to play for Eddie Robinson, then returned to Big D and signed with his hometown team, moving back in with his mother. He was a long shot to make the Cowboys. He was among the eighty rookies the Cowboys annually brought to training camp. They didn't do it just to help out a hometown kid, and he wasn't supposed to be much more than a training camp body. Defensive ends, it seemed, ran the 40 faster than Walls. But forget the measurables. He had a knack for being around the ball and being able to catch it.

Receivers often become cornerbacks if they can't catch. Walls may have had the best hands on the Cowboys. He picked off Montana twice in the championship game and recovered a fumble by Easley, but he was trailing Clark on one of the most memorable plays in NFL history and wound up with his picture all over the front pages of sports sections the next day. Still, he refused to let his existence be defined by The Catch. "My life is more fulfilling than that," he said.

He actually had played a great game until The Catch. He had perfect position on both of his interceptions and was in the right place to recover the fumble. Three turnovers in a championship game. And nobody remembers. Montana kept going at him. He would win a few and lose a few. Walls was not fazed. It was almost as though he dared Montana to bring it. If the quarterback went the other way, then how was he going to pick it off? Up until the moment Clark caught that pass, Walls might have been the best player on the field. "I feel sorry for any defensive back that has been in that situation," Ronnie Lott said. "He played a very good game. The thing that always amazed me about Everson is that he was always around the ball. Joe threw it in a place where maybe Kareem Abdul-Jabbar couldn't get to the ball. Dennis Thurman used to tell me you can't stop the perfect play no matter how great you are at that position."

It takes a special demeanor to play cornerback. Walls was so easygoing that he had the immediate ability to put the last play behind him and move on to the next one, which was a good thing, because Montana threw in his direction ten times that Sunday in Candlestick Park, many of the passes complete. In addition to the 2 INTs and the fumble recovery, Walls had a team-high 9 tackles. He never concerned himself with getting beat. It was part of the job description. But so was bouncing back. That was a real gift. He would just get Montana on the next play. Only in that game, there was no next play for him after Clark's catch.

It wasn't until nine years later, when Jimmy Johnson cut him in Dallas after his first season as the Cowboys coach, that Walls made up for getting beat by Clark. He was playing for the Giants in Super Bowl XXV. Thurman Thomas was killing New York on the ground as Bill Parcells and Bill Belichick conceded Thomas his yards and flooded the passing lanes with nine defenders in an attempt to slow down Jim Kelly's explosive no-huddle offense, which had just scored 51 points on the Raiders in the AFC Championship Game. On Buffalo's last drive, Thomas was running free in the open field with Walls the only defender who could prevent a long touchdown run or, at the very least, stop him from gaining another 20 yards. Walls was not a physical corner. But he squared up and took Thomas down after a 22-yard gain to the Buffalo 41-yard line. It was the most important tackle of his life.

It was his personal redemption for The Catch, but it was not a Kodak moment such as Clark literally had when the famous shot of The Catch was used in the company's advertisements. In fact, Walls's tackle was all but forgotten when Scott Norwood was wide right from 47 yards in the closing seconds in the Bills 20–19 loss. Just like nine years earlier, Walls again wound up on the cover of *Sports Illustrated,* only this time instead of his futile jump to stop Clark, he was jumping in triumph, with his arms outstretched.

"He's really a nice guy. He was a great player," Clark said. "He had a great game that day against us. That's just one of those weird moments where he thought the ball was going out of bounds. He was right beside me. He had me covered. That was the brilliance of Bill Walsh."

Clark and Walls never became best friends, but they were friendly. They didn't make appearances together like Ralph Branca and Bobby Thomson, who hit the Shot Heard 'Round the World for the New York Giants off Branca to beat the Brooklyn Dodgers in the 1951 playoff game for the National League championship. But they would bump into each other at various events. At an awards banquet in 1985, Clark was hanging out with Walls and his family. Clark told Walls that Kodak had paid him $15,000 for the right to use the picture of The Catch in print and television ads. And then he told him that he managed to get Montana some money because he was the one throwing the pass, even though he wasn't even in the picture.

Walls recounted the conversation:

"Hey, man, did you get your money?"

"What money?"

"I'm the guy making The Catch, and you're the guy I caught it on. We're all on the same team with this."

Walls wound up suing Kodak. They settled out of court. Walls said he got a $25,000 check and took an expenses-paid trip to Super Bowl XXII, where his friend and fellow Grambling alum Doug Williams was named MVP for the Redskins. "I made a good living off that play," he said.

Walls once signed a picture for Clark of the 49ers receiver making The Catch over him by writing, "You were out."

"I think he was hoping I was out of bounds when I landed," Clark said. "I ran into him at a Super Bowl soon after that. He said that he had to have a picture of him higher up than me. So he got up on a chair and was reaching up. He's a really good guy. He must be. He gave up a kidney for his buddy. The thing that I feel bad about is, he's in that picture, so it always looks like he's getting beat."

Walls was just getting started on his career, and he had a lot of confidence, so he didn't let himself get down after the loss to the 49ers. He knew he had a lot of years to play in the NFL, although he was perhaps naive about the significance of what had just taken place. He went to Hawaii for the Pro Bowl, and as far as he was concerned, Clark's catch might as well have been ten years earlier. Walls had put it out of his mind. But he was the only one. It's all anybody wanted to talk about.

"The Cowboys have been in some big games before," he said. "Why is this something? I was almost ignorant of it. To me, I thought it was a good play. I just looked at it as another heartbreaking loss.

One thing I learned with the Cowboys . . . is, every loss was astronomical. The reaction to every loss was overblown. Everyone expected us to win every game. And win the Super Bowl every year. I've always been very surprised by the reaction to it, to this day. I thought it was a great game. A helluva game."

Walls, even after time passed, could never understand why it was considered such a landmark game in the history of the two franchises. In a sense, he was in denial like Danny White, although that was about all those two had in common. Though a young guy, Walls always said what was on his mind. That rubbed a lot of his teammates raw, especially the ones who had been around for a while. Here was this rookie free agent who walked around like he was a ten-year veteran. He took losses hard, but it was never the end of the world for him.

"For one team to be judged so harshly by one game and for one team to be elevated so highly by one game, it still baffles me," he said. "Even with that, everyone sees me reaching up in futility trying to knock the ball down. I was so surprised that everyone thought that play was *the* play. When you look at that game, as you do with any game that is so great like that, it never comes down to that one play. It just never does. Plays not made by some people still stand out to me. Plays that were made still stand out, maybe even more so than the catch itself."

White could have bailed out Walls if he hadn't fumbled two plays after The Catch. "The end was so anticlimactic," Walls said. "Everybody was looking at me as some type of scapegoat. You know me—it takes more than a bunch of criticism to make me question myself. I cannot back off the fact that, except for maybe the Super Bowl for New York, that was probably the best game I ever played."

If Ed Jones, Larry Bethea, or D. D. Lewis, who were all desperately trying to get to Montana, had been able to hit him or get in his face or bring him down, then Walls never would have been in this position. He stayed with Clark about as long as a defensive back can stick with a receiver on such a short field. Given enough time, Clark eventually was going to break free.

"The play took so long. I didn't know what was going on," Walls said. "By the time I looked up, the ball was already in flight. As opposed to watching Joe release it, I didn't know what the flight of the ball was. I don't know the trajectory. That's when it looked like it was going out of bounds. And all of those things happened in a fraction of a second."

All of a sudden, Walls was grouped with some of the Cowboys goats of the past. Jackie Smith dropped the touchdown pass when he was wide open in the Super Bowl against the Steelers. Jethro Pugh got plowed out of the way by Jerry Kramer, allowing Bart Starr to score the winning touchdown in the Ice Bowl. Don Meredith threw an end-zone interception against the Packers the year before the Ice Bowl in the NFL Championship Game in Dallas. Walls was just a twenty-two-year-old kid. Why couldn't Jones knock down the pass? Why couldn't Bethea shove Montana before he released the ball instead of after? Then it would have been fourth and 3, and Walsh would have had to make a decision: Go for the first down or go for the touchdown. Instead, Candlestick Park was complete mayhem. Clark had jumped higher than he ever had in his life, and Walls looked like his cleats were stuck in cement.

"The guy rose up. He made a great catch," Dennis Thurman said.

Walls once told NFL Films, "My entire career has been to avoid a highlight film. Of course, I got into the ultimate one—one of the most exciting plays in playoff history."

Walls was stubborn, didn't back down to the Cowboys machine, and was a training-camp holdout one summer, but his character was never questioned. His family nicknamed him Cubby as a kid because he looked like bear cub with lots of hair over his body. It was a heartwarming story when he came back from Grambling, made the hometown team, and was able to go to Mom's for lunch if he wanted. Springs was a fifth-round pick of the Cowboys from Ohio State in 1979. He was loud and outgoing and funny. When Walls arrived, they became immediate friends. Walls would bring Springs over for a home-cooked meal and Springs would take Walls under his wing and teach him about the NFL. Springs had a tail-back's mentality: He wanted the ball in his hands. But that wasn't going to happen often with Dorsett on the team. Landry played him at fullback, where he was an adequate blocker and occasionally was given the opportunity to run the ball. When Landry was in the mood to be cute, he allowed the left-handed Springs to throw an option pass, and he threw for two touchdowns in his career.

Springs had some off-the-field issues in a strip club, and Landry cut him in 1985. He was too big an influence in the locker room for a player the Cowboys considered a replaceable part. By the time Springs packed up his stuff and went to play for the Bucs, the Walls and Springs families were extremely close, and they stayed that way long after they were done with football. Their wives were like cousins. Their daughters were like sisters. Walls's son and Springs's younger daughter looked out for each other. And Springs's older son, Shawn, from a previous relationship, was a football player. He ran around the Cowboys locker room as a kid and wound up follow-ing in his dad's footsteps to Ohio State, but he played Walls's posi-tion and wore his number. Unlike Walls, who had to play his way onto the Cowboys, Springs was a first-round pick for Seattle in 1997.

After he finished his career with two seasons in Tampa, Ron Springs did some college coaching for a while, working for former Cowboys teammate Steve Wilson at Howard University. One sum-mer, he worked for the Giants and Dan Reeves in training camp in the minority internship program that Walsh started with the 49ers. Walls finished his career with the Giants and Browns, and when everything settled down in their lives, Springs and his family settled back in Dallas and Walls's family never left.

"When he was looking to move back to Dallas, he stayed in my guest room; he was driving my car," Walls said.

But in 1990, at the age of thirty-four, Springs was diagnosed with diabetes. He was told it was genetic. That was also the most satisfying year of Walls's NFL career. Johnson had no use for an outspoken thirty-year old cornerback as he was attempting to rebuild the Cowboys with young players. Up in New York, Parcells was positioning the Giants for a Super Bowl run, a long shot considering the 49ers were coming off back-to-back championships and a 55–10 beating of the Broncos in the Super Bowl. Parcells loved collecting players toward the end of their career who still had something left to give and a lot left to prove. He did it with Ottis Anderson, who turned out to be the MVP of the Super Bowl that season. Walls fit the profile of what Parcells wanted—a playmaker in the secondary, an experienced veteran who had played on the big stage, and a good guy in the locker room. He got exactly what he needed. Walls led the Giants with 6 interceptions that season. It's not easy going from one side of this fierce NFC East rivalry to the other, but Walls fit in perfectly and was accepted right away.

He was worth every penny to the Giants simply for the tackle he made on Thomas in the Super Bowl. He played one more year with the Giants, but that was a disaster. Parcells had retired for the first of three times with three different teams. Belichick had already accepted the Cleveland Browns head coaching job right after the Giants beat the Bills, but even if Belichick was still on the staff, George Young had his mind made up long ago that he would not promote him. He didn't think Belichick had the proper communication skills to run an NFL team. That was good news for the rest of the

NFC East, who were happy the defending champs were now without their head coach and the defensive coordinator who was the brains of the operation. Young instead promoted little-known running-backs coach Ray Handley, who was an egghead just like Young. Handley might have been the worst head coach in Giants history. Young fired him after two years, and he never coached again.

Walls was gone after one year with Handley and then played two years for Belichick in Cleveland and retired after thirteen years in the NFL—four Pro Bowls, one first-team All-Pro, one Super Bowl, and three times leading the league in interceptions. He played for Landry, Johnson, Parcells, and Belichick. Not bad for a kid from Dallas nobody drafted.

But he's never had much support for the Hall of Fame. Jerry Jones has not put him in the club's Ring of Honor. And it wasn't until he and Springs were honorary captains for the 2007 season opener against the Giants that he was honored at Texas Stadium.

"I always look at it as they knew me as being a helluva ballplayer," Walls said. "Now they know me for something other than being an athlete. That blows my mind because, hell, I think I'm more heroic for trying to go in there and hit Earl Campbell head-on than I am for giving a freakin' kidney to somebody. I couldn't afford to be hitting Earl Campbell, but giving a kidney, I could afford to do that. When you look at the sacrifice I made for athletics, to me, it's a greater sacrifice than I made for Ron. I sacrificed a lot to be a professional athlete."

In each case, it was a choice he made. He always wanted to play pro ball. When his career was finished, he was fanatical about staying in shape. It wasn't with the idea that one day his peak physical condition would make him an excellent candidate to be an organ donor. But it helped. Nothing could make Walls's mother, Ouiga, endorse her son's decision. She worried that one day she might need Everson's kidney for herself, and obviously her son couldn't give up the second one. She worried that he wouldn't come out of the surgery. She was mad because Springs had never called her to see how she was handling what her son was doing or to thank her.

"She was on the warpath," Walls said.

Walls started working out with Springs to make sure Springs' body was in prime condition in the event he was a match. All he knew for sure is both of them were O positive blood types. Each time there was a possibility of a donor from within the Springs family, it fell through. Walls had given blood at the Carter Blood Bank, and when they discovered they had the same blood type, Walls said, "Let me get checked out, man. Let me see what I can do. We kind of talked about it very casually. It was no epiphany."

He started to make phone calls. He went for further tests and found out he was a match but didn't tell Springs right away. He didn't want Springs to pressure him to do the surgery tomorrow. Walls finally broke the news to him, but there was still a long way to go. He went for psychological tests, in which he was asked all the basic questions, such as: Did you hate your mother? Have you ever been suicidal?

"Man, when you answer, don't just go yes, no, yes, no, yes, no," Springs said. "They try to fool you."

Ron's son Shawn found out Walls was a match and was going to donate his kidney and spoke to the *Washington Post* about it. Walls was incensed. He hadn't told his daughter, didn't think he had yet told his mother or his sisters, and only remembers he'd told his wife and father. He never wanted it to become so public prior to the transplant. Ron never wanted Shawn to get tested. "Like I said, I could afford to do it," Walls said. "When you make a decision like that and your families are so close, it's a sacrifice. It's not the ultimate. To me, the ultimate sacrifice is giving your life. But it's not like pulling teeth, either. It's not like I gave him a molar or something. I had never done major surgery, that was my main thing."

When he woke up, he was still a bit groggy and made the un-usual pronouncement that he thought he saw Bill Parcells. He was either dreaming or hallucinating. He never told Parcells he was one of the first people he thought of when he was in the recovery room. "I wouldn't give him the satisfaction," he joked. "Everybody was thinking, 'My God, he's still on drugs.'"

Walls is a hero even though the story does not have a happy ending. He and Springs had formed the Ron Springs and Everson Walls Gift for Life Foundation to raise awareness about diabetes through education and early detection and to raise awareness about organ donation. Walls has also spoken to Congress and had a bill in-troduced supporting organ donation. Springs loved his new kidney. He just didn't get to enjoy it long enough.

"You should always try and surround yourself with people who truly have your best interests at heart," Walls said. "There may be a time when you really have to call them on the love they have for you. That's the nice way of saying it. The other way is you better be nice because you never know when you might need them."

Friends like Walls are hard to find. "Hopefully, you've got a friend like that somewhere," he said.

9

I LEFT MY HEART
IN SAN FRANCISCO

49ERS OWNER Eddie DeBartolo felt like a real horse's ass. This was no time to give up on his team, but he did. They were trailing 27–21 and were backed up at their own 11-yard line, and just under 5 minutes remained. It was going to take a drive for the ages against a veteran defense with a lot of playoff experience to get San Francisco to the Super Bowl. Joe Montana had had a great season, but he wasn't having a great game. He had already thrown three interceptions and lost a fumble.

This was just the warm-up act for the 49ers and DeBartolo. He was a kid at thirty-five and planned to be in this for the long haul. He was building an organization that would last. He had Montana, a franchise quarterback. He had Walsh, a state-of-the-art coach. He had the intense Lott, who would never let the players quit. He had enough quality young players to build around to ensure the 49ers would be contenders through the rest of the decade. But with 89 yards to go, DeBartolo wasn't feeling confident. He thought the game was over. This was going to be a tough loss to handle, especially after the Niners had embarrassed the Cowboys by 31 points on the same field just a few months earlier. Still, after winning just fifteen games in the first four years he owned the team, this was an historic turnaround for the 49ers, no matter how this game finished.

DeBartolo left the owner's box at decaying Candlestick Park to start the long trip down to the field. He wanted to be inside the locker room door when the game ended so he could shake the hands of every one of his players and coaches and address the team and thank them for a great season. He made his way to the lower-deck concourse, then walked down the aisle through the stands and onto the field. The 49ers were slowly working their way to the Cowboys end zone. The atmosphere was electric, and DeBartolo was hurrying so he could see what was going on.

He wasn't carrying a white flag when he settled in, right in front of the baseball Giants dugout behind the end zone on the opposite side of the field from where Montana was driving the offense. The 49ers had a real chance of pulling this out. Three minutes were left. The 49ers were dinking and dunking the Cowboys, but had not crossed midfield. Walsh was crossing up Dallas by giving the ball to journeyman running back Lenvil Elliott. He was outcoaching Landry, who had pulled all three of his starting linebackers, put in two extra defensive backs and a nickel linebacker, all designed to stop Montana and the passing game. Who knew that Lenvil Elliott, a no-name on a team of overachievers, would ignite the fire?

Elliott played his first six years for the Bengals, where he overlapped with Walsh. He was a tenth-round pick in the 1973 draft, a round that no longer exists. His most productive year in Cincinnati was 1975, in Walsh's final season with the Bengals, when he carried 71 times for 308 yards. Walsh brought him to San Francisco in 1979, where his stats continued to be alarmingly unspectacular. He had only seven carries for 29 yards during the 1981 regular season. But with leading rusher Ricky Patton out with a sprained knee against Dallas and Paul Hofer already out for the season, Walsh pulled Elliott out of storage and turned him loose on the biggest drive of the game, not that the strategy scared the Cowboys at first. It just confused them. Elliott wound up with more carries (10) and more yards (48) against Dallas in the championship game than he had had all season.

His number was called three times on the first five plays of the drive, and he picked up 24 yards to help advance the ball to the San Francisco 41. Montana also threw incomplete to him twice in the first six plays, with Elliott dropping the first one. Montana passed five yards to Earl Cooper, and then Walsh confused the Dallas defense again with a 14-yard end around to Freddie Solomon that had been set up by Elliott's sweeps. He then hit Clark for 10 and a wide-open Solomon for 12 to give the 49ers a first down at the Dallas 13 with 1:15 left. On first down, Montana missed a wide open Solomon in the left corner of the end zone. Solomon had beaten Walls by about a mile.

When the CBS broadcast of the entire game on three DVDs was delivered to Montana at his home in California in 2008, he used it as a teaching tool for his sons, Nathaniel and Nicholas, who were both quarterbacks, big surprise. One was on his way to Notre Dame as a walk-on and the other was a standout in high school in southern California who would later commit to play at the University of Washington. Watching the game at a hotel restaurant in Phoenix, one day before the Giants upset the Patriots in Super Bowl XLIII, Montana agonized when he reviewed that pass to Solomon. That was the game right there, he thought. He had a chance to win it. But he airmailed the ball right over Solomon's head. Walls was barely in the same zip code. Walsh was animated on the sidelines.

"I jumped as high as I've ever jumped in my life," Walsh told *Sports Illustrated* after the game. "I thought that was the championship right there. We were never going to get that open again. It had worked perfectly to get Solomon free in the end zone, and we missed it."

Montana said the timing was off. And, yes, he did catch Walsh's reaction. "He looked pretty disgusted," he told *SI.*

Walsh went against the book again on second down and ran a sweep around the left side with Elliott that picked up seven yards.

Sadly, it was the final carry of Elliott's career. Patton was back for the Super Bowl two weeks later against the Bengals, and Elliott was gone from the NFL by the time the 1982 season started. Tragically, he died of a heart attack in 2008. He was only 57. He did leave a legacy: He was the unknown and unsung hero on the drive that led to The Catch.

Now it was third and 3 at the Cowboys 6 with 58 seconds remaining. Walsh took a time-out. Sprint Right Option was the call. DeBartolo was a hundred yards away, standing behind the end zone on the other side of the field. He would have to rely on the reaction of the crowd, because he could not see a thing. Maybe he was too nervous to move, but he had the worst vantage point in the house.

"Funny story," DeBartolo said, twenty-six years later. "I never saw The Catch. I was standing in front of the dugout behind a San Francisco policeman who was on a horse, and he had just moved in front of me. There must have been eight or ten policemen on horses."

DeBartolo's view was literally blocked by the horse's ass. "I will never forget it," he said. "I heard this gigantic roar and the stadium just erupted. Think of being a horse's ass. That's probably what I was. I was absolutely behind this gigantic horse, and I'm not tall to begin with. I heard everybody go nuts. The policeman said, '49ers touchdown!'"

DeBartolo never saw Montana's pass. He never saw Clark's catch. He saw and heard the fans going insane. He missed the whole thing. DeBartolo was soon in the locker room, just as he planned, but the tone of his speech was a little different than he anticipated.

"You guys earned it and deserved it because you are the best team in football," DeBartolo said. "You deserve it because of what you and everybody else have done. I'm so proud. I don't think anything can top this in my life. I love you all, and I thank you."

DeBartolo was twelve years younger than his coach and not that much older than many of his players. He wanted to be one of them or at least be loved by them. These were his guys. It was not the typical owner-player relationship. Clint Murchison, the Cowboys owner at the time, was hardly ever seen in public. He gave Schramm and Landry everything they needed to succeed, but he stayed in the background. Murchison was the anti–Jerry Jones, who always manages to make his way to the sidelines every week and does everything but call the plays, although that's something he certainly would like to do. It was the era before Robert Kraft of the Patriots would get face time almost as often as Tom Brady, as New England was winning three Super Bowls in four years from 2001 to 2004. It was a coach-and player-driven league in the early eighties. The owners signed the checks, paid the bills, and stayed out of the way. But DeBartolo was different. He loved the camera and the camera loved him.

He wanted to be around. His players wanted him around. He lived in Youngstown, Ohio, but had a place to live in San Francisco and was a strong presence around the city and the team. His father, Ed Sr., and the DeBartolo Corporation are credited with being instrumental in the development of shopping malls as an American way of life. On March 31, 1977, Ed Sr. bought the 49ers and handed them to his son to operate. Turning thirty is tough. Might as well celebrate the landmark birthday with your very own professional football team. Thanks, Dad.

DeBartolo's team stank when he took over, but he set about changing the culture. Walsh turned out to be one of the great innovators in NFL history, and DeBartolo became one of the most generous and controversial owners the league had seen. It was the pre–salary cap era, so when the 49ers won Super Bowls, he was not afraid to spend it on his players. He treated them like royalty; they rewarded him with rings, and he rewarded them with a trip to Hawaii. It was a trade-off he embraced.

He won them over early in the 1981 season. The 49ers were 2–2 with a road game coming up in Washington. Walsh was only 10–26 in his third season, and there were not a lot of indications he was turning things around. "We're at the airport and we're not leaving," Randy Cross said. "There is no plane. The United Airlines guy is there, and he tells Keith Simon, who made all our arrangements, 'I'm sorry. We've had a problem with our equipment.' We're all standing around and Keith goes, 'I'll tell you what: There better be a fucking plane at the gate in twenty minutes.' Out pulls a DC-10. We all had our own row."

The 49ers beat the Redskins 30–17. "We're in the locker room, and Eddie is in there," Cross said. "We're all chanting, 'DC-10, DC-10.' "

"OK," DeBartolo said. "You got it on the way home."

The DC-10s became the only way to fly the friendly skies for the Niners. Their cross-country trips became a ride in luxury, and whether it was psychological or physical, the wide-body aircraft worked. So did the gourmet food. "Eddie was a great guy. Superstitious," Cross said. "We kept flying DC-10s, and we kept wearing people out."

It was in training camp that summer of '81 that DeBartolo began to get close to his players. Maybe too close. There has to be a line drawn between management and its players, but the last thing DeBartolo wanted was to be stuck in a stuffy office and be distant from the guys whom he hoped would win him a championship.

"When these guys were drafted in '79 and '80, I started to become more of a players' owner," he said. "I spent time with these guys. We'd go out and have a beer together, and I'd have dinner with them. I changed the way things were done on the airplane. We went to a large-body plane. Everybody got two seats. We had a chef that would come on board from United and a local guy from a restaurant. We had food cooked for the guys on the plane. The players knew that. It was just an absolute transformation of attitude. We didn't have the greatest football team in 1981. We won the Super Bowl and beat the Cowboys in that playoff game. I don't think we had as good a team as the Dallas Cowboys. I truthfully don't. If you ask any of the top players on the team, they would probably agree."

He learned from his father to take care of the people working for him. The DeBartolo company had six-hundred employees in Youngstown. From the time his father was building roads and duplexes, he treated his workers like they were part of a family. They were not afraid to come to Eddie Sr. for anything. He was tough, much tougher than Eddie Jr. But he cared. His son wanted to carry that approach over to the NFL. He treated all those who worked for him with respect. And his players appreciated it. When DeBartolo was inducted into the Bay Area Hall of Fame in 2008, former team president Carmen Policy and a few players threw a cocktail party for him. He was touched when nearly fifty players showed up.

"We remained close over the years. All the players, not just with superstars like Joe Montana and Ronnie Lott," he said. "I had a Super Bowl reunion of the five Super Bowl teams in Las Vegas. We invited front-office people, coaching staffs from all five Super Bowls. I'll tell you something: It was almost like a love-in. I guess we had five or six hundred people. We picked up the tab. It was an unbelievable three-day event."

It cost DeBartolo a couple of million dollars. He loved every penny of it. "I had dreams and you all made them come true," he told his guests.

DeBartolo was amazed by what the 1981 team achieved. This was the pre–Jerry Rice and pre–Roger Craig era. This was a team that had won 6 games the previous season and 2 games in each of the two seasons before that. Walsh took over after a 2–14 season and promptly went 2–14. But that victory over Dallas early in the '81 season convinced the 49ers they could play with anybody. After starting

1–2, they won seven in a row, lost to Cleveland by three, won their last five regular season games, and then beat the Giants, Cowboys, and Bengals in the playoffs.

"There was just an attitude. They felt confident," DeBartolo said. "C'mon now, we had Freddie Solomon, who was a really good receiver, a really great guy. We had Mike Wilson, another possession receiver who had decent speed. Mike Shumann. Lenvil Elliott from the Cincinnati Bengals. Bill had them running reverses during the playoff games and the Super Bowl. That team won in spite of themselves. There was talent on the team. You saw that talent get a lot better as they matured over the years. They did it with talent, but with a lot of heart and soul, too. And with Bill's coaching."

The 49ers won titles again in 1984 and 1988 with Walsh. Then he stepped down, and they won again in 1989 and 1994 with George Seifert in charge. The Niners became the first team to win the Super Bowl five times, but after that last championship run, tough times were ahead for the franchise. They won a thrilling wild-card game against Green Bay in 1998 when Steve Young hit Terrell Owens with a 25-yard touchdown pass in between two Green Bay defenders with eight seconds remaining for a 30–27 victory. But the Niners lost the next week in Atlanta. Young was forced to retire in 1999 after he suffered the last in a series of concussions in a game against the Cardinals in Tempe when troubled running back Lawrence Phillips missed a block on Aeneas Williams.

Walsh always second-guessed himself for leaving too soon. But he would be back with the 49ers, just not on the sidelines. He kept rotating jobs between Stanford and the 49ers, where he ran the front office for a while and found ex-CFL quarterback Jeff Garcia as the potential successor to Young. Garcia turned back the clock to the Montana days when he led an incredible comeback against the

Giants in the 2002 wild-card game, bringing the 49ers from a 38–14 third-quarter deficit to a thrilling 39–38 victory. But the Niners could not sustain success and lost to the Bucs the next week.

The 49ers had a tremendous run from 1981 to 1994. Walsh left after '88. Montana left after '92. Young was gone in '99. Coaches and players come and go all the time. But it was the exit of DeBartolo that really shook up the franchise. The 49ers had what was considered the best organization in the NFL, but once DeBartolo was forced out and his sister, Denise DeBartolo York, and her husband, Dr. John York, took over, the franchise became dysfunctional. They knew little about running an NFL team.

DeBartolo got himself involved in a casino-gambling licensing scandal that eventually led to a change in ownership of the 49ers. He pleaded guilty in October 1998 to not reporting a $400,000 extortion attempt by former Louisiana governor Edwin Edwards, who allegedly wanted a bribe in exchange for a riverboat casino license. In December 1997, he turned over control of the team to his sister, Denise, as he concentrated on his legal issues. He was given two years probation and fined $1 million in the case. NFL commissioner Paul Tagliabue fined him $1 million and suspended him for the 1999 season.

DeBartolo never returned to the team. He settled with his sister in 2000, giving her the 49ers while he took control of other family holdings. "Knowing what he had done for this team and organization and what he meant during that period of time—it's hard to see that happen to guy you like, a friend," Montana said. "He was an owner that felt like a player. You could feel a different sense of love from him. The ups and downs were his ups and downs."

It was a humiliating end to what had been a glorious time in DeBartolo's life. "Nobody wants to go and leave something they love under circumstances that aren't perfect," he said. "I must tell you one thing: When my sister and I decided to split the company, I had an opportunity to take the 49ers side. I don't think there's any way the NFL could have stopped me if I would have taken this side, being the 49ers. I just really and truly don't."

Even if he would have faced challenges from Tagliabue and other NFL owners, DeBartolo believed he could have returned. "The best thing was to take the separation agreement and take the side that I did take and let Denise and her husband have the 49ers and run the 49ers," he said. "I would have rather have bowed out in a different way. It is what it is. Play the hand that you're dealt." It was an interesting choice of words by DeBartolo, considering that it was his involvement with owning a casino that started the chain of events that led to the end of his NFL days.

"Everybody knew that Tagliabue might have fought the situation," DeBartolo said. "The last thing I wanted to do was be in a protracted court battle with the league. Things turned out for the best. It may have been time. Being involved in the NFL, especially as an owner, is a full-time job. It takes its toll on you. I think in the long run, I probably am better off."

DeBartolo had a falling out during that time with team president Carmen Policy, who had been his friend for thirty years. Policy left the 49ers in 1998 to run the Cleveland Browns, which reentered the NFL as an expansion team in 1999. Policy took Clark with him as his general manager. Clark had proven himself to Policy during the tumultuous final days of Montana's time with the club in 1993. The pressure and tension of DeBartolo's fall from grace with the Niners led to battles between him and Policy, with speculation that Policy was trying to take control of the team, but years later they settled their differences and became good friends again. One day they may try to buy another NFL team together. There are always rumors about DeBartolo buying the Raiders from Al Davis and moving them to Los Angeles. But San Francisco is where DeBartolo's heart is.

"It was extremely tough for him to give up the Niners," said Policy, who returned to the Bay Area as a winemaker after he left Cleveland. "But it was an extremely tough time. He was going through a horrendous period in his life. He was facing serious problems in Louisiana, he had serious financial problems, he was in the middle of a major controversy with his sister and brother-in-law. Nothing was going right. On top of it, to lose his absolute identity was almost too much to bear. You have to understand, it was the Niners that distinguished him from his dad. It was the Niners that allowed him to come out from under his shadow that was so broad and so long and so dark."

DeBartolo has spoken about getting involved in a syndicate to buy an NFL team. "Maybe owning twenty to thirty percent and then having a group you put together. I don't know if that will ever come to pass," he said. "I like what I'm doing now, and I like the time that I have to myself. I'm doing real estate, sports representation, marketing, and hospitality companies. I'm involved in a company that makes automotive parts."

DeBartolo lives in Tampa, and his name has surfaced over the years in regard to buying the Bucs. "I think he's bored. Very bored," Policy said. "Even though he is doing fine, how do you leave showbiz once you've been at the top? He obviously regrets what happened in Louisiana. I do think he didn't understand what was happening at the time. If he had better advisors, it wouldn't have happened. Whatever happened was the result of being careless, not bad intentions."

DeBartolo and Walsh were a team, and they revived a dead franchise and won three Super Bowls together, but by the 1988 season, their relationship was strained. DeBartolo had not always agreed with Walsh's personnel decisions, and that season he stripped Walsh of the team presidency and assumed the job himself. The Niners were only 6–5 with 5 games remaining, and not only did it look like this was going to be Walsh's final season, but it didn't appear it would even end in the playoffs.

The one regret Walsh carried through the rest of his life was that he quit coaching the 49ers too early. Al Davis always believed ten years was the maximum a coach could stay in one job and keep from going stale. This was Walsh's tenth season.

Somehow, the Niners rallied at the end of the season to finish 10–6 and win the NFC West. They beat the Vikings at Candlestick in the divisional round, making up for the embarrassment of the previous season, and then dominated the Bears 28–3 at brutally cold Soldier Field in the NFC Championship Game. This wasn't Walsh's best team, but it had a lot of heart. It refused to quit.

In the Super Bowl two weeks later, Montana took the Niners 92 yards and threw the winning 10-yard touchdown pass to John Taylor with 34 seconds left in a 20–16 victory. Montana attempted nine passes on the drive against the Bengals. His only incompletion came when he uncharacteristically hyperventilated—this was Joe Cool?— at the line of scrimmage, nearly passed out, but still had the presence of mind to heave the ball out of bounds.

The drive is legendary as much for what Montana said in the huddle before it even started as it is for Montana's throw to Taylor. He was the king of practical jokers, and he sensed there was a bit too much tension around him. But he wasn't kidding when he turned to right tackle Harris Barton, who worried enough for the rest of the team.

"Hey H."

"Yeah," Barton responded.

"Look down there in the far corner of the stands. That's John Candy."

"That *is* John Candy. What's he doing here?"

It loosened everybody up. "I kind of thought to myself, *If Joe Montana can be so loose and sure about himself, maybe I should stop worrying,*" Barton said.

Montana and the Niners had defeated the Bengals seven years earlier to win their first Super Bowl. Cris Collinsworth was a rookie wide receiver for Cincinnati in 1981. Montana was about to cost him another ring. "He's taken more from me than the IRS," he said.

There was 3:20 left on the clock, way too much time. "Our defense had stopped them all day. They hadn't done anything," Collinsworth said. "We were sitting on the sideline, and one of our rookies looks over to me and says, 'We got them now. It's over. We got the ring.' I said, 'Will you please shut up? Have you lost your mind?'

"I said, 'Please look in the huddle and see if number sixteen is there.' He said, 'Yeah.' And I told him, 'Then shut up.' It happened so fast, it was ridiculous. The only regret we had is, he didn't score faster so we could get the ball back with a little time."

Walsh was extremely emotional in the locker room after the game. He knew he was done. He had to step away from a television interview and embrace his son Craig in an attempt to regain his composure. He was crying. "I never should have left," Walsh told the *San Jose Mercury News* in 2002. "I'm still disappointed in myself for not continuing. There's no telling how many Super Bowls we might have won."

He once said if he had just taken one month off after the Super Bowl and gone to Hawaii, he could have continued coaching. But at least Walsh hadn't quit in his second season in 1980. After an eighth straight loss in Miami, he said he'd made up his mind he wasn't going to make it as a head coach and planned to move into management. The 49ers then won three in a row, and there was promise going into 1981.

But after the huge comeback victory against the Bengals in the

Super Bowl seven years later, he was emotionally spent. Walsh had created an atmosphere of unrealistic expectations for himself and his franchise. Getting to the playoffs wasn't good enough. Getting to the championship game wasn't good enough. Walsh put incredible pressure on his team and the organization to win the Super Bowl every year. Anything less and the season was judged a failure. It was a product of Walsh's huge ego. He never could accept that he was trying to outsmart brilliant coaches who had Hall of Fame–caliber players. The other team never won; the 49ers lost. It's what made the 49ers great, but it also led to their unraveling. When Montana hit John Taylor to beat the Bengals, the first Super Bowl to be decided on a last-minute touchdown pass, Walsh had his third title in eight years and also what seemed the perfect exit strategy: Not even Lombardi walked away on top.

"He would not have lasted another season," Policy said. "He broke down three times in 1988. I was there in his house on two occasions, and he barely made it through. If it wasn't for Joe Montana, Ronnie Lott, the team, and his assistant coaches being there for so many years, we would have never made it to the playoffs that year. Once we got in the playoffs, it was almost like a shot of adrenaline. The pressure had gotten to him. He was almost unable to carry on that season. The doctors knew he couldn't have gone another season."

Walsh said during the 1988 playoffs that coaches often become the victims of their success. He set the standard so high for his players that nothing but championships was expected or accepted.

That was true for him, as well. Every team goes into the season setting the Super Bowl as its goal, but the 49ers truly believed that if they didn't win it, then the season was a complete failure and waste of time. In the years immediately following the '84 Super Bowl, the Niners lost to the Giants in the playoffs in back-to-back years, each time scoring only 3 points and the second time giving up 49. Then there was the humiliating loss to the Vikings in the playoffs following the strike season, which was the start of the Montana-Young quarterback controversy.

"Everybody expects nothing but wins," Walsh said. "They ignore that twenty-seven other franchises have equal desires and opportunities and that so-called parity gives winning teams tougher schedules and poorer positioning in the draft."

Once Walsh left the 49ers, he was like a lost soul. He just didn't know what to do with himself. He went to work for NBC for three seasons on NFL and Notre Dame games. But he was unable to carry his glib personality into television. He had built a reputation for his innovative approach to offense by scripting the first twenty-five plays, but on TV he came off as too scripted, which isn't a good thing when you are announcing unscripted football games. Walsh clearly missed coaching, but he wasn't going back to the 49ers. He returned to coach at Stanford in 1992, a move that came out of nowhere. He stayed for three years, had two stints in the 49ers front office, and then went back to Stanford in 2004 to work in the athletic department, where for a short time he was the athletic director.

He lived in the Bay Area but enjoyed going to his vacation home in Monterey with his wife, Geri. He was extremely dedicated to Geri, who suffered a major stroke in 1999. She had gone from being an athletic woman to requiring nearly round-the-clock care. Walsh would take care of her at night, and two women would come in during the day to attend to her needs. Walsh experienced more heartache when his son Steve, the oldest of his three children, died in 2002 at the age of forty-six after battling leukemia for nearly twelve years. Steve was a reporter for ABC News. Sadly, ironically, Walsh would be diagnosed with the same disease in 2004. It wasn't until late in 2006 that he went public with his illness. He was dead less than one year later.

In his final months, The Genius hosted a lot of his former players and colleagues from his 49ers days. Montana, Lott, and Keena

Turner spent a lot of time with Walsh at his house in Woodside in the Bay Area. DeBartolo and Policy paid a visit together. Walsh spent more time talking about some of the tough losses than the exhilarating victories. "Maybe we could have gone to two or three more Super Bowls and won a couple of more," he told DeBartolo.

On the day DeBartolo and Policy showed up at his house in the spring of 2007, Walsh had made arrangements for lunch to be served. He had been prohibited from drinking wine, one of his favorite things, because of the medication he was taking. Nevertheless, he had white and red wine for his guests. DeBartolo and Policy were most appreciative. Disobeying the doctors, Walsh hoisted a glass or two with his old friends that day.

"We talked football and old times," Policy said. "Absolutely no mention of his health came up. When it was time for us to leave, reality set in. We were all very clumsy with it."

Policy said Walsh had put a "game plan" together for his death. One last script. He brought in old friends to clear the air on any lingering issues. He called in a public-relations official from his 49ers days to, as Policy said, "orchestrate the funeral. He was scripting the first twenty-five plays. It worked in typical Walsh fashion."

Montana spoke at the funeral. He owed so much to Walsh. Even though Montana was confident he would have been a successful NFL quarterback if he played in another system, he became a Hall of Famer and the greatest NFL quarterback in history because he and Walsh formed the perfect marriage. If Walsh had had the skills to be a quarterback instead of an amateur boxer, he would have been Montana. He was always using boxing analogies, telling his players the key to football was "beating the opponent to the punch," an art Montana perfected.

"People always tried to drive something between him and me," Montana said. "He taught me a completely different level of playing. He prepared his quarterback to be perfect. That's what he did."

Turner, the linebacker who played the '81 championship game after contracting chicken pox, was Walsh's constant companion during the final months of his life. He still doesn't know how he got the chicken pox, usually a childhood malady, although he suspects it might have happened when he visited a school in the Bay Area. Because of all the rain before the Dallas game, Walsh took the 49ers to Anaheim to practice at the Rams facility. That's when the chicken pox broke out all over Turner's body. It broke out on the Thursday before the game.

"I had them everywhere. Literally," he said. "Had them in my mouth, in the crack of my butt. I couldn't eat for a while. It was uncomfortable more than it was being sick. By the time Sunday came, I was just so preoccupied with the game. I made the decision I was going to play. I just had to get through it."

He lathered his body in calamine lotion. He put layers of plastic on his skin so his uniform and shoulder pads wouldn't rub up against him. His teammates were teasing him unmercifully. "I can't remember how I played other than I played," he said.

He had only two unassisted tackles. "It was a tough game," Turner said. "It set us on a totally different track for years to come."

There was a lot of reminiscing as Turner settled in for his talks with Walsh over the last few months of his life. He last saw him on the Thursday before Walsh passed away at his home. He died four days later, on July 30. "Sometimes men don't like to tell other men they love them," Turner said. "In all of those conversations over the last few months, we always ended by saying, 'Hey, I love you, Coach,' and he would say, 'I love you, Keena.' It was very sincere times. We spent a lot of times laughing and joking. There wasn't a lot of room for anything else. He would take the lead with the tough conversation, about his situation, what he was feeling, where he was with it.

"What do you say? You listen and appreciate and remember all the good times."

10

THE CATCH

ONE PLAY changed it all. The 49ers became a dynasty, and the Cowboys went into storage for a decade. Bill Walsh became the Genius, and Tom Landry became a sympathetic figure. Joe Montana became Joe Cool, and Dwight Clark became the hero of overachievers. Everson Walls became admired for the class and dignity with which he handled getting burned by the greatest pass and catch in NFL history. One play did all that on January 10, 1982.

Candlestick Park was rocking so hard, it felt like it was about to fall into San Francisco Bay. Lenvil Elliott, the journeyman running back who had been cut in training camp and brought back during the season, had just run a sweep around the left side for 7 yards to the Cowboys 6-yard line. Walsh was mixing up the Cowboys nickel defense by continuing to call 18 Bob, a sweep to the right, and 19 Bob, a sweep to the left. It was Walsh's version of the old Green Bay sweep, and Elliott kept picking up big chunks of yards. And when Walsh sensed that the Cowboys were overpursuing against Elliott in the middle of the drive, he called Fake 18 Bob Z Reverse Left, which was a reverse from Montana to Elliott, who was sprinting to his right faking another sweep before handing off to Freddie Solomon, who then picked up 14 yards around the left side.

Just 58 seconds remained. It was third and 3. Walsh called the second of his three time-outs. Montana came over to the sidelines and stared intently at Walsh. It might have been frantic all around them, but Walsh and Montana could just as well have been chatting about what to order for dinner in the coach's office. White wine or red, Coach? A little brie? There was no panic. Walsh spoke calmly, matter-of-factly. Montana hung on every word. It was not an all-or-nothing down. Not yet, anyway. Walsh was going for the touchdown, but the 49ers could still pick up a first down if the play broke down, even though he never mentioned that to Montana. As long as the 49ers didn't turn the ball over for the seventh time, they still had fourth down as insurance. "We all knew it was two-down territory," guard Randy Cross said. "You have to have the thought *We're going to score.*"

Walsh outlined the same play that Solomon scored the 49ers' first touchdown on, back in the first quarter, which now seemed months ago. Solomon again was the primary receiver. Dwight Clark was Montana's second option. Walsh took off his headset and looked directly into Montana's eyes.

"We're going to call a Sprint Option pass. He's going to break up and break into the corner. You got it? Dwight will clear," Walsh said.

"OK," Montana said.

"As soon as you see the angle he's breaking, then just drop the ball up there. If you don't get what you want, simply throw the ball away. You know what I mean?" Walsh said.

"OK," Montana said.

"Hold it, hold it, not there, away it goes," Walsh said.

"OK."

"Be ready to go to Dwight. You got it?"

"OK."

Montana returned to the huddle. This was why the 49ers and Cowboys pushed themselves through two-a-days in training camp, lifted all those weights, sat in all those meetings, practiced four times a week during the season, played sixteen games, one divisional round playoff game, and 59 minutes and 2 seconds of the NFC Championship Game. This was money time. This was a test of wills.

Who wanted it more? The Cinderella 49ers, who'd won six games the previous season and two each in the two years before that, or the arrogant Cowboys, America's Team, who always expected to be in the Super Bowl. Who could handle the enormous pressure? The 49ers were 13–3 in the regular season. The Cowboys were 12–4. San Francisco's regular-season victory over Dallas was the difference in who earned the home field for the championship game. Now was the time for the Niners to use it to their advantage.

The 49ers were 6 yards away and 6 points down.

Montana licked the fingers on his right hand as he approached the huddle.

"Sprint Right Option," he told his teammates.

"He was the calmest in the huddle when he should have been the most nervous," Clark said. The moment was not too big for him. He had been taking injections all season to relieve the tendonitis in his right elbow. He was in the trainer's room before the championship game. Early in the third quarter he took a hit on a fourth-down quarterback sneak and was slow getting up. Trainers lifted up his shirt on the sidelines, looking in the area of his ribs.

"I do not remember the injury, so I am sure it was nothing serious," Montana said.

It was serious enough that backup Guy Benjamin, who played for Walsh at Stanford, was warming up on the sidelines. They were going to have to line up the cops two deep on the Golden Gate Bridge if Montana didn't pull this one out. The 49ers believed this game was theirs because everything Walsh had told them before had come true. If he said a play was going to work, they had no doubt. Sprint Right Option would work, they were convinced. The Cowboys believed there was no offense capable of driving 89 yards on them with a spot in the Super Bowl on the line. And certainly not the 49ers. "We didn't know their names," Charlie Waters said. "There were no Tony Dorsetts on their team."

The 49ers walked to the line of scrimmage. Montana stood over center Fred Quillan, took the snap, and set off the most frantic, exhilarating, compelling, and amazing 7 seconds the NFL had ever seen.

Montana was never the most physically gifted player. But he was focused and smart and extremely coachable and had great instincts. He could block everything out around him, and now that ability to push distractions to the side was being put to the ultimate test. Back at Notre Dame he had shown his mental toughness when he'd battled through the flu and hypothermia in that miraculous Cotton Bowl comeback. A little coffee and chicken soup, and he was good to go. He was not among the 49ers who were slowed down by the flu in the week before the championship game. When he arrived at Candlestick, he had nothing on his mind but trying to take his team to the Super Bowl and prove to the Cowboys that it was foolish for them to come back for more punishment after what San Francisco had done to them in October.

Montana had gone through the pregame warm-ups, gone back with his teammates to the two-tiered locker room, and then run on the field to a standing ovation as he was introduced with the 49ers offense. But just as Montana was set to play the biggest game of his life, he was jolted by disturbing news that was delivered to him on the sideline. Professional athletes always have to be wary, even a bit paranoid, about whom they associate with away from the field; it's always wise to be on the lookout for swindlers and kooks, especially when you are Joe Montana.

Montana played hurt. He never played scared. But no one

could have blamed him if he'd been looking over his shoulder for three hours on this otherwise glorious January afternoon in the Bay Area. Some moron had phoned in a death threat. The stadium was packed with 60,525 fans. It was the pre-9/11 days, before fans were subjected to pat-downs by security as they entered stadiums. Times were different then. Did someone sneak a handgun into Candlestick with a plan to splatter Montana on the field? Was the person sitting in the upper deck? The end zone? How about right behind the 49ers bench? Or will he just bust through security, run onto the field, and shoot Montana point blank at the 50-yard line? Was he a crazed Cowboys fan or a gambler with big money on Dallas who just wanted to shake up Joe Cool a little bit?

It would be years before Monica Seles was stabbed in the back by a crazed fan of Steffi Graf at a 1993 tennis tournament in Hamburg, Germany, but phoned-in death threats were nothing new to celebrities. They were just something athletes had to put out of their minds if they were going to perform. Not that it was an easy thing to do. Montana doesn't recall whether this was his first death threat, just that it wasn't the last. None of them were dismissed. The timing on this one, however, was horrendous. DeBartolo had once hired Jim Warren, a 49ers security man, to live at Montana's house with him after someone threatened to kill him. Montana had been instructed to turn the lights on outside the house and to keep them off inside unless he really needed them. There was no hiding this Sunday, however. Everybody knew where he was all the time, except perhaps the Dallas Cowboys defense.

"They told me on the sideline that there was a death threat," Montana said. "Nobody wanted to stand by me. People scattered quickly. They told me right before the game or right at the start of the game. Somebody was going to try and shoot me during the game." Montana tried to put it out of his mind, although he admits it was somewhat disconcerting. His offensive linemen could protect him from Too Tall Jones and Harvey Martin, but if some nut had a gun in the stands and was looking to put a bullet in his back between the 1 and the 6, there wasn't much Randy Cross or Keith Fahnhorst were going to be able to do for him. "It didn't really matter at that point, right?" Montana said. "Once I'm out there and you are alone, there isn't a whole lot that could be done. You just hope that it wasn't true. It went through my mind a couple of times."

He convinced himself to concentrate on the game. There, he knew, "people were trying to do physical harm, that's for sure," meaning the Cowboys defense. "The other one," meaning the supposed gunman, "I'm not so sure."

When the Cowboys played a Sunday night game in Anaheim in 1986, a death threat was phoned in on Tom Landry before the game. He stood on the sidelines wearing a bulletproof vest, but not with a lot of people around him. None of the players or coaches were taking a chance of getting in the line of fire. "I wasn't going over by him," Tony Dorsett said.

Tony D had his own experience with death threats. It happened before a game at Texas Stadium during his second year, in 1978. Gil Brandt told him about it and tried to calm him, assuring him he would be safe. Dorsett wasn't so sure.

"They killed the president of the United States down here," Dorsett reminded Brandt. "What makes you think they won't shoot my black ass?"

The Cowboys surrounded Dorsett with a security detail on the sidelines, but his teammates had no desire to be around him. Tony Hill ran away any time Dorsett got close. "If I'm going to get shot," Dorsett joked. "Somebody is going to go down with me." But the threat was taken seriously. Even when Dorsett was taking a shower after the game, security men protected him. "Fuck, who is going to come in here that we ain't going to know?" he said.

Dorsett's car was brought around for him, so he didn't have to walk through the parking lot. "If somebody wanted to kill me, they could just ride up beside the damn car and *Bang!* blow the window open," he said.

There was another death threat on Dorsett that season in the week before the Cowboys played the Steelers in the Super Bowl in Miami. The Cowboys responded by moving Dorsett to the same floor in the team hotel where the team's administration was staying.

"It's an awful feeling," he said.

Not many of Montana's teammates were aware that he played the championship game after learning his life had been threatened. But all they had to do was look at the tape of the game and fast-forward to the very last play.

It started with 27 seconds remaining at the 49ers 47-yard line after Dallas called its final time-out following Danny White's fumble. It was second down. Montana took a few steps back and kneeled down, just as he had on first down. Dennis Thurman came around from Montana's left and tried and failed to wrestle the ball away from him. Montana got back on his feet, and with about 19 seconds remaining and no way for the Cowboys to stop the clock, he began to jog off the field with the ball tucked under his left arm and his right index finger pointed to the sky, signifying that the Niners were number one. Guard Dan Audick started to jog with him. Montana did not stay long enough to shake any hands, not his teammates' nor the Cowboys'. He began to pick up the pace. The fans were quickly storming the field.

By the time Montana was inside the 10-yard line and nearing the end zone, the fans had completely swarmed the field, and Montana was weaving his way through them like a car driving 50 mph in bumper-to-bumper traffic on Interstate 101. The ball was now tucked under his right arm, and Montana was in a full sprint for the baseball Giants dugout right behind the end zone. The dugout had a tunnel that led to the 49ers locker room. He did not have a police escort, and if security was assigned to him, he outran the coverage. It might have been the fastest Montana ever ran.

"He's lucky he got off the field," Cowboys tight end Doug Cosbie said. "That was a mob. My dad's side of the family has been in San Francisco since the pre–Gold Rush days, 1840. I spent a lot of time in Candlestick watching the Giants. I come from a long line of San Francisco cops. One of my first cousins was a cop who was working the game. I didn't even see him until the game was over. He grabbed me. He was a big guy, maybe six four, and he grabs me and starts taking me off the field. Some guy comes running up to me, and my cousin takes one of those nightstick things and jams it into his stomach. I swear I thought it was going to come out the back side."

The police escorted Walsh off the field. Lott bumped hard into one of those police horses that had blocked DeBartolo's view. Montana never forgot what he was told before the game. Somebody was out to get him. Nobody said it wouldn't happen on the field after the game. "I got the hell out of there," he said. "I wasn't taking a chance."

The next anybody saw of Montana, he was sprawled on the floor of the 49ers locker room, completely drained, as Amos Lawrence leaned over to say something to him. "It was an exhausting game," Montana said. "I was so tired, physically and mentally. It was just one of those games that took everything out of you. It's not like me to lie on the floor."

Charlie Waters was the Cowboys' third-round pick out of Clemson in 1970 and had seen it all. He played in five Super Bowls in the seventies, winning two and losing three. He was the heart, soul, and brains of the Cowboys defense. The coaches loved him. His teammates loved him. He knew this was his last game if Dallas lost. "I was playing crippled," he said. "My knee was shot. I was playing on a torn ligament in my right knee."

He's lost count of the number of surgeries he's had. "Probably fifteen or seventeen," he said, and not all of them came when he was playing. In 2000, it was determined that he had broken his back twenty years earlier. By now, it was cutting into his spinal cord and he was losing the feeling in his legs. They warned him that if he didn't have it taken care of pretty soon, then he could lose control of his legs and his bowels within one year. "That's just the game," he said. "It's what we paid."

The price got higher in 2003, when he had his right knee replaced. "Best operation I ever had," he said.

The NFC title game was his last chance to get back to the Super Bowl. Not too many retire on top holding the Vince Lombardi Trophy. Waters had given his body to football, the game he loved; the least the game could do in return was let him go out a winner. When the 49ers took over at their 11-yard line with 4:54 remaining, he knew defensive coordinator Ernie Stautner was making a mistake playing the Prevent Defense. "I said bring the four-three in, and when they get past the 50-yard line and moving towards the 40, when the field is smaller, go ahead and go nickel," he said.

The Cowboys stayed in the prevent until third and 3 at the 6-yard line. There was no panic in the Dallas huddle. Waters was so sure the Cowboys would come up with the stop, that no team was driving 89 yards on Doomsday II, even if he didn't agree with the defensive call. Landry kept telling Waters during the drive that the defense would make a play. And Waters had faith in Landry. "I loved him," he said. "He was a test. He'd haunt you."

One game early in his career, before Waters moved from cornerback to safety, he was beaten for three touchdowns by Philadelphia's Harold Jackson. Waters had based his pregame preparation on the Cowboys' precious computer printouts. The Eagles happened to cross up that report, and Waters had a miserable game. At the team meeting the next week, Waters was ready to take his medicine from Landry. "You can't just stick your head in the dirt," Waters said. "You've got to sit there and take it like a man. So I sat there and took it like a man. It was rough. That's where I learned to deal with adversity." Landry showed the film of the game. Waters sat there and cringed. Then Landry spoke. He told the forty-five men in the room that Waters had had a tough game, but if everybody tried as hard as he did, the Cowboys would never lose a game. "I was on board with him forever," Waters said.

He was already convinced Landry knew everything and his word was gospel. Now he knew he could count on him to have his back. When Landry finally moved him to safety, he became an All-Pro. "All was right with the world," he said. "There's where I was originally supposed to be. I was a pretty good strong safety, but I couldn't play corner."

The 49ers had put up 45 points on the Cowboys in the October game, but Waters was one of those Cowboys not convinced the 49ers were for real. He thought the game was a fluke. He gained respect for Montana, but he still wasn't the type of quarterback Waters feared. He didn't like playing against guys like Terry Bradshaw, who had a big arm. He didn't mind playing against quarterbacks who tried to outthink him. It was a matchup he always felt Dallas would win. He didn't fear the 49ers, but he did learn to appreciate their offensive approach to the game. "The brand the 49ers played, I was just not aware how genius it was," Waters said. "Their job was not to throw the ball down the field. Their job was just to get it to the open man and get three to five yards and that was a successful play for them in the passing game."

Joe Montana to Dwight Clark ended Waters's career, face down in the painted end zone in Candlestick Park. "Here I am with my face buried in that frickin' red kitty litter," he said. But giving up the

three touchdowns to Jackson, losing that game to the 49ers, and all
the surgeries suddenly meant nothing to him on December 4, 1995.
He was now the defensive coordinator at the University of Oregon
after spending seven years on the staff of the Broncos, where his
friend Dan Reeves brought him into the coaching business. He had
wanted to work for Landry after his playing career ended, but
Landry wanted Waters to take a psychological test that was required
for all of Landry's coaching candidates. The tests are very popular
before the draft as teams try to gather as much information about
players as possible. No player was ever closer to Landry than Waters.
They had been together for twelve seasons. Waters was insulted. If
Landry didn't know everything about him by then, what was some
test going to show? Waters refused to take it, and Landry didn't
hire him.

He went into the real estate business in Dallas but was excited
when Reeves called and hired him in 1988. Coaches lead a vaga-
bond existence, going from job to job, city to city, wherever the next
opportunity might present itself. After Reeves was fired by the Broncos following the 1992 season, Waters remained and worked two
years for Wade Phillips, until Phillips was fired too. Waters had
coaching in his blood. He wanted to stay in the NFL, but the next
opportunity came from Oregon coach Mike Bellotti, who had just
been promoted from offensive coordinator. He asked Waters to be
his defensive coordinator.

Waters and his wife, Rosie, had three sons. The oldest was Cody.
He was seventeen years old and would be a senior at Cherry Creek
High School in Denver in the fall. A few years earlier, the Clemson
head coaching job opened up, and Waters would have loved to return to his alma mater, but he couldn't even get an interview because he had no college coaching experience. Playing in five Super
Bowls and having Tom Landry as his mentor all those years wasn't
enough. He knew Oregon would look good on his résumé, but he

was torn when the offer came. He didn't want Cody to switch schools for his senior year. Still, he wanted the job. He needed the job if he was going to be a head coach in college one day. The family reached a compromise. Rosie and the kids would stay behind until Cody finished high school and went off to college. Things changed after Cody accompanied his father on a trip to Eugene shortly after he started working. "Dad, we're a family. We've got to do this together," Cody said.

The week after Cody was born in 1977, Waters intercepted three passes in a playoff game against the Bears, an NFL postseason record. He told the story of that game to Cody many times as he was growing up. "I had my greatest game as a player," he proudly told him.

The entire family moved to Eugene. Cody Waters, six three, 180, played high-school soccer and football, had been accepted to the University of Texas, and planned to be a walk-on as a kicker. On December 3, the family took a road trip into the woods of Oregon to cut down a tree for Christmas. Cody had had two never-explained seizures in the previous three years, the most recent during the family's last year in Denver. Waters was scared for his son. He took Cody to every doctor he could find. "There is nothing wrong with him," he was told. "Some guys go through this. Kids go through these growing pains."

The doctors did not put Cody on any medication. "He wasn't into drugs or anything like that," Waters said. "He was at a Catholic school. He was strong in that world."

Cody didn't wake up on the morning of December 4, and Waters still doesn't know why. His death was attributed to undetermined natural causes. It was nothing associated with his brain, his heart, or any disease. His father never stopped blaming himself. "I could have not trusted the doctor's opinion and taken Cody to the Mayo Clinic," he said. "I could have just done a little bit more, researched a little bit more. But, man, they convinced me this guy was healthy as a horse."

Burying one's child is a pain that never goes away. It hasn't for Waters. "I was brain dead," he said. He's tried to understand why Cody could be taken from him and Rosie and his other two boys just two weeks before his eighteenth birthday. He had his whole life to live. He's confused about why doctors told him there was nothing to worry about and then his son doesn't wake up one morning.

"I think about him every day," he said. "I hate the pictures that I have of him in my head. I can still remember the morgue. It was so gruesome. It's your child."

Less than one month later, Waters fulfilled his obligation to Oregon and coached in the Cotton Bowl on New Year's Day. Cody had been looking forward to returning to Dallas, the city where he was born. He would have been in his familiar spot down on the field by his father's side holding the cord to his headset. His younger brother Ben held the headset instead, and Cody's initials were on the helmets of every Oregon player. And when the season ended and Waters took a deep breath, he knew he had to leave his job. Rosie needed to go home to Dallas, where she had a lot of family. Cody was buried in Tyler, about ninety minutes from Dallas, and moving back to Texas allowed the family to be closer to the grave site. Waters left coaching and has never returned. He had opportunities to join Jackie Sherrill's staff at Mississippi State, Steve Spurrier wanted him to run his defense at Florida, Jeff Fisher wanted him to be his defensive-backs coach with the Tennessee Titans, and former teammate Drew Pearson offered him the opportunity to be the head coach of the team he was running in the XFL. But Waters couldn't bear the thought of the late nights breaking down film and the recruiting trips that took him away from home too often. He was overwhelmed with guilt about not being there for his children.

The Waters family moved back to Dallas by the end of February. Roger Staubach hired Charlie and Rosie to work for his real-estate firm. Rosie was doing real work. Charlie was given a token position, just collecting checks, still not sure why his life was had been torn apart. Charlie eventually branched off and teamed up again with Cliff Harris, his old buddy from the Cowboys, in the energy business in Dallas. Waters and Harris were quite a pair when they played safety together, and it had to be comforting to be back with his friend while coping with the most tragic period of his life. Charlie had even named his third son after Cliff.

Waters was suffering and was struggling to find ways to become whole again. "Grieving is such a personal thing," he said. He would pick up the Dallas newspaper, turn to the obituaries, look for families that just lost their child, and attend funerals for kids he didn't even know. Over a sixth-month period, he went to more than ten funerals. He never told Rosie what he was doing. It's something he even considers doing now. It was not done out of morbid curiosity. Somehow, it helped the healing.

"Why did I do it? I don't know," he said. "It's amazing that a funeral lasts forty-five minutes to an hour. It's a person's whole life. Then *poof,* it's gone. I had a craving to just let the parents know that other people cared. I would go to the receiving line. I never let them know it was me. I didn't go in as Charlie Waters, ex-football player. It's hard to explain. I just had a desire to go, not just to see how other people handle it. It was to just make it a little more reverent, a little more special, for the son that was gone."

By the end of 1996, Waters had stopped looking in the newspaper. "I didn't mean to do anything disrespectful to Rosie," he said. "I needed it for myself."

His office near downtown Dallas is filled with family pictures. He points proudly to the many pictures of Cody, his oldest. "There is no such thing as closure," he said. "I'm OK, but I'm pissed. I think it might be the world's worst tragedy. Losing your spouse might be, but losing a child before their time when they hadn't had a chance to live. Why didn't my child get to experience all this stuff? Cliff's kids are all doing this stuff. But you know what, it's just like everything else—it made me a stronger person—but I certainly don't offer that as any kind of reason for why it happened, and I would trade my life in a second for him being able to experience life. He was a great person."

Waters was interested when SMU, which is in Dallas, was conducting a coaching search late in 2001. He had been out of coaching six seasons and had only one year of experience at the collegiate level. They passed him over. Waters would have been a terrific recruiter and would have helped restore to prominence a program that had been shut down by the NCAA "death penalty" in 1987 for making improper payments to players and their families. Waters may not have had much college coaching experience, but he knew what it meant to try to rebuild when you've gone through an unspeakable tragedy. Rebuilding a football program would have been easy compared to how Waters had to rebuild his life.

Dwight Clark was one of the many 49ers battling the flu the week before the championship game. It really got him bad that Tuesday and Wednesday. Cross was so sick, he was throwing up the entire game. He was drinking fluids to keep from dehydrating, but was having trouble keeping anything down. Just as the 49ers huddled up to start the last drive against the Cowboys, Cross could not control himself.

"People always say, 'What was the mood like in the huddle? It had to be special. Was it like that drive in Super Bowl XXIII?' " Cross said. "I was puking my guts out. It had gotten to the point where I didn't even leave the huddle anymore. You kind of sit there and go 'Ugghhh.' "

The huddle moved a few yards to escape Cross's vomit, but that didn't exactly get the 49ers into the right frame of mind to drive the ball down the throats of the Cowboys. "Oh man, R.C., what are you? Crazy?" his teammates said as they backed away from him.

Clark was exhausted. When Walsh called his first time-out with 1:15 remaining after a 12-yard pass to Solomon had moved the 49ers to the Dallas 13, Clark was slumped over, down on one knee as the medical staff came running out onto the field to take a look at him. Clark had missed Wednesday's practice but returned the next two days.

The trainer was talking to Clark, asking him if he was all right. Clark was concerned about just staying on his feet. "Everybody was worn out," he said. "That had been a grueling game, and to drive that distance, most of it being running plays, everybody was pretty worn out."

The Cowboys defense was drained as well. At the two-minute warning, Randy White and Harvey Martin were each on one knee at midfield, sucking air. This was now a test of survival—last team standing.

Third and 3 from the Dallas 6. Montana comes over from his meeting with Walsh and called Sprint Right Option. Solomon was lined up in the right slot, with Clark just outside of him. Clark's initial job was to pick off Solomon's defender, which was Dennis Thurman, forcing him to turn his head and allowing Solomon to run free underneath. Clark was to sprint toward the end line near the goal posts—but not too close, because he didn't want to run out of bounds—then plant hard and reverse field to the right. He also wanted to leave himself room to come down with the ball and not be out of bounds.

"We will never run this play on fourth down," Walsh told

Montana and Clark in training camp. If Montana had to go to Clark, his second option, Walsh told him, "Joe, you throw it high enough where it goes out of bounds or Dwight can jump and catch it, but don't throw an interception, because we will still have another play."

Montana took the snap from Quillan and began sprinting to his right. Immediately, the Cowboys made a huge mistake. Ed Jones was at left end and Larry Bethea was at left tackle. Bethea was playing because Buffalo's Conrad Dobler had leg-whipped John Dutton in a game on November 9, and he was unable to go against the 49ers. "He got a blood clot in his thigh, and we had to play Bethea in his place," Waters said.

Bethea was supposed to run a stunt with Jones. Too Tall was supposed to take the inside route, and Bethea's assignment was to loop to the outside, taking Jones's responsibility, and prevent Montana from getting outside the pocket.

"Bethea didn't execute the stunt," Waters said. "Ed executed it perfectly, and then when he saw Joe scrambling out, you saw D. D. Lewis and Ed moving into the picture. Why is Ed moving into the picture? Bethea is already supposed to be out there. He had a clean shot [but] he didn't run the stunt. Bethea is chasing him from behind, but he should have been the wall to keep him closed in." Jones actually started to execute the stunt, but when Bethea didn't loop around, Jones started his pursuit of Montana.

But then the 49ers made a mistake too: As Solomon was making his break, he slipped and threw off the timing of the play. Thurman was step-for-step with Solomon. He was no longer an option for Montana. "It was very moist and wet in the corner," Solomon said. "I was told to stay in the corner. If I didn't get open, just stand there. I would hold the defensive back in place."

Montana was following Walsh's instructions. He kept rolling to his right. Rolling, rolling. "Hold it, hold it," Walsh had told him on the sidelines.

Up in the coaches' booth, Sam Wyche was sitting next to George Seifert, the defensive-backs coach. "Right then, every nerve ending in my body is alive," Wyche said. "There goes Joe rolling to his right. Freddie Solomon is covered. I'm yelling, 'Keep it alive Joe, keep it alive.' I could see Dwight coming open. We had worked on it all week long. I leaped forward just one moment with a burst of energy. I swear to this day I would have gone out of the booth, but George reached over and grabbed the back of my pants. He saved my life. I know my heart was pounding like everybody else in the stadium."

The play began with Elliott and Earl Cooper in a split backfield behind Montana, with Cooper to Montana's right. Thurman was 2 yards off the line in front of Solomon, who was lined up a yard behind the line. Walls was right in front of Clark and gave him a solid bump to the outside as soon as the ball was snapped, but Clark was only momentarily diverted. He was still able to cut toward the middle of the end zone.

Once Solomon slipped, Montana kept sprinting toward the right sideline. He was by the 10-yard-line number on the field, between the hash mark and the sideline, when he pump-faked. He was in full retreat, moving backward and toward his right. Bethea, who had avoided Cooper's cut-block attempt, was bearing down on him. Cross was trailing Bethea with no chance of taking him out of the play. Jones was two yards directly in front of Montana. He pump-faked again, which got Jones in the air. He is six nine, a formidable obstacle to throw over, but he was on his way down when Montana released the ball. If Jones had been at the top of his leap when Montana let the ball go, it would have been like trying to throw over the Empire State Building. Bethea was also in front of him and trying to summon the energy to leap. The two of them created a huge wall. Montana was within 3 yards of the sideline, his right foot was just shy of the 14-yard line, and his body was leaning backward when he released the ball, throwing it off his back foot. It was a spectacular throw.

"I came close to getting him," Jones said, right after the game. "He had to put a big arc on it to prevent me from batting it away."

Given the benefit of nearly thirty years to think about it, Jones isn't so sure Montana was following any script. "I would bet my last hard-earned dime that Joe Montana didn't have the poise to see who was in pursuit and wait for me to come down. I thought he was throwing it away to get them to the next play," he said.

Montana never saw what happened next. Bethea pushed him down after the ball was gone, and he was buried in the Candlestick dirt. "As big as they are, they made you change the direction and flight of the ball," Montana said. "I had to at least try to get it over their hands. This is a guy who is six foot nine. And with his hands up, he's pretty damn big. So I couldn't throw it like I wanted. I had to put a little more air under it."

Clark had taken Walls to the middle of the end zone, where he was met by safety Michael Downs. Waters was a few yards to the left. Walls looked back to see where Montana was scrambling. Clark was briefly tangled up with Downs, but Walls had time to get back on Clark when he made his move to the right. "We had practiced this," Clark said.

Clark was just a bit deeper and a step ahead of Walls when the ball came flying their way. "I knew he was scrambling, but I had to find Clark," Walls said right after the game. "I thought the ball was going out of bounds, but he made a great catch. There wasn't much I could do. I thought it was out of the end zone."

Clark airlifted himself. Did he have rockets in his cleats? He caught the ball with both arms extended as far as possible over his head. The ball actually rattled around in his hands, and for one moment, he lost control and only had it with his left hand, but he quickly secured it with his right hand—all this while he was in the air—and came down with it just in front of the back line. It went beyond acrobatic. He then spiked the ball and it rolled away. If The Catch was a classic, so was Montana's throw.

"I remember thinking, 'That is high. I got to get up,'" Clark said. "But you just kind of react to it. I didn't know it was a double catch until I saw the still photograph of several frames. It's scary to think that ball was not in my hand the whole time. I'm too nervous to think about it. We had practiced that play so many times. Joe would either throw too long and get picked or I would have to jump or he would throw it over my head. It was never right in practice. But under duress, he put it in a perfect spot. Any lower and Walls would have knocked it down. He threw it off his back foot with three guys in his face."

Cross had one of the best vantage points in the house. "All I know is, it's Sprint Right Option, and the sprint is right outside the tight end," he said. "The ball should be out of his hands by the time he gets outside the tight end, unless the first receiver is not open—then he's going to have to keep going. You always thought with Joe you had to block exactly the way the play was called. And then you better keep blocking because there was no telling where he was going to end up.

"I had a perfect view. I'm blocking Bethea—Fahnhorst and I," Cross said. "As it keeps getting wider, I'm thinking that it's not going to keep going. Bethea keeps running. I'm looking at him, and he and Too Tall are chasing Joe. He throws the ball, and I look straight back. Dwight came out of nowhere. It looked like it was heading to the top of that back wall or the first row. They had practiced the play. Not quite like that."

Thurman remained with Solomon. They were in front of the

end zone, out of the play. Thurman's job was to follow Solomon, even after he slipped. "I look at the ball and it appears to be a thousand feet over my head," Thurman said. "So, I'm watching, then, holy shit, he caught the ball. Did I realize it was going to be given a name? No. When you are playing in a game, you don't feel like you just witnessed something that is going to go down as part of history."

Montana couldn't see a thing. He was down and blocked by a bunch of big bodies. He relied on the reaction of the crowd to tell him what happened. It was New Year's Eve at Candlestick, just ten days late. All Montana knew from the sound of the crowd was that Clark caught the ball, but he had no idea what really happened.

"When I let it go, I thought it was just above his head," Montana said. "I got knocked down, and I got to the sideline, and I still remember our old equipment manager, Chico Norton, came to me and said, 'Man, your buddy saved your ass that time.'"

"What are you talking about, Chico?"

"He jumped out of the stadium."

"Chico, he's white. He can't jump."

Up in the coaches' booth, Mike Ditka, one of Landry's offensive assistants, who was known for getting a little emotional, took off his headset and slammed it down. Ray Wersching came on for the extra point. Montana was the holder. Jones and Harvey Martin were in the middle of the Cowboys line, but Wersching's kick easily sailed over Jones, who launched his six-nine body trying to keep the score tied.

San Francisco 28, Dallas 27.

Clark made a once-in-a-lifetime catch. Montana's throw was spectacular. But the Cowboys weren't buying it. They were convinced then and are even more convinced now that Montana was throwing the ball away, that the upper deck was more of a target on that pass than

Clark. He threw it off his back foot as he was leaning backward. Jones, Bethea, and Lewis were in his face. Montana let it fly from the 14-yard line. Clark was 24 yards away at the back of the end zone.

There is footage from the 49ers practices showing Montana and Clark practicing that play, but it never worked. Montana never put it in a spot where Clark could catch it. But when the adrenaline is pumping and a ticket to the Super Bowl is at stake, athletes are capable of making plays they would not make under more mundane circumstances. Dallas never could accept the fact that Montana shredded them on the way down the field. And when Sprint Right Option broke down, they refused to believe that Montana's throw and Clark's catch were right out of Walsh's playbook. They believe Montana was playing for fourth down.

"You know what's funny about that play?" Montana asked. "Bill having the intuition—we never threw the ball to Dwight on that play. And we'd run it for three years."

But in camp that summer, Walsh had made Montana and Clark practice that part of the play over and over again, as if he knew that the 49ers were going to the NFC title game, would drive down the field, and need Sprint Right Option to run against a tired Dallas defense to win the game. He was The Genius, after all. He predicted before the game that the winning team would score four touchdowns and the losing team would score three. He was exactly right. The Niners were the first NFC team since the 1970 merger to win thirteen regular-season games. They are also the only team to win an NFC playoff game despite 6 turnovers. True, Houston won an AFL playoff game in 1961, Baltimore beat Dallas in Super Bowl V, and the Steelers beat the Raiders in the 1975 AFC playoffs, all overcoming 7 turnovers. But giving the ball away on 6 out of 15 possessions usually gets a team eliminated in the playoffs.

"They had six turnovers and two pass-interference penalties. When that happens, you're supposed to lose," Drew Pearson said.

"They were lucky to win this game. They were lucky they were even in position to win it at the end. If we had taken care of business and played a better offensive football game, we would have won that game going away."

But Danny White completed only 16 passes in the game, and just 5 went to his wide receivers, Pearson, Hill, Butch Johnson, and Doug Donley. They combined for only 103 yards receiving. Dallas converted the 6 turnovers into only 14 points.

Walsh made sure Montana knew he should throw the ball away rather than risk tossing his fourth interception. He might not have seen Clark catch the ball, but he saw him when he released it. And he sure knew he wasn't throwing in a spot where Walls could get his third pick. "I wasn't throwing it away," Montana said. "If I was throwing it away, I'd have thrown it a helluva long time before then. Everybody is yelling and screaming, 'What a great play.' I just threw it, and Dwight caught it. How can it be that great? I didn't know until after the game when I saw the replay."

Pearson bumped into Montana at an autograph signing in Anaheim in the summer of 1982. He said Montana made a point of stopping by to see him. "He told me then he was throwing it away even though it was a designed play," Pearson said. "He was throwing it away. Maybe he said it to comfort me. Maybe at the end of a designed play, he was throwing it away. Here's Dwight Clark, who came out of nowhere. Even if Everson was on him, I think it was one of those moments. I don't think Dwight Clark could get that high again. You are in a zone. The momentum and adrenaline takes you to another level of your ability."

Maybe it's just the Cowboys' way of rationalizing the loss, but they are convinced that he was trying to heave it out of the end zone and it didn't go far enough. "He may swear up and down that he wasn't," said Thurman, who was a student of the game even before he became an assistant coach in the league. He says Clark was supposed to pick him to set Solomon free, but didn't. "The way that play has been run, from what I see right now, Dwight pretty much screwed it up," he said. "He did nothing he was supposed to do on that play except catch the ball and win the game."

As if that wasn't enough.

Pearson thought Walls played the coverage incorrectly. Knowing he had inside help from Downs, Pearson felt he should have protected more to the outside. "He was still a rookie," Pearson said. "They were going to try and exploit that. A little adjustment like that would've made the difference. Maybe Everson didn't know he had that inside help. Maybe he did, but didn't know the best way to take advantage of that was to line up to the outside. In that game, they were attacking him. They were going deep on him."

Does it really matter that Walls says he is "convinced" Montana was throwing the ball away? "You know how legends grow legs? All of a sudden he's not throwing it away. Then all of a sudden they are practicing that play in training camp," he said. "Then there's documentaries. It really cracks me up. Dwight is just pouring it on."

Clark has repeatedly told a story that after he caught the ball, either Too Tall or Harvey Martin turned to Montana and said that they had just beaten America's Team, and Montana responded that the Cowboys could watch the Super Bowl like the rest of America.

"Are you going to tell me anybody's falling for that crap?" Walls said. "Do you really think that while that play is going on, with all the hoopla, the crowd's going crazy, that Joe is going to stand still and listen to what anybody has to say? Do you think any of our defensive linemen, especially Ed Jones, is going to say, 'You just beat America's Team'? That's when people really get carried away and too full of themselves."

Landry, who was always gracious in defeat, had a hard time hiding his frustration right after the game and took a swipe at the team that had just prevented him from going to the Super Bowl. "The

49ers are not a better team than us, but the game ended at the right time for them," he said. "Montana has to be the key. There's nothing else there except him."

It was a game for the ages, one remembered with the simplest of names: The Catch. The Cowboys had four Hall of Famers on that team: Tex Schramm, Landry, Dorsett, and Randy White. The 49ers also had four: Walsh, Montana, Lott, and Fred Dean. But nobody enjoyed the perks that came from winning that game more than Clark. Life was already pretty good for him. He was dating Shawn Weatherly, otherwise known as Miss Universe.

"I started dating her in college. She was at Clemson," he said. "She was the homecoming queen, she won the Miss Clemson pageant, then she was Miss South Carolina, Miss USA, and then Miss Universe."

She once said her three favorite players were Dwight Clark, Dwight Clark, and Dwight Clark. "I dated her four years," he said. "She left shortly after The Catch. She wanted to be in television. I wanted a family."

It doesn't get much better than making the most famous catch in NFL history and dating Miss Universe at the same time. They broke up in March 1982. "Now I'm single, and I get a new contract. I have a Super Bowl ring," he said. "All the 49ers are hot."

A real estate developer approached him with a proposal. He had built a huge complex in Los Angeles and put a few movie stars in it, who became magnets for new clients to buy his property. Now he wanted to attempt the same approach in San Francisco. He built a complex at 101 Lombard Street in downtown San Francisco and paid Clark to live there. He had a lot of free time early in the 1982 season when the players went on strike for fifty-seven days. But that didn't slow Clark down. "It was like being a rock star. I was rockin' an' rollin'," he said.

He never really stopped. That play has followed him his entire adult life. He made $12,000 in 2005 when Gatorade used the footage of The Catch with a surprise ending: the ball slipping through his hands. He didn't know what they planned to do with The Catch until he saw the commercial on television. "Did I just drop that?" he asked. It was found money for Clark.

"I'm still making appearances and doing autograph shows from a play that happened more than twenty-five years ago. To me, that's pretty remarkable," he said. "The cool part about that play is, the Dallas Cowboys had beaten up the 49ers team two or three times to knock them out of the Super Bowl in the early seventies, and to be able to give the 49ers fans that one signature play, I'll forever be that guy. The story is passed down from generation to generation. It becomes bigger than life. That is definitely my football identity. And I'm fine with that. I actually like it a lot."

Montana was excited about cashing in on his celebrity, too, but Walsh was concerned. He didn't want Montana to burn himself out. He also didn't want him to be a one-hit wonder. "I was doing everything off the field," he said. "[Walsh] said, 'Look, just remember, I know it might be a one-time opportunity, but I'm just telling you, the more scarce you are, the more people will want you.'" He told Montana he had two reasons for giving him that advice. It was true. And he wanted him to spend as much time as he could on football. "We're still just beginning here," Walsh said.

Montana did benefit long-term from one endorsement deal. He met his future wife, Jennifer Wallace, while they filmed a Schick commercial together in January 1984. He proposed that summer, and they were married in 1985.

The 49ers became such a high-profile team that even Cross, an offensive guard, was able to cash in and became a media star. When he dislocated his foot, tore all the ligaments in his ankle, and broke his leg on Memorial Day in the off-season following the first Super Bowl victory over Cincinnati, he received a call from a friend who was in radio, asking if he was interested in getting into the business. Cross had a huge cast on his leg and was on crutches, but his friend promised he would send a limo to pick him up every morning. He took a job reading sports on KSFO. He soon turned that into his own radio show and television show, which he did for the last six years of his career, until he retired after his third Super Bowl title in 1988. Then he turned television and radio into his second career with a job analyzing NFL games on CBS and his own radio show on Sirius.

"My dad, Dennis Cross, was an actor, and I grew up in the business," he said. "He told me a long time ago, when I was in high school, that when I was approached by sportswriters in Los Angeles, to have something interesting to say. During the 1960s, there was a television show called *The Blue Angels* that was on for a couple of years. If you watched television from 1965 to 1974, you saw my dad die innumerable times. He was either an Indian or a Mob guy. He was one of the few people to ever die on *Get Smart*. He was in *The Rifleman, Wanted Dead or Alive, The Virginian*."

The 49ers were a start-up company with Walsh, in an area of the country that specialized in these type of businesses. They were just doing it on a national stage, growing up fast, trying to be taken seriously. January 10, 1982, was the coming-out party for Joe Cool and the 49ers, and the going-away party for Landry and the Cowboys. Walsh was building a team that would last in San Francisco, winning four more Super Bowls in the next thirteen seasons, the greatest run for any team in the Super Bowl era. If they had not defeated Dallas in that landmark game, the 49ers might never have gone on to win all those Super Bowls; they could have been nothing more than a shooting star, flashing across the sky and disappearing. It's happened so many times in NFL history. That game convinced them they could be great. Montana may have gone on to be the best quarterback in NFL history anyway, but that game proved he was a special talent. As Cross says, "Would Larry Bird still be thought of the same way without the steal and the basket? Would Babe Ruth be thought of the same way without the home run for the little kid or the mythical called shot? No, probably not. For Joe, it was one of the first bricks in that legend."

Montana, an overlooked third-round draft pick, and Clark, a tenth-round pick nobody in San Francisco other than Walsh even wanted, teamed up on one of the most sensational plays in sports history. It prevented Landry from reaching his sixth Super Bowl, a goal he never attained. Adding to the pain of losing to the 49ers, he coached many of them three weeks later in the Pro Bowl in Hawaii after the 49ers defeated the Bengals 26–21 in the Super Bowl. The 49ers had to show their resilience in that game after taking a 20–0 lead at the half. The Bengals got within 20–14 after they had missed an earlier opportunity when the Niners put on the greatest goal-line stand in Super Bowl history. Even so, that game almost seemed anti-climactic. The real Super Bowl had been played two weeks earlier at Candlestick Park. The Cowboys surely would have beaten the Bengals, too, and then could have tacked another Super Bowl onto Landry's plaque in the Hall of Fame. The tears were flowing in the Cowboys locker room in Candlestick Park. They were so close. They knew they missed out on a brilliant opportunity. Landry did not say much to his players after the game.

"All I remember after the game is, I had gotten twenty-two tickets because I grew up out there," Cosbie said. "My friends were waiting outside for me after the game. One of them that I went to high school with was jumping up and down smiling. He said, 'What a great day. You scored a touchdown and the 49ers won.' I was like,

'What?' I turned around and got on the bus. What are people thinking? Obviously, someone was a diehard 49ers fan that I got a ticket for."

Over the course of the decade, Landry went from football icon to football martyr. The Cowboys were growing old, and Landry was growing old with them. He was fired in 1989, and Jimmy Johnson had the Cowboys in the Super Bowl by 1992. Dallas then became the first team to win three Super Bowls in a four-year period.

The 49ers were 6 yards away and 6 points down with 58 seconds remaining. Montana took the snap and rolled to his right on Sprint Right Option. Clark jumped as high as he could, right into the beautiful San Francisco evening, and when he came down with the ball, everything had changed.

A dynasty was born. A team was destroyed. One play. The Catch.

Acknowledgments

DWIGHT CLARK and I were sitting in the eighth-floor lobby of the Marriott Marquis in midtown Manhattan early on a Monday morning during the 2007 football season. He had flown up from Charlotte, where he was living at the time, to watch the 49ers play the Giants the previous day in the Meadowlands. I came with my portable DVD player and three discs CBS was nice enough to send me of the original television broadcast of my all-time favorite game.

Dwight came with his memories.

I fast-forwarded the third disc to the spot where just 4:54 was left in the 1981 NFC Championship Game. The 49ers were trailing the Cowboys 27–21 and were backed up at their 11-yard line. As the hotel guests around us scrambled to check out or head off for a meeting, Clark sat on the edge of his seat watching the drive of a lifetime against America's Team.

Finally, we reached The Catch.

As Joe Montana rolled right, Clark was surprisingly anxious watching the broadcast as the ball sailed toward him, almost afraid he was going to drop it. When he caught the pass, I looked over to check on his reaction. He actually got choked up, and I thought he was about to cry. It was just the beginning of my journey researching this book, and I knew right then this compelling moment in NFL history would evoke strong emotions from everybody it had touched.

I was in my first month as the Cowboys beat writer for the *Dallas Morning News* when I was in the Candlestick Park press box that day. It's still the greatest game I've ever seen. I had no idea, of course, that one day I would be writing a book about it. For that, I want to thank Sean Desmond, my editor at Crown, former Dallas resident, and still a huge Cowboys fan. He conceived the idea of using this game as a way of telling the story of the emergence of the 49ers dynasty and the fall of the Cowboys empire. Sean and I quickly discovered we share the same passion for this game.

It would have been impossible, of course, to tell this story without the cooperation of Montana and Clark, who were incredibly generous with their time and insights. Joe was so enthusiastic about the project he accepted my offer to write the foreword. I have learned by covering the NFL for more than thirty years that when you want perspective, you start with the offensive line. That's why 49ers guard Randy Cross was my first interview. Ed DeBartolo, Carmen Policy, and John McVay were very helpful reconstructing the good and bad times of that era. They shared great stories about Bill Walsh, whom I got to know well in the years before his death.

I've always enjoyed my visits back to Dallas after working there for nearly eight years, but it doesn't get any better than a two-day trip in April of 2008. I spent the first morning with Tony Dorsett and the afternoon with Roger Staubach—lots of great football talk and memories. Staubach's career ended one year before I arrived in Dallas, but I quickly learned you can't cover the Cowboys without developing a relationship with Roger the Dodger.

The second day in Dallas had a different tone as I listened to Drew Pearson recount a series of tragedies in his life that led to depression, and then a few hours later I sat with Charlie Waters and had chills as he spoke about the unexpected death of his eighteen-year-old son more than ten years earlier. I appreciate Pearson and Waters trusting me and opening up their souls.

Pearson, Dorsett, Everson Walls, Dennis Thurman, and Doug Cosbie were always my go-to guys in the locker room when I covered the Cowboys. A beat writer couldn't ask for anything more. And nearly three decades later, they were my go-to guys once again.

Just one note about Tom Landry. Games and events tend to blend into each other after many years. But I will never forget the morning after Landry was fired. I drove to his house and waited hours trying to get the first interview with him. When it appeared a good idea was not going to produce a positive result, I audibled and went to the Cowboys headquarters at Valley Ranch, where the previous evening Jerry Jones announced he had fired Landry. It was a longshot Landry would be there, but at some point he was going to clean out his office. In those days, the media had free run of the building, and I walked over to Landry's office. He was sitting by himself packing all those years into boxes. He invited me in and we talked for over an hour. He was as gracious after getting fired as he was following a big victory.

I appreciate the support of my editors and colleagues at the *New York Daily News*. Thanks to the public relations staffs of the Cowboys and 49ers and my old friends at the *Dallas Morning News* for their assistance. And thanks to my wife, Allison, for not cleaning out the attic, where I have every one of the stories I wrote in my nearly eight years at the *Morning News* packed into boxes.

The Catch was one of those classic moments where everybody knows exactly where they were when Joe Montana threw it and Dwight Clark caught it. I was in Candlestick and hope I was able to put you right there with me.

Index

About the Author

GARY MYERS started covering the NFL in 1978 and was in the press box at Candlestick Park for The Catch, on January 10, 1982, as the beat writer covering the Cowboys for the *Dallas Morning News*. In 1989, he joined the *New York Daily News,* and began a thirteen-season run as the inside information reporter for HBO's popular *Inside the NFL*. In addition to writing for the *Daily News,* Myers also cohosts the YES Network's *This Week in Football.* Myers graduated in 1976 with a B.S. in newspaper journalism from Syracuse University's Newhouse School of Public Communications. He lives in Westchester County, New York, with his family.